DESERT ROSE

DESERT ROSE

The Life and Legacy of
CORETTA SCOTT KING

Edythe Scott Bagley

with Joe Hilley

Afterword by Bernice A. King

The University of Alabama Press • Tuscaloosa

The University of Alabama Press
Tuscaloosa, Alabama 35487-0380

Typeface: Garamond
Cover photograph: Courtesy of the Coretta Scott King Estate
Cover design: Gary Gore

∞

The paper on which this book is printed meets the minimum
requirements of American National Standard for Information
Sciences—Permanence of Paper for Printed Library Materials,
ANSI Z39.48-1984.

Library of Congress Cataloging-in-Publication Data

Bagley, Edythe Scott.
    Desert rose : the life and legacy of Coretta Scott King / Edythe Scott
Bagley with Joe Hilley ; [afterword by Bernice A. King].
        p. cm.
    Includes bibliographical references and index.
    ISBN 978-0-8173-1765-2 (trade cloth : alk. paper) — ISBN 978-
0-8173-8612-2 (ebook) 1. King, Coretta Scott, 1927–2006. 2. King,
Coretta Scott, 1927–2006—Influence. 3. King, Coretta Scott, 1927–
2006—Political and social views. 4. African American women civil
rights workers—Biography. 5. Civil rights workers—United States—
Biography. 6. African American women political activists—Biography.
7. African American women—Biography. 8. King, Martin Luther, Jr.,
1929–1968. 9. African Americans—Civil rights—History—20th
century. 10. Perry County (Ala.)—Biography. I. Hilley, Joseph H. II.
Title.
    E185.97.K47B34 2012
    323.092—dc23
    [B]
                                                    2011052587

In loving memory of our parents, Obie and Bernice McMurry Scott,
who taught their children by example the enduring values, and
Yolanda Denise King, who embodied the creative energy of the theatre.

And dedicated to Bernice Albertine King, Dexter Scott King,
Martin Luther King III, and Arturo Scott Bagley: heirs of the legacy.

Contents

Preface

Work on the manuscript for this book began in 1966, at the insistence of my sister, Coretta. At the time, our family was deeply involved in the Civil Rights Movement. There was much for me to write about, and although I was not living in the South at the time, my heart was very much there. The awakening spawned by the Civil Rights Movement was something for which we and our forebears had longed since the beginning of slavery. Our family was keenly aware of the Movement's work and intimately involved in its development.

The events of the 1950s and 1960s did not occur in a vacuum but were rooted in people and places stretching back to the days of emancipation and beyond. Much of the momentum for the Civil Rights Movement originated with the American Missionary Association (AMA), an organization that worked in the South after the Civil War building schools and providing teachers for newly liberated African Americans. Lincoln School in Marion, Alabama, where Coretta and I received our secondary education, was one of those AMA schools.

Lincoln School had many teachers who were social activists. Two of them, Frances and Cecil Thomas, were our mentors. Under their tutelage, we developed a social conscience that even at a young age set our eyes on the issues of social and economic justice. Later we attended Antioch College where that conscience was strengthened and nurtured.

From an early age, Coretta was comfortable taking charge. When she gave someone an idea or an assignment, she did so for a purpose, and she followed through with support. When she suggested I write about our family's involvement in the Civil Rights Movement, it was not a casual matter to her. At the time, however, I had a busy toddler who needed constant attention. To allow time for research and writing, Coretta offered to provide a sitter to look after my son, Arturo, three hours a day. With Coretta's assistance, I hired a young student named Maria who was attending nearby West Chester State College.[1]

Maria was a blonde white girl who I liked right away. My son, Arturo, also liked her, and she adored him. While I worked on this book, Maria pushed Arturo in his stroller around the black neighborhood where we lived. I am sure the sight of them together raised many eyebrows, but she never reported any trouble and I never asked any questions.

The organic structure for this book—soil, seed, bud, blossom, fruit—was inspired by *My Brother's Keeper,* a biography of James Joyce written by his brother, Stanislaus Joyce. I read that book in preparation for the production of *Exiles* that I produced while attending graduate school at Boston University, and the structure seemed fitting for my sister's story.

The title, *Desert Rose,* was derived from my knowledge of the region and culture in which Coretta and I were born and reared. We grew up under the harsh and withering restrictions of the Jim Crow South. Coretta was determined—through education, art, faith, and social activism—to do all she could to create a better life for herself, her family, and people around the world. In so doing, her life was like a rose pushing up from the parched, dry ground, and springing forth in a beautiful blossom.

Work on this project began with interviews of Coretta, our father, and other family and friends. At the same time, I collected and read every book, newspaper article, and magazine story I could find that had any bearing on the subject.

From the beginning, my husband, Arthur, was supportive and helped in ways only a husband can. Jessie Treichler, director of the Office of Development at Antioch College and Coretta's adviser when she was a student there, provided copies of documents from Antioch's archives. Along with all the other assistance Coretta gave me, she also found an interested publisher.

Work on the initial draft took almost two years of reading, interviewing, and combing through family documents and school archives, and hours seated at my desk putting it all on paper. In the end, I compiled an account of Coretta's life from birth through the Montgomery years. Doing that afforded me the opportunity to sort through memories I had almost forgotten and to hear the memories of those few outside our family knew. But it had been work. I was ready to see the results in print.

On Thursday, April 4, 1968, I put the manuscript in the mail to the publisher. Having finished a long and arduous task, I went home and sat down to relax. Late that afternoon, on a balcony outside his motel room in Memphis, Tennessee, Martin Luther King Jr. was shot and killed.

Martin's death brought many changes to our lives. In his absence, Coretta was thrust into leadership roles she had intentionally avoided while he was alive. One of her first commitments was to write her own story, *My Life with Martin Luther King, Jr.* As a result, publication of my manuscript was put on hold and then canceled.

Except for writing an addition covering the period of mourning associated with Martin's funeral, I put the manuscript aside. Then, in 2004, while visiting Coretta in Atlanta, she asked about it. As we discussed the manuscript, she once again insisted that I finish it.

The effort to complete this book, both my initial work and now this final version, has been a labor of love, learning, inspiration, and growth. Without this, I would have missed so much of the meaning of the civil rights revolution and its continuing relevance today. How grateful I am that God, through his servant Coretta, chose me for this task. However, no one could complete a work of this magnitude without the support and encouragement of friends and family.

My son, Arturo Bagley, himself a student of the Civil Rights Movement, was an enormous help with information and research.

Steve Klein, Communications Coordinator for the King Center, provided unwavering support. Steve joined the staff of the King Center in 1971, and in his professional capacity, he assisted my sister with many writing projects. He helped me gain essential insight into her leadership role and the importance of her influence.

On one occasion, while looking for a book to give as a wedding gift to friends, Steve suggested *Standing in the Need of Prayer,* a book produced by the Schomburg Center for Research in Black Culture at the New York Public Library. I found Coretta's heart and soul in the foreword she wrote for the book. In it she observed, "It is said that every prayer is heard and every prayer is answered in some way . . . I believe that the millions of prayers spoken by African Americans from the Middle Passage on down to today have been heard by a righteous and loving God."[2]

No one knew better than Coretta how much the success of the Civil Rights Movement depended on prayer and on God's divine intervention.

Another person who gave me encouragement and support was Kathryn Johnson. An excellent journalist, Ms. Johnson reported on civil rights issues and events for the Associated Press during the 1960s. She is one of many southern white women whose hard work and strong character helped usher in a new day in the South, creating a healthier climate for all its inhabitants, whites as well as blacks. She graciously provided research for the segment of this book on the history of the Fox Theatre.

Bernice Cosey Pulley, a World YWCA representative to the United Nations and a social activist, shared valuable materials and pictures, many of which I had not previously seen.

Answers to questions on the Scriptures were researched by Elder E. Richard McKim and his wife, Joanne.

During the final phase of my work on this manuscript, my niece Bernice King gave me assignments that kept me moving toward its completion. I wish to thank her for her assistance and support.

I have enjoyed the typing assistance of Karen Roache and Margie Dudley-Kornegay. Both of them took delight in helping me prepare the manuscript. Margie was most diligent in typing the final portions of it.

Again, I appreciate the support of all these people.

When Joe Hilley came on board to assist in preparing the manuscript for publication, he became a partner in what has been for us a noble task. Though he joined me in the late stages, his contribution to the final version of the manuscript made the book a more compelling work. For his diligence and dedication, in my heart I remain deeply grateful.

Bernice, Martin, and Dexter King have waited patiently for the story I have written about their mother. It is for them and baby Yolanda Renee, and for posterity, that I have struggled all these years to record the personal history of Coretta Scott King.

DESERT ROSE

I SOIL

I will make them and the region around my hill a blessing; and I will send down the showers in their season; they shall be showers of blessing.
—Ezekiel 34:26

1

Slavery

Sweat trickled down Willis's back as he slowly made his way between the chest-high rows of cotton. Picking first on the left, then on the right, he slipped his fingers between the coarse, prickly leaves and plucked cotton bolls from the stalks, then stuffed them into a sack that hung from his shoulder. Using both hands, he worked in rhythmic motion, picking and stuffing and turning and picking, keeping his hands constantly moving back and forth across his body as he twisted from side to side.

Almost three times the size of Willis's young body, the picking sack was made of heavy canvas and trailed behind him on the ground. Already it was more than half full. The weight of it pulled down on the strap across his shoulder, making it dig into his collarbone. He paused long enough to shrug the strap over to a different spot, then set his hands moving once again. Stopping, even for a moment, was dangerous. Pickers got the whip for working too slowly.

By mid-morning, the hot September sun had turned the field into a steaming cauldron that stretched for half a mile, from the willow trees by Macy's Pond all the way to Jemison Road. Farther north, in places like Virginia and Maryland, cooler weather made the mornings pleasant. In Maine and New Hampshire, leaves already were turning red, yellow, and golden brown. Up there, the nights were cold enough for a fire. But where Willis worked, on Scott's Plantation, deep in the heart of Alabama, the branches on the pecan trees were still heavy and thick with dark green foliage. Red maples growing by the pasture along Dry Creek still cast a dark shade. First frost was months away.

In the fall of 1862, Willis was all of fourteen years old, but already he was an experienced hand. He had started his first job almost as soon as he learned to walk. He filled the wood box by the stove in the kitchen at the big house, drew water from the well for the house servants, and fed the chickens. When he was six, Mr. Scott's overseer sent Willis to the field to carry the water bucket. All day he followed slowly behind the pickers with the bucket and a gourd ladle, ready to offer them a drink. The next spring, they handed him a hoe. He had been working the cotton harvest since he was big enough to drag a sack.

That September, war raged across much of the South. Virginia, Mississippi, and Tennessee saw heavy fighting. Almost every week, folks arrived in Marion, having fled the war in wagons loaded with trunks and chests and wardrobes. Children and servants rode on top. Mules and livestock were tethered behind. Isolated and of little strategic value, Alabama had escaped the devastation many other states had suffered. Perry County, where Willis lived, would not see Union troops for another two years.

As Willis picked his way across the cotton field that September morning, events were happening that would one day change his life. A thousand miles away in Washington, D.C., Abraham Lincoln sat at his desk on the second floor of the White House. Before him was a sheet of paper, and on it was the draft of a preliminary proclamation declaring his intention to bring slavery to an end. If Lincoln had his way, emancipation would come the following January to all states that remained in rebellion against the Union. That morning, he read the draft aloud for his cabinet.

News of Lincoln's decision spread rapidly through the North and sparked a heated debate. Down South, word of what he had done moved much slower but was met with an equally vigorous reaction. By the time Willis heard about it, the cotton was picked and sold, and he was chopping firewood, butchering hogs, and tending the smokehouse. Even then, after word got around and everyone was talking about it, not much in his life changed. At Scott's Plantation, the daily routine continued to follow the age-old ritual of work, sleep, and work some more—just as it had for years.

The harsh and cruel reality of a slave-based economy had held the South in its grip for over two hundred years and would continue to do so for another hundred. While enslaved, blacks were not allowed to own property, enter into contracts, or travel freely without permission. Illiteracy was strictly enforced with laws that prohibited anyone from teaching slaves how to read.[1] Deference to whites was the order of the day and would remain so until the twentieth century was well over half gone. Blacks were obliged to give a white person whatever they wanted or to suffer the consequences for failing to do so. Any deviation was met with a reprimand, often delivered at the end of a whip, a club, or worse.[2]

Emancipation did not reach Alabama until 1865, and then only in stages. On April 2 of that year, Federal troops under General James H. Wilson's command fought their way to Selma, several miles east of Perry County. Ten days later, Montgomery surrendered and on May 4, Confederate general Richard Taylor surrendered all of Alabama to Union control. With the war effectively ended and Federal troops occupying the major cities and towns, only pockets of slavery remained in the state, most of them confined to rural areas where a few owners stubbornly clung to dreams and hopes of a return to the past. Finally, on December 2, 1865, the Alabama legislature formally ratified the Thirteenth Amendment to the US Constitution, officially ending the practice of slavery.

No longer bound to his former master, Willis faced the daunting prospect of life on his own. In 1865, making a living was not a foregone conclusion, especially for a black man in a county still dominated by white landowners. Conditions were much the same in other states throughout the Deep South. Faced with that, many former slaves journeyed north, supposing metropolitan areas like New York and Boston offered a better life. Others went west in a determined bid to explore the full reach of their newly granted liberty. Some simply took to the road, wandering from town to town, sleeping in the woods, and enjoying the luxury of unfettered travel. And some, like Willis, settled down right where they had always lived.

Though white landowners—the same men who just months before had owned Willis and thousands like him—still controlled the means of production, they faced the same uncertainty as their former slaves. With hundreds of thousands of acres to farm and no one to tend it, plantation owners needed labor to work their land. Former slaves, though now free, still needed a way to earn a living. To solve their dilemma, landowners divided their plantations into individual farms and rented them out to their former slaves in a sharecropping arrangement. Men and women who in the previous year had worked the land beneath the heavy hand of slavery found themselves working that same land as tenants, paying their rent with a portion of the crop they produced. It was still slavery only this time the chains were economic, not iron and steel.

As was the case with most former slaves, Willis entered freedom without a surname. Slaves were known only by their first name. To make his way in life, Willis needed a family name. In one of the many paradoxes that defined the South, he chose the name of his former owner, Scott, and became known as Willis Scott.

After the end of the war, things moved rapidly in Willis Scott's life. By 1880, he occupied a farm at the northern end of Perry County near the community of Heiberger, and was married to a woman named Delia. Together, they had a family of nine children. One of their children was a son named Jefferson. He was our grandfather. Jeff Scott's son Obie was our father.

Many who survived the plantation life were simply lost in the years that followed, swallowed up by the passage of time and the obscurity of American society. Others drifted listlessly from one thing to the next. Some learned to cope with the system, applying the survival skills they had developed on the plantation to the challenges of living in the segregated South. And some found a way to prosper. We were blessed with industrious and courageous parents, grandparents, and great-grandparents. They not only endured, but they did so without compromising their sense of dignity and worth. Their indomitable sense of purpose and their deep desire for justice was carefully passed from generation to generation until it came to rest in full measure on my sister, Coretta.

2

Scotts and McMurrys

By temperament, Coretta was most like her grandmother, Cora McLaughlin Scott, for whom she was named. Grandmother Scott passed away before Coretta and I were born, but we heard plenty of stories about her from family and friends. Through their memories, she was a real and vital presence in our lives.

Constantly working and always active, Grandmother Scott was an eternal optimist with a compulsion for orderliness. She operated her household in a systematic and methodical manner, and she believed in following a schedule. As a matter of routine, she awakened her family at four in the morning and served breakfast by candlelight. Afterward, the beds were promptly made, the dishes washed, and the house put in order. Most days, she and her older children went to the field shortly after sunrise.

With her day structured around a schedule, she maintained discipline and order by the imposition of rules. One she most consistently enforced was a prohibition against returning to bed before nighttime, even on rainy days. Grandmother Scott had a place for everything and everything was in its place, including her children.

Driven to succeed, she was determined that those in her care would have a better life than the one she lived. Key to that effort was ownership of her own home, a goal she and Grandfather Scott achieved before her untimely death at the age of forty-two. She spent her short lifetime bearing children, working in the fields, tending to the many chores of the farm, and maintaining a home.

In contrast to Grandmother Scott's obsessive and disciplined nature, our grandfather, Jeff Scott, was gentle, affable, and levelheaded. Whereas Grandmother was frank and outspoken, Grandfather Scott was careful and cautious. An inwardly strong man, he had learned well the art of weighing his words and using them in tactfully constructed sentences. It was a skill essential for survival in a segregated society that forced black men to adopt a dual persona: the strong, determined men of ambition they knew themselves to be and the subservient, demurring ones that whites of that day expected.

A farmer by occupation, Grandfather Scott owned three hundred acres and lived well for his time. Cultivated and harvested by members of his large and expansive family, that farm provided a dependable, solid life. He was the father of thirteen children by his first wife, Cora, and ten by his second wife, the former Fannie Burroughs.[1]

Though hampered from his youth by a stuttering problem, he never allowed that speech impediment to intimidate him or deter him from public leadership roles. Instead, he regularly sought and accepted prominent positions in the church and community. Like his father before him, Grandfather Scott was determined to give his children and grandchildren a better life and did not shrink from using his influence for that purpose. He attended Mt. Tabor AME Zion Church where he was chairman of the board of trustees, preacher's steward, Sunday school superintendent, and church secretary, positions he sometimes held simultaneously. Devoted and honest, he was a natural leader who discharged his duties and responsibilities with a degree of unselfish service few could match.

Beyond the local church, Grandfather Scott was district Sunday school superintendent, responsible for Sunday school programs in all churches within our region. In addition, he was chairman of the board of trustees of Crossroads School, the elementary school that served three African American communities in our section of the county.

Though Grandfather Scott was concerned about the needs of the mind and spirit, he understood the importance of temporal issues as well. After the Civil War, benevolent societies sprang up among African American communities all over the South. Known in our area as Rising Star Societies, their purpose was to care for the sick and bury the dead. In effect, they were poor people's insurance companies. For as little as ten cents a month, a member received a small weekly benefit during illness and a modest funeral upon death. In Perry County, almost every church was associated with one of those societies. The one in our community was called the Mt. Tabor Rising Star Society. Grandfather Scott was president of that society as well as the Perry County Association of Rising Star Societies. He helped found the Rising Star Association in nearby Hale County and served as its president, too.

Because of his many positions, Grandfather Scott was one of the most widely traveled black men in our community. At a time when many blacks struggled with illiteracy and cultural isolation, Grandfather Scott attended church conferences in distant places and was a strong lay leader on the national level. To keep up with affairs beyond our county, he subscribed to the *Birmingham Age-Herald*, the daily evening paper from Birmingham, which he received every afternoon. Most mornings, he sat near a window and read the previous evening's paper before going out on his farm to work.

One day in the spring of 1941, Grandfather Scott was busy hauling fertilizer to the farm in preparation for the planting season. Near the outskirts of Marion, he lost control of his pickup truck, ran off the road, and struck a large tree. The force of the crash caused severe head and chest injuries. A passerby found him slumped over the steering wheel unconscious. He died en route to the hospital.

All who had known Jeff Scott remembered him as a most remarkable man. He lived to be sixty-eight years old and resided not far from our home. I have fond memories of him. Coretta did, too, and she often remembered him in conversation. From his example, she acquired an interest in the broader issues of the day and a cosmopolitan perspective that guided her throughout her life.

❦

From our mother's side of the family, Coretta inherited a unique mix of captivating beauty and strong character. Grandmother McMurry, who was Molly Smith before she married, was already fifty years old by the time Coretta and I were old enough to remember her. A gracious and kind lady, it was obvious even then that as a younger woman she had enjoyed a nearly perfect figure. Of African American and Irish lineage, she had a delicate beauty and was the quintessential lady—always patient, soft, and deferential.

Like the typical wife and homemaker of her generation, Grandmother McMurry mastered the domestic arts of sewing, cooking, childcare, gardening, and animal husbandry. When we knew her, she always had at least two lovely cats. With eight children to care for, making clothes and quilts was a necessity, but she continued to sew long after her children were grown. She used needlework as an outlet for her wonderful sense of creativity.

When she was not sewing or cooking, Grandmother McMurry worked in the yard. She had a passion for plants, especially flowering ones, and maintained a home filled inside and out with all varieties. Though she knew almost nothing of scientific gardening methods, the plants in and around her house responded to her touch and flourished under the same love and care that she gave us. Plants were so much a part of her life that in our memories she was often standing beside a flowering hydrangea, a row of zinnias, or a bed of phlox.

Martin McMurry, our grandfather, was the antithesis of his lovely and graceful wife. He was stern and unyielding; children feared him, and adults stood in awe of him. He was a man who exuded strength and authority simply by the manner in which he carried himself. Neighbors and strangers alike knew from his determined gait that he had a clear sense of purpose.

Born in 1862, Grandfather McMurry was the son of a slave woman and a white slaveholder. His mother was part African American and part Native American. His father, a white man, never acknowledged our grandfather in any way. Because of his rich racial blend, he had the skin color, hair texture, and facial features of a Caucasian, but those who expected to find in him a man aspiring to be white often found themselves the recipient of his more tempestuous side. Martin McMurry might have been light skinned, but he had the heart and soul of a proud black man. He and his wife taught their children, all of whom were light skinned, to love the race of their black ancestors. For members of the McMurry family, race was less a matter of genetics and more one of intentional, emotional cultural identification.

Throughout his life, Grandfather McMurry did his best to remain self-sufficient. An industrious and diligent man, he worked his 280-acre farm with only the help of his family. He could do everything from digging a well to making molasses. Innovative and untiring, he raised some of every kind of plant and animal that grew in the South. From goats to guinea fowl, scuppernongs to sugar cane, his farm was always full of surprises. He even grew his own tobacco, a rarity in Alabama. Of all his traits, Grandfather McMurry was best known as a wise and shrewd man. He had a reputation for being the most astute man in the community. White and black people alike sought his counsel. With an insatiable thirst for knowledge and a keen intuition, he had a unique understanding of the problems faced by his generation.

Born two years before slavery ended, Grandfather McMurry grew up in a southern society where blacks were intentionally denied educational opportunities. As a result, he attended school only one day. Instead of formal education, he taught himself to read, and when he was not busy with chores around the farm, he was usually reading. For him, reading was the key to a vast storehouse of information and knowledge to which no rule or law could prevent him access.

On Saturday afternoons while other people were fishing, shopping in town, or relaxing, Martin McMurry could be seen sitting on his front porch, poring over a book. And on Sunday afternoons, he could usually be found in the same position deeply absorbed in Bible study. He spent a lifetime studying Scripture. His library consisted almost entirely of Bibles and Biblical reference books. Among the laymen of his church he was considered the leading authority on Biblical questions.

Many African Americans of his generation had the same intense interest in reading and learning. Having been denied access to education for so long, they saw their personal freedom as inextricably tied to knowledge and enlightenment. They had witnessed firsthand the effects of ignorance and the intellectual and spiritual myopia that resulted, not just among their fellow slaves but among the white plantation owners as well. Liberated from the plantation culture, they had no intention of returning to it. Ignorance and lack of understanding were chains that could tie them to the past. Knowledge and understanding opened doors of opportunity for those of their race. They spent their lives working to ensure that they did not return to the life of servitude from which they had been set free.

Coretta took to heart Grandfather McMurry's interest in education and his understanding that knowledge was the key to social and economic freedom. She pursued her own education with diligence, then spent the remainder of her life educating others and opening doors of opportunity for them. Her belief in the importance of education took hold right there on Grandfather McMurry's farm as she observed the manner in which he conducted his life and the importance he placed on learning, improving himself, and trusting in God to see him through.

3

Perry County

Perry County, where Coretta was born, is located in the heart of Alabama's Black Belt region. Then, as now, the term Black Belt carried a double meaning. A dark strip of rich farmland that stretched across the center of the state, the area first acquired its name from the color of the soil. During the nineteenth century, the Black Belt was home to numerous cotton plantations. The land was worked by African slaves. As a result, the Black Belt was populated by a preponderance of African Americans, giving the term "Black Belt" its secondary meaning.[1]

After the Civil War, African Americans in Alabama participated in local, state, and national politics, voting in large numbers. They helped elect men of color to public offices at all levels. Perry County produced A. H. Curtis of Marion, one of the most outstanding black lawmakers of this period. He was elected to the Alabama state legislature in 1870 and later served on the Alabama State Board of Education. Through his efforts, the Alabama Colored University was opened in Marion in 1874 as part of Lincoln Normal School, which had begun in 1867. In the fall of 1875, Curtis was a Perry County delegate to the state convention that drafted a new Alabama constitution.[2]

Then, in 1901, white Democrats revolted against the changes brought by Reconstruction. They convened a state convention to write a new constitution, one designed to specifically disenfranchise blacks.[3] Using devices such as the poll tax, the so-called literacy test, and other racially motivated provisions, the new constitution led to the wholesale disfranchisement of blacks and brought black participation in Perry County politics to an end. As a result, during the first half of the twentieth century, the number of African American voters in the county dropped to inconsequential levels.

For most of the period between the end of the Civil War and the early twentieth century, Perry County's economy was based on farming and agriculture, and life continued in much the same fashion as it had during the days of slavery. Then, following World War I, northern timber companies brought sawmills to the area, creating new jobs and ready cash for all residents, both black and white. With virgin forests and sufficient manpower, sawmill owners prospered. Many local businesses did, also. Enterprising black businessmen benefited from the economic boom.

Erroneously expecting the good times to last, most people lived for the moment and made no provision for the future. That brief period of prosperity came to an end with the economic crash of 1929. During the Great Depression, everyone suffered, but the plight of those who did not own their homes was worse.

While the timber industry brought new prosperity to the region, it also created a new group of dependent workers. Something of an industrial tenant, a sawmill employee had a relationship to his employer that was comparable to that of the sharecropping farmer to his landlord. Though not held in chains, sawmill employees were nevertheless economically enslaved by the mill owners.

Most sawmill owners operated commissary stores that sold general merchandise. Through those stores, sawmill owners provided their laborers with food and clothing. Often they provided the house in which the employee lived. All of which employees paid for from their earnings. The employer kept the books and deducted the charges from the worker's wages. All too frequently the employee owed more than he earned. During the Great Depression, most workers never got out of debt.

In spite of tough economic circumstances, some African Americans found a way to thrive. For many years, the best-known black business in Perry County was Childs' Bakery. It was still there during Coretta's high school days. Established during Reconstruction and located in Marion's main shopping district, the Childs brothers' bakery had a virtual monopoly on the county's retail bread and pastry trade. As time passed, however, other merchants began to import bread from national bakeries, eventually underselling Childs'. In the late 1940s, the store went out of business.

Though most of the county's population was black, most of the land was owned by whites. In spite of advances offered by the timber industry, cotton was still king until long after World War II. The majority of blacks were tools of a plantation economy and were subject to its attendant evils—economic exploitation, political disfranchisement, and cultural deprivation—just as their forebears had been for centuries under slavery. However, with the mass migration of blacks to urban centers during World War II, the plantation economy was greatly disrupted. Some of the large farms that previously had been worked by black tenant farmers and sharecroppers lost much, if not all, of their labor force.

In the northern section of the county where Coretta and I grew up, African American families such as the Scotts, Tubbs, McMurrys, Smiths, and Osburns owned the land on which they lived. Our paternal and maternal great-grandparents, members of the generation liberated from slavery, acquired farms and worked hard to accumulate the capital necessary to operate them. Several owned farms of three hundred acres or more.[4]

Like the Founding Fathers who were concerned about life and liberty, black freedmen saw the ownership of land as the prerequisite to independence and middle-class status, and they were willing to struggle and sacrifice in order to acquire it for themselves and their families.

Of equal importance to the continued independence and freedom of blacks was their desire for education. African American property holders were more inclined to seek education—the means to real and lasting liberty—than those whose lives were more dependent on white landlords. And, although largely disfranchised until enactment of the Voting Rights Act of 1965, blacks in Perry County who owned their own land had a degree of economic independence and pride that their less-fortunate neighbors who were tenant farmers and sharecroppers could not enjoy. Before 1945, only the propertied class of blacks regularly sent their children to high school and college, often at great sacrifice. Incomes were small, families were large, and education was costly. Consequently, the number of blacks who finished high school was comparatively small, and only the determined made it through college.[5]

This was the tradition and culture into which Coretta Scott was born and the soil into which she was planted. Later in life, when Coretta spoke of bigotry and oppression, she did so from a deep well of experience that began on the day she was born. Yet, it was not a life that left her bitter or angry. Instead, she learned from the people around her that the only way she could fail was by giving in to the demands of oppression. She saw the misery and majesty of life in the people around her, and she understood the sacrifices freedom demanded. From the example of family and neighbors, she learned to draw energy and strength from the circumstances that would have held her down. When Coretta was born, Perry County was a miserable place for African Americans but a perfect place to cultivate a leader who would work to alleviate the misery in the lives of blacks across the nation.

II SEED

Still other seed fell on good soil. It came up, grew and produced a crop,
multiplying thirty, sixty, or even a hundred times.
—The Gospel According to Mark 4:8

4

Parents

Our mother, Bernice McMurry, was the youngest child in a family of eight children. A picture-book image of a farmer's daughter, she had large bones and heavy limbs. She had high cheekbones and a light but flushed complexion that reflected her father's Irish and Indian heritage. Her eyes were large, dark, and dewy. Her lips were thin, her nose was pointed, and her hair was long, straight, and black.

During her childhood, Bernice learned to do all the things that farm girls of that era did. She helped tend the family farm and cared for the farm animals, some of which became her pets. Her chief companion and playmate was her older brother Alonzo. Under his watchful eye and guiding hand, she engaged in what were normally considered boys' activities. She and Alonzo spent their days romping across the pasture, wrestling in the grass, and tending to their chores.

After studying at the local elementary school, several of Bernice's older siblings had attended boarding school at the Tuskegee Institute. The school, founded by Booker T. Washington, was located on the opposite side of the state. Bernice was not as fortunate as they. She completed all of the grades taught at the local Crossroads School, but that was the extent of her formal education. In 1921, Bernice married a young man from the community named Obie Scott. At the time of their marriage, Bernice was seventeen. Obie was twenty-two. A year later their first child, Eunice, who did not survive childhood, was born. I came along two years later, when Mother was twenty. She was twenty-two when Coretta was born and twenty-five when she gave birth to Obie Leonard, her youngest child and only son. We were all born at home.

For childbirths, most people in our community used the help of an older woman who had experience in delivering babies. We referred to her as a midwife, but she had no formal training, just years of experience helping to bring babies into the world. Our great-grandmother Delia Scott was the midwife when Coretta and I were born. People often think of slavery and the plantation life as something in a history book, a time long ago and far away. When Coretta and I were delivered from our mother's body, the hands that first held us were the hands of a woman who was born a slave.

Our parents were young and permitted us freedom of expression, which often made them seem more like a big sister and big brother than adults. Their world and ours were not that far apart. Although we had reverence for their authority, we honored and respected them without the fear many children have of their elders. Our parents encouraged us to pursue whatever interests captured our minds and never let Coretta or me avoid something simply because we were girls. Dad used to tell us, "You can do anything anyone else can do." These were more than mere words; our parents modeled that attitude in their lifestyle.

In the 1920s, Mother became the first black woman in our community to drive a car. Later, she learned to operate a truck. At the same time, she taught herself the art of barbering and assisted Dad in his part-time barbershop, which he operated in our home. For many years, a rumor circulated that she hauled lumber, too, driving a heavy trailer truck. She seemed to enjoy the cachet that rumor created and did little to quell it. In reality, she was never quite able to drive a lumber truck, though I think she might have tried on several occasions. However, for three years while her two younger children were still in high school, she did drive a school bus, making the thirty-mile round-trip twice each day. Later, when Dad opened a general merchandise store, she helped operate that, too. Our parents encouraged us to pursue our dreams without preconceived limitations.

Though Mother and Dad worked side by side, Mother was a person in her own right. She was an active churchwoman who made her strongest contribution in the area of music. Blessed with a good, clear soprano voice, she was a soloist in the Mt. Tabor Church choir. Musically inclined from an early age, she was not formally trained until the age of thirty when she fulfilled a lifelong dream of studying the piano. In time, she achieved enough proficiency to play simple hymns during church services. She continued to study and eventually gained the confidence to play for the church adult choir, a position she held for a number of years.

Raising three children in an increasingly complex society, Mother's attention was divided in many different directions. Children, home life, and church took most of her energy and limited her opportunity to pursue other interests. She loved gardening but never gave it the attention needed to achieve the kind of success her mother had enjoyed. A member of the Eastern Star, she was the Worthy Matron of her chapter for many years, a position that reflected the confidence and respect others in the community had for her. She attended meetings of the Perry County Civic League, was active in a women's farm club, and was a member of the Matron's Social and Literacy Federated Club of Marion.

Our father had a temperament much like our mother; together they made a good pair. They grew up in the same community, had similar backgrounds, and were reared under comparable economic and social conditions. The Scott and McMurry families had lived in the northern end of Perry County since the end of slavery. Mother and Dad grew up knowing each other.

While many other black children experienced daily reminders of their family's economic dependence on remnants of the southern white plantation system, our parents grew up as children of independent black farmers. Mother and Dad were surrounded by people who instilled in them a sense of confidence and a feeling that they could compete on a comparable basis with whites. Growing up as they did, without the necessity of showing deference to white people, our parents learned to believe in themselves, their own worth, and their ability to determine their own destiny.

As a boy, Dad was popular among his peers. Most of his male counterparts wanted to be his friend. Girls in the neighborhood liked him, too. At the same time, he had an easy rapport with older people. Adults were impressed by the fact that he was never satisfied doing only what was required. Second place was never good enough for him. He wanted to be first, and he worked hard to make it happen. That attitude was most notable in school where he excelled academically and ranked near the top of his class.

When he completed classes at the local elementary school, his teacher asked if he could be given the opportunity to obtain further schooling. That request presented a problem. If Dad were to continue his education, he would have to go away to boarding school. The nearest high school for blacks was Lincoln School, a private school in Marion.

At the time, the county provided no free education for blacks beyond the sixth grade. Perry County Training School at Uniontown, the county's sole black high school, was not opened until 1925.[1] Even then, many of Perry County's black students did not live close enough to reach it. Black children were not bused to and from school until the 1940s. To attend high school, families had to either transport their children each day or provide a place for them to stay during the week, both of which involved inconveniences and additional expenses. Because of that, high school education was not available to most black children in the county.[2]

In spite of the obstacles, Grandfather Scott decided to make the sacrifice and sent Dad to Lincoln. The school had dormitories for students in those days, but they found a room for him with a family near the school. It was cheaper than the accommodations on campus.

As an eager student, Dad was grateful for the privilege of continuing his education and felt fortunate to attend a good school like Lincoln. Its excellent campus, classrooms, and faculty, composed largely of white women from the North, made it an ideal place to study.[3] Dad's teachers were impressed with his scholastic ability, especially his work in mathematics.

Unfortunately, Grandfather Scott was unable to send Dad back to Lincoln for a second year. Tuition and fees, plus room and board, were more than the family could spend on one child. Other children in the family also needed attention. After a single year at Lincoln, Dad's formal education came to an end.

Though disappointed, Dad did not give up. Instead, he went to work on his father's farm and set about helping his sisters and brothers. He stayed on the farm until 1919, when he went to work as a fireman in the community's first sawmill. Taking his earnings from his job home, Dad gave it all to his father to help the family survive.

As a man destined to earn a livelihood working with his hands, Dad quickly realized that achieving economic success required both brains and brawn. He learned from hard work at the mill that a man who depended solely on muscle power would never get anywhere in American society. Still, the jobs available to him required physical labor. To get ahead, he would have to work smart.

5

A Black Man in a White Man's World

With a willingness to work and a desire to do so in the most productive manner, Dad began to look for ways to supplement his income as a sawmill employee. By then he and Mother were married, and their first child was on the way. Extra income was a necessity, not a luxury.

Before long, he tried his hand at barbering. Back then, most people who were interested in cutting hair learned the trade by practicing on the heads of their neighbors. Using a pair of hand clippers, Dad found a friend willing to let him try and started to work. The business was small at first but as word spread around the community, he soon had more customers than he could handle. We were never sure whether they came for the haircuts or the conversation, but they always found a way to pay and that was what mattered. Before long, he was working several nights each week and on weekends. Many Sunday mornings he cut the hair of men who stopped by on their way to church. As the barbering business grew, Mother learned to cut men's hair and worked with him.

A few years later, Dad made one of the riskiest decisions of his life. It turned out to be one of the smartest. After years of unloading trucks at the mill, he decided to give up his job as a sawmill employee and work for himself hauling logs and lumber. To do that, he had to purchase his own truck, which meant finding someone who would finance the transaction and allow him to pay for it over time. Hauling logs and lumber was hard and hazardous work, but trucking was a lucrative business. Drivers who delivered to the mill made a good living, and they worked for themselves. Dad liked the idea of being his own boss.

Embarking on his first real business venture, he bought a truck and began delivering logs to the sawmill where he had previously worked as an employee. He was the only black driver-owner at that sawmill. Some of the white drivers made derogatory comments about him, but through the 1920s no one seemed unduly concerned. Jobs were plentiful then, and Dad did his best to avoid causing trouble.

Like many other people, we enjoyed the 1920s. Mother and Dad bought a Victrola record player and filled the house with music. During our most impressionable years, Coretta and I were introduced to the voice of Bessie Smith.[1] This period was when they bought our first car, too; it was a Baby Overland that Mother learned to drive.[2] Like many women of that era, Mother had long hair that hung to her waist, but as times changed, she changed with them and cut her hair for the first time. It seems rather tame now, but those were dramatic changes for our community—a young couple with a fast car and a wife with short hair. Later in life, neither Coretta nor I cared much for automobiles, but music and drama stayed with us. I concentrated on theatre. Coretta was captivated by music.

The Roaring Twenties brought a time of lighthearted prosperity and joy, yet Mother harbored feelings of discontent. Her four sisters had left home and gone to live in large cities. Three of them lived in Michigan. She often thought and spoke of moving north. Like all southern blacks, she had been led to believe that the northern section of the United States was a haven of freedom and opportunity. Above all else, she wanted her children to obtain a good education, and she felt it would be easier for us to do that in the North.

Doubtless, too, there were other good reasons why Mother considered leaving Alabama. Segregation was the law, and whites were becoming more heavy-handed in enforcing it. Opportunities for blacks to advance socially and economically were all but nonexistent. Any place that offered us a chance to grow and expand was a place that interested her.

After months of discussion, she eventually succeeded in convincing Dad that a man with his intelligence and initiative should go north where, she thought, he would encounter less discrimination and find greater opportunities. He was aware of the injustices that ambitious blacks in the South encountered when competing with whites in the same market for the same jobs. He experienced it every day. In the segregated society of the South, blacks, for the most part, competed with other blacks for jobs. Blacks of little ambition did not experience as many difficulties as those who, like Dad, were highly intelligent and aspired to succeed beyond their assigned station in life. Dad wanted the same opportunity to climb the economic ladder as anyone else. He wanted to compete as a man, not merely as a black man. Finally, after endless conversations on the topic, he agreed to give the North a try.

In the fall of 1929, Dad heard rumblings of an impending economic catastrophe, but like many others he ignored the early warnings. He parked his truck at the house and went to Detroit. This time his adventurous spirit brought disappointment. Shortly after he arrived, the nation was plunged into an economic depression. For months he walked the streets looking for work. The only job he found was shoveling snow. Like most other large cities, Detroit had thousands of unemployed workers and very few new jobs. With a family depending on him for support, Dad did not have time to wait for the economic situation to improve and soon returned to Alabama.

Back home in Perry County, a few jobs were available, but wages were low. Hard times echoed across the countryside. Dad was offered a job hauling lumber for a large company in one of the adjoining counties. He readily accepted.

A year later Dad needed to replace his truck. Once again, he needed a way to finance the purchase. A plantation owner we knew as Mr. Belknap agreed to buy the truck for Dad with the understanding that Dad would make payments on it out of his weekly earnings.[3] Instead of paying Dad for hauling timber to the mill, the mill owners sent their payments to Mr. Belknap. He, in turn, deducted the amount due for payment on the truck from the mill's checks and gave Dad the balance.

In time, Dad needed a trailer. Mr. Belknap was happy to supply that as well under the same arrangement. In addition, Dad purchased gasoline, oil, staple food items, and other household goods from Mr. Belknap's general store. As wages were low and there was not a great demand for lumber during the Depression years, Dad's earnings were small. Starting out in debt, it was easier to fall further behind than to get ahead, and that's what happened. For seven years he ended each week owing more to Mr. Belknap than he did the week before. His only consolation was the knowledge that everyone he knew was suffering through the same circumstances. Despite the precarious economic situation, our family was better off than most other families in our community.

All of Dad's earnings on his regular job went to his creditor, but having ingenuity and a truck, he was able to pick up extra money on the side. On Saturdays and other days when he was not hauling lumber, he hauled cross-ties, collected and sold scrap iron, transported furniture and other belongings for people who were moving, and made trips to town for those who did not have their own means of transportation. The money he earned from those extra jobs made a big difference in our lifestyle.

In 1938, after years of struggle, Dad was approaching the day when he would be out of debt. Then, he and Mr. Belknap were involved in a terrible accident. Rounding a curve from opposite directions, Dad in his truck and Mr. Belknap in his car, they crashed headlong into each other. Both the car and truck were damaged. Dad was not hurt, but Mr. Belknap was injured. Though there was some question as to who was responsible, Dad agreed to pay $1,000 as the cost of the accident. Mr. Belknap added that amount to what Dad already owed, which delayed his plan for financial freedom.

As the Great Depression continued to take its toll on Perry County's economy, jobs became scarce. Harassment from white truck drivers increased. Dad's presence at the lumberyard was a threat to the status quo. More jobs would be available to whites if he were not around. A black competitor, when well-paying jobs were scarce, was more than they could take. To make matters worse, Dad hauled more lumber per load and more loads per day than they did. When demand for lumber allowed it, Dad often left home around three o'clock in the morning and seldom returned before nine or ten at night. While other truckers hauled three thousand board feet per load, Dad hauled four and five thousand. If they hauled three loads per day, Dad hauled five. Truckers' pay was based on the number of board feet of lumber hauled. The more they hauled, the greater their earnings. That was all the motivation Dad needed to excel. The mill foremen soon found that Dad counted his own lumber accurately and honestly, and before long they accepted his calculations without bothering to check the count themselves.

As harassment on the job began to rise, rumors circulated that if Obie Scott did not quit hauling lumber, the white people were going to kill him. They also began saying he was a reckless driver. One white woman said that she had to drive her car into a ditch to get out of the way of his truck. Dad had friends across the county who heard the rumors and warned him, but he kept driving, hauling as many loads each day as the sawmill allowed.

When rumors proved ineffective to deter him, white drivers made actual threats on his life. For a while they told him that if he returned to the lumberyard, he would be killed. Dad knew he was not doing anything wrong, so he ignored them and each day returned to the job. When threats didn't work, the white drivers became more belligerent and aggressive.

One day, as Dad was hauling a load of lumber, a group of them drove alongside him in their car. Armed with shotguns, they forced him to stop. Guns drawn, they sprang from the car and ordered him out of his truck. Dad's two helpers bailed out of the cab through the door on the opposite side of the truck and ran into the woods, leaving him to face his assailants alone. Unfazed, Dad slowly climbed from the truck. They grabbed him by the shoulder and shoved him toward the car. Dad started calmly in that direction. All the while, the white men were cursing and making threats against him, assuring him they had come to take his life.

When he reached their car, Dad turned to the man who had ordered him from the truck and looked him in the eye. Calmly and in an even, measured tone he asked what he had done to offend them that would require him to pay with his life. Dad's simple question sparked a discussion that soon became a vigorous verbal exchange. As the conversation continued, the men began to argue point after point. Soon, the white men who had been riding in the car lost enthusiasm for the confrontation. In the end, they let Dad go but warned him to stay away from the lumberyard.

Despite being disturbed by what had happened, Dad was not intimidated in the least. The following day he informed the owners of the company about the trouble. They were certain the threats were meant only to scare Dad away and assured him that if he returned to the lumberyard, he would not be harmed. Dad knew his assailants better than the company owners, and he knew the men who had attacked him were capable of doing almost anything. But he braced himself and went back to the woods for a second load to take to the lumberyard.

True to their word, a few days later the white drivers staged a repeat performance of the earlier incident, making more violent threats. For a second time Dad reported his trouble to the company owners. This time, they were forced to take action. Dad hauled more lumber than anyone else on the job. He was the last trucker company officials wanted to lose.

To alleviate the trouble, they sent Dad to haul from a different location. He worked there by himself, hauling as much lumber as his truck could carry. Dad's refusal to cower or retreat in the face of threats and challenges, though difficult at first, was well rewarded. Working alone, he was able to haul as many loads as he wanted, which meant more income.

Tensions between Dad and the white truckers eased, but rumors of Dad's "uppityness"—a slang expression indicating he was living beyond his station—persisted until the war years. Then, more serious national issues clouded the personal and localized tensions of racial relations. The economy again thrived and competition for jobs became less pronounced.

White truck drivers were not the only ones who gave Dad trouble. Traveling around Perry and surrounding counties, Dad had several skirmishes with the law. Several times while trying to establish himself as a truck driver, he was forced to pay fines for traffic violations that were not clear-cut breaches of the law. White policemen, like white truck drivers, seemed determined to break his spirit. Although Dad was not a man to bring his problems home to his family, he did not deliberately hide things from us either. He regularly told Mother about the difficulties he encountered during conversations that Coretta and I often overheard.

After his encounters with the white drivers, one important discussion Mother and Dad had was about whether Dad should carry a pistol in the glove compartment of his truck. Although Dad bought the pistol and for a while carried it, he never used it. He and Mother decided that one man with a pistol could never be equal to an armed mob bent on killing him. Consequently Dad resorted to the most effective weapon—nonviolent direct action, though he did not call it that. He used to say, "If you look a white man in the eye, he won't harm you." It was a theory that worked for him, but one that caused his young children considerable concern.

As children, Coretta, Obie Leonard, and I learned to live with uncertainty. For most of our childhood, we never knew whether our father would return alive from his job. Each night we waited up to eat supper with him, knowing he might not come home. Fortunately for us, our father always returned home, though often it was so late that we already had fallen asleep. Sometimes on those lonely nights, we saw Mother wiping tears from her eyes, trying her best to keep us from noticing.

6

Opposition

In the early 1940s, Dad finally paid off his debts to Mr. Belknap. At the same time, he began operating a taxi service in the nearby town of Greensboro, twenty miles from our home. With a winsome personality, he was soon the busiest black cab driver in town. Because he gave the other black cab drivers strong competition, they supported the local police and highway patrolmen in an effort to drive him out of town. For several months, he received traffic citations for the slightest, and sometimes imaginary, violations.

As the taxi business grew, Dad purchased a new car. Taxis were regulated by the state and required a different license plate from those for personal use. Dad inquired at the highway patrol office in Greensboro to make sure his new car was properly licensed for taxi service. The patrol chief in Greensboro told Dad he could write to Montgomery to transfer the for hire license from the old cab to the new one. A few days later, Dad received a reply from Montgomery telling him how to effect the change. On that very day, a Greensboro policeman noticed the new cab parked outside an African American barber shop without the For Hire sign showing. The officer called Dad out of the barber shop and began to berate him for this. Dad started to explain, "The law in Montgomery wrote me that I should—"

The patrolman would not let him finish. He blurted out, "Damn the law in Montgomery. I'm the law here!"

And with that he struck Dad with a blow that knocked him unconscious. When Dad regained consciousness, he was lying on the sidewalk with the patrolman standing over him, kicking him, and telling him to get up. After the patrolman left, Dad's friends helped him to his feet and urged him to leave town immediately. Dad listened, but he refused to go home until his usual time.

A few days later the patrolman brought charges against Dad in court. When the court date arrived, Dad and the patrolman appeared before the judge. Already aware of what had taken place, the judge declared, "Obie Scott works hard, pays his debts, and is law abiding. Case dismissed."

Dad walked away feeling like a winner. He continued to operate his taxi in the town until some years later when he took on other responsibilities.

For Dad, the lean years of the 1930s were followed by the green years of the 1940s. With the beginning of World War II, the demand for lumber increased. Dad added a second truck and later a third. With a crew of six men and three trailer trucks, Dad could keep a small mill operating at full capacity.

In 1946, he left Greensboro Lumber Company to haul for Akron Lumber Company, which was owned by a Jewish man from up north. In Dad's words, the owner was "a real friend to the colored man. I learned to like him a whole lot." Seeing my father's great potential for business, he encouraged Dad to establish his own sawmill. He would be just as happy buying lumber from a black sawmill operator as he was getting it from white operators. Since Dad owned his trucks, he could haul his own lumber and do his own logging.

Finally, it seemed Obie Scott, the grandson of a slave who lived in the backwoods of Alabama, was ready to make the big leap to owning an entire mill operation. With quiet determination, he set up a mill. Because no black sawmill operator was available to oversee the day-to-day work, Dad hired a white man for the job. That was more than whites in Perry County could take. A black sawmill owner was difficult for them to accept, but a black owner employing a white operator was more than most would tolerate.

All went well for the first few weeks. Then one day the operator took Dad aside and tried to persuade Dad to sell the sawmill to him. Dad refused, but the operator persisted. When Dad still refused, the operator ended the conversation with the admonition, "If you don't sell it to me, it won't ever do you no good." Dad replied that he had no intention of selling the mill.

On the following Sunday afternoon, under mysterious circumstances, the sawmill burned to the ground. With all the indications of an inside job—a watchman was supposed to be on duty to guard against just such an occurrence—the fire was almost certainly the result of arson.

Dad reacted to the destruction of his sawmill as he always had to acts of bigotry leveled against him. The anguish, frustration, and defeat he felt was only temporary. He never permitted those feelings to destroy his faith in himself or of the ultimate triumph of good over evil. Either he would replace the sawmill or try something else. When black men of his generation sang, "There's a better day a-coming, hallelujah!" they were singing out of experience and from a desire that made those words a prayer.

After taking a few days to think about it, Dad contacted the company from which he had purchased the sawmill. They agreed to replace it, and Dad decided to give it another try. Now he had to find an operator. From talking with people in the community, he learned that David Billingsley, a black man from Marion, was available. Billingsley was a good sawmill operator and had years of experience. Dad approached Billingsley about the job, and Billingsley agreed to do it. His enthusiasm for the task lifted Dad's spirits, and he began making plans to restart the mill.

Before long, news of the plans to rebuild the mill reached the former operator. Two days before the saws were scheduled to start turning, he came to Dad, a bit intoxicated, and told Dad that if he started the sawmill again, he would have the same kind of trouble he had before. Dad knew he faced daunting circumstances.

Although Dad was certain the mill had been destroyed by the operator, he had no way of proving it. The sheriff's office was reluctant to investigate harassment of blacks and even less inclined when the accused was a white man. As Dad weighed his options, he knew the harassment would continue and there was no way to stop it. More than that, his family might be at risk. After assessing the situation, Dad came to the conclusion that the losses he would suffer would outweigh the gains. So he decided to let the sawmill go. Besides, he already had another business venture in mind.

A few months after the sawmill was destroyed, Dad opened a small grocery store in a building next to our home. To us it seemed as though customers were waiting outside before the shelves were stocked. As soon as he put up the Open for Business sign, they filled the store. Within a year Mother and Dad were convinced that a general merchandise store was a business that would do well in our location, and they began making plans for expansion. A new building and additional supplies, including gasoline, oil, and automobile accessories attracted larger numbers of customers.

The grocery business was an instant success, but it had its challenges, not the least of which was the problem of credit. Ordinarily, the owner of a large country store could not demand cash sales for all purchases. When the proprietor was a generous person like Obie Scott, a man who found it impossible to turn away anyone who needed food for his family, unpaid accounts piled up. Dad never let it bother him. He and Mother did most of the work themselves, and with a large volume of customers, they kept the business operating at a profit while helping those in need. In addition, Dad still had his lumber trucks, which he kept in operation every day.

In the 1950s, changes in the timber industry made it necessary for most truckers in the industry to shift from hauling lumber to hauling pulpwood. The change increased the responsibilities of the truckers who now had to locate, cut, and haul the pulpwood they took to the mill. It was a time-consuming operation that required the work of several men. Hauling pulpwood and operating the store kept Dad busy sixteen hours a day, six days a week.

Yet, like Mother, Dad managed to find time for church, fraternal, and civic responsibilities. An ardent church member, he also was a Mason and served on committees for civic improvement. Dad's obligations to his church came first. He was the church's chief fund-raiser and joyously contributed his time and means to what he considered the most important institution in the world.

Dad was a success by any American standard. Yet material gain for its own sake was not his primary motivation. Generosity was the central ingredient in his personality. He always said, "God blesses us in order that we may be a blessing to others." If there was anyone who ever lived by the dictum, "You have what you give. Bread cast upon the water returns," it was Obie Scott.

Dad's vitality and vigor came from the philosophy by which he lived and the habits he followed from his youth. He ate wholesome foods in moderate amounts and stayed away from alcoholic beverages. Instead, he drank water, and plenty of it. In between meals, when he was home, he would often drink a glass of fresh buttermilk. During the summer months, he enjoyed cool lemonade. He worked sixteen hours a day most of his life and had no major illnesses. He died shortly before his hundredth birthday.

The expression that Dad used most often was, "I've been lucky." And indeed he was blessed. The grandson of a former slave, he lived to see his state transformed from a plantation society into one in which black people could freely enter any establishment they liked—and do so through the front door. Children of every color had access to education, and though the quality might not be as good as one would like, they could not be turned away because of their color or ethnic origin. The machinery of government could no longer be used to enforce the racist policies Dad had endured.

On March 26, 1965, Dad joined Coretta and Martin for a march that ended in Montgomery. There, he sat on the platform with them as Martin addressed a crowd of over fifty thousand people, black and white. Seeing that crowd and hearing that speech, Dad caught a glimpse of America's true potential. For the first time, he saw the possibility that America could become one nation under God. Filled with joy and gratitude, he said, "This is the greatest day in the whole history of America."

This was the family from which Coretta sprang. Born into a dual society where two worlds lived side by side in an uneasy and often tumultuous existence, she had the opportunity to see firsthand the complete spectrum of social relations—white landed aristocracy and black and white tenant farmers, sharecroppers, and sawmill workers. Through the efforts of our parents and grandparents, she had the advantage of spending her formative years immersed in rich diversity from the most die-hard conservatism to the most altruistic idealism. Planted in fertile soil and blessed to have come from strong and hardy stock, she was well on her way to changing the world before she ever set foot out of our house.

Coretta and my mother's side of the family, the McMurry's. Our mother, Bernice McMurry, is sitting in our grandmother Molly McMurry's lap. Our grandfather Martin McMurray is seated next to Molly, c. 1904. Courtesy of the Coretta Scott King Estate.

Coretta and my father's store and gas station in Marion, Alabama, c. 1988. Courtesy of the Coretta Scott King Estate.

Taken in June 1927, shortly after Coretta was born. Coretta is sitting in mother's lap, and I'm standing next to them. Courtesy of the Coretta Scott King Estate.

Coretta's mentors and lifelong friends, Cecil and Fran Thomas in their early days at Lincoln School, c.1942. Courtesy of the Edythe Scott Bagley Estate.

JUDSON COLLEGE
Established 1838
MARION, ALABAMA

Office of the President

February 11, 1943

Mr. Cecil Thomas
Lincoln Normal School
Marion, Alabama

My dear Mr. Thomas:

It was our pleasure recently to have the
Little Chorus of the Lincoln School render a
special concert in the Judson auditorium. This
concert was of the highest order, and met with
a most enthusiastic reception on the part of all
of our students, administration, and faculty. I
can recommend the chorus most heartily to churches
or organizations desiring an outstanding musical
attraction of this type.

Most sincerely yours,

Leroy R. Priest, President

Letter from the President of Judson College in Marion, Alabama, to Cecil Thomas of
Lincoln School praising the Lincoln Chorus for its performance at Judson College,
February 1943. Courtesy of the Coretta Scott King Estate.

From left to right: Coretta (right) and me (left) with Fran Thomas, our Lincoln School
mentor, c.1942. Courtesy of the Coretta Scott King Estate.

Coretta (right) with unidentified classmates at their Lincoln School graduation in 1945.
Courtesy of the Coretta Scott King Estate.

Coretta enjoying a leisurely moment biking during her early Antioch days, c. 1948.
Courtesy of the Coretta Scott King Estate.

Coretta with college boyfriend Bob Madison, c. 1947. Courtesy of the Coretta Scott King Estate.

Coretta in the home of Mr. and Mrs. Elmser Lawson, the Scott sister's "adopted" family while in school at Antioch College. Courtesy of the Coretta Scott King Estate.

Coretta with our brother, Obie Leonard, at the Lawson's house during his visit with Coretta at Antioch College. Courtesy of the Coretta Scott King Estate.

Martin and Coretta share a special moment during their courtship, c.1953. Courtesy of the Coretta Scott King Estate.

Coretta and Martin with their wedding party at our parent's home in Heiberger, Alabama, on June 18,1953. Courtesy of the Coretta Scott King Estate.

Coretta in recital in 1956 at Dexter Avenue Baptist Church in Montgomery where Martin pastored from 1954–60. Courtesy of the Coretta Scott King Estate.

THE USHER BOARDS
AND THE
YOUNG MATRONS COUNCIL
OF

Dexter Avenue Baptist Church

PRESENT

CORETTA SCOTT KING
SOPRANO

In Recital

MINNIE KIMBROUGH SCOTT
ACCOMPANIST

MONTGOMERY, ALABAMA

Sunday, September 30, 1956 — 5:30 P.M.

Rev. M. L. King, Jr. _____*Pastor*
Mr. L. W. Smiley _____*Chairman*
Mrs. Norman Walton _____*Co-Chairman*
Mr. R. D. Nesbitt _____*Advisor*

Program from Coretta's recital at Dexter Avenue Baptist Church, September 30, 1956.
Courtesy of the Coretta Scott King Estate.

Enjoying a moment after one of Coretta's concerts. From left to right: me; Martin's sister, Christine King Farris; Coretta; and an unidentified woman. Courtesy of the Coretta Scott King Estate.

Family picture at their Johnson Avenue home in Atlanta. From left to right: Yolanda, Coretta with Bernice in lap, Martin holding Dexter, and Martin III, c. 1963. Courtesy of the Coretta Scott King Estate.

SOUTHERN
CHRISTIAN
LEADERSHIP
CONFERENCE

Presents

CORETTA SCOTT KING, *Soprano*

Accompanied by JONATHAN BRICE

in

A 'Freedom Concert'

Also Appearing

LEON BIBB, Folk Singer

At

TOWN HALL—113 West 43rd St., N.Y.

✦

Sunday, November 15th—5:30 P.M.

CORETTA SCOTT KING, Soprano
(Mrs. Martin Luther King)

Mrs. King, wife of the internationally famous civil rights leader, Dr. Martin Luther King, Jr. who recently was awarded the 1964 Nobel Peace Prize, tells a moving and beautiful story of the "Freedom Struggle" since the days of the Montgomery Bus Boycott to the present. At the side of her husband since those early days, few persons know the full story better. Her telling of that story is done in song and narration.

Tickets are available:

Southern Christian Leadership Conference
312 West 125th Street, N. Y. — Telephone UN 6-2000

Box Office — Town Hall
113 West 43rd Street, N. Y. — Telephone JU 2-4536

Southern Christian Leadership Conference
Office of Louis & Rowe
200 West 57th Street, N. Y. — Telephone CI 7-3136

HARYOU-ACT, INC. (Both Offices)
180 West 135th Street and 179 West 137th Street
Telephone: AU 6-4100, AU 6-1100

New White Rock Baptist Church
600 West 153rd Street, N. Y. — Telephone WA 6-7666

PLEASE MAKE ALL CHECKS AND MONEY ORDERS PAYABLE TO: **FREEDOM CONCERT**, Mrs. Marian Logan, Treasurer.

Price Range of Tickets **$5.00 — $10.00** and **$25.00.** Boxes **$150.00** (six seats at $25.00 each)

Student Tickets:
$2.50
Available at S.C.L.C. office — 312 West 125th St.

Proceeds:
S.C.L.C. and Goodman, Chaney, Schwerner Memorial Center,
Meridian, Mississippi

Program from Coretta's concert at Town Hall in New York City, November 15, 1964.
Courtesy of the Coretta Scott King Estate.

Above: Coretta
helping Martin
get dressed for the
Nobel Peace Prize
Ceremony in Oslo,
Norway, December
1964. Courtesy of the
Coretta Scott King
Estate.

Left: Coretta holding
the resolution and
Martin displaying the
Nobel Peace Medal
while posing for a
picture with the King
family during the
Nobel Peace Prize
ceremony weekend,
December 1964.
Courtesy of the
Coretta Scott King
Estate.

Coretta joins Martin for the third Selma-to-Montgomery march with James Bevel (far right front), March 1, 1965. Courtesy of the Coretta Scott King Estate.

UNITED WORKERS FOR CHICAGO

present

Coretta Scott King

FREEDOM CONCERT

MRS. MARTIN LUTHER KING, JR

3:00PM SUNDAY
OCTOBER 16, 1966

DUNBAR HIGH SCHOOL
3000 SOUTH PARKWAY

Notice for Coretta's concert in Chicago, October 16, 1966. Courtesy of the Coretta Scott King Estate.

Coretta and Martin at home in Atlanta celebrating the birthday of Dora McDonald, Martin's secretary. Front row from left to right: Dora with Dexter in her lap and Bernice sitting; back row from left to right: Coretta, Martin III, and Martin, c.1966. Courtesy of the Coretta Scott King Estate.

Memphis City Hall on Monday, April 8, 1968, the day before Martin's funeral. From left to right: unknown gentleman, Rev. Bernard Lee, Rev. Ralph D. Abernathy Sr., Coretta, Yolanda, and Harry Belafonte. Courtesy of the Coretta Scott King Estate.

Coretta with Robert and Ethel Kennedy at the King home in Atlanta after Martin's funeral on April 9, 1968. Courtesy of the Coretta Scott King Estate.

III BUD

The most beautiful rose is one hardly more than a bud wherein the pangs
and ecstasies of desire are working for larger and finer growth.
—Carl Sandburg

7

Crossroads School

Coretta was born on April 27, 1927. As proud parents, Mother and Dad set about selecting a suitable name for her. With what must have been prophetic insight, they named her after two women from Dad's side of the family—his mother Cora and an aunt named Etta. They combined the two names and decided upon the name Coretta.

This method of naming children was widely practiced among African Americans of our generation. An expression of something deep in the psyche of the early twentieth century black, it was an attempt to remember those who had gone before us and a reminder that what we attained was attributable to their sacrifices. Names like Velberta, Mattiwilda, Leontyne, and Margarella were derived in a similar manner. In addition to showing deference to older relatives, the sound of those names reflected the poetic soul of the African American—and an ability to create something new out of existing forms. Names were important, and they had a way of taking on added significance when they were reminiscent of our forebears.

Coretta was the strong-willed, free-thinking granddaughter of Cora Scott, an imperious and energetic woman, and the serenely beautiful Molly McMurry. An unusual mixture of strength and serenity, Coretta combined in her personality the temperament of both women.

As a toddler, Coretta was always busy, carrying buckets, bags, and boxes filled with whatever she could find. Often they seemed much too heavy for such a small person, but somehow she managed to move them around the yard. She loved Grandfather Scott and followed him to the fields whenever Mother allowed. She insisted that he permit her to help him chop cotton and hoe the corn. Physically, Coretta was a beautiful blending of our parents. She was a hardy youngster, with a symmetrical face, flawless olive brown complexion, pug nose, thin lips, and long, thick, wavy black hair.

Our mother believed that a child's formal education should begin sooner rather than later. Consequently, she enrolled each of us in school after our fifth birthday. I think she would have enrolled us earlier, but the school building was located three miles from our house. We had to be old enough to walk there and back by ourselves every day.

The school in our community was called Crossroads School, which derived its name from the intersection where it stood. That was the school Coretta and I attended. When Coretta began there at the age of five, she was physically developed enough to withstand the rigors of the walk to school and the long day in class, but intellectually, she was not quite ready. That became evident during her first year.

At the time, children spent their first year in a grade called primer. Unlike kindergarten, primer activities were comparable to those of the first-grade level today. During the primer year, the teacher's objective was to help the child develop visual and auditory discrimination to a point that enabled her to read. Normally, by the time a child finished the year, she would have mastered the primer reader and learned to write and count.

As the year began, Coretta had great difficulty learning to read. Mother and Dad worked with her at night, reviewing each day's lesson. With their help, she performed acceptably at home. But by the time she reached class the following day, she had forgotten everything she had learned the night before. This persisted throughout most of that first year. Then, rather suddenly, everything clicked in place. When she was about six years old, she began to read and understand numerical concepts and relationships. By the end of the first grade, her rate of learning was so rapid that her teacher permitted her to skip second grade.

Crossroads School was a Rosenwald School. Construction of the building was financed by the Julius Rosenwald Fund, founded by the part-owner of Sears, Roebuck. Established in 1917, the Rosenwald Fund constructed rural schools for black children in the South. The actual work of erecting the structure was performed by parents from the community under the supervision of a local carpenter. Parents also served as trustees with responsibility for maintaining the building. Our grandfather, Jeff Scott, was chairman of the board. With the help of the Rosenwald Fund and the interest of the community, Crossroads School was somewhat more comfortable, functional, and aesthetically appealing than rural schools for blacks in our area that had been built solely with public funds.

A two-teacher school when we attended, it had been constructed as a single classroom with a stage at one end. There were two rooms for storage and large windows that allowed natural light to enter from the right side of the building. Later, by partitioning the single room, the school was divided into two classrooms; one was used for the grammar grades, the other for the primary department. In a time when schools for black children were routinely unpainted, Crossroads School was painted inside and out. Though sparsely furnished with blackboards constituting the bulk of the educational equipment, the teachers were diligent, resourceful, and committed to the task of educating children.

Because of their commitment to education and desire to foster lifelong learning habits in their students, our teachers achieved amazing results. That they did so in a system created by whites for the purpose of reinforcing mediocrity among blacks made their work all the more remarkable. While the school term for white children in the county was nine months in length, ours was five. White children were bused to school. Black children walked, which meant most African American children who lived more than four or five miles from the school had poor attendance records. At Crossroads, the total enrollment was a little over one hundred students. The average daily attendance was approximately seventy-five to eighty.

In elementary school, Coretta was an earnest and excellent student. She went through the six grades as the brightest child in her class. She enjoyed singing and often sang or recited poems in school programs. Singing and dramatic reading followed her throughout her life and became an integral part of her later work. Both in and out of school, Coretta received the admiration of friends, neighbors, and relatives. To all except her rivals, she was an adorable child.

During those elementary years, she was a tomboy and liked to run, jump, and climb. She also was a fighter who believed in striking first. Until the time she entered high school, Coretta had an uncontrollable temper. Not only would she attack Obie Leonard and me with anything at hand, she found her chief antagonist in Willie Martin McMurry, a mischievous cousin one year her senior. In addition to scuffling and fighting together, Coretta and Willie Martin played all kinds of games, the most dangerous of which was hitting wasp nests then running away. Once while playing that game, Coretta received so many stings that she became ill.

Coretta's aggression as a child was a basic part of her personality. She always met problems head on. When we were youngsters, I tended to be more imaginative and introspective. She was inclined to be cerebral and objective. As a young child, I was afraid of worms. I didn't like to look at them or touch them. When we went fishing, which we often did during the summer months, Coretta always baited my hook.

She had no qualms about killing the earthworms we used for bait and did not mind their slimy skins. Curious and confident, Coretta was positive, direct, and persistent. When she became involved in an argument, she would not let it end until she proved her point. She believed in letting people know exactly where she stood.

When she began attending Crossroads School as a five-year-old, I was already seven. For the previous two years, I had walked to and from school by myself each morning and afternoon. The Tubbs boys, three brothers who lived up the road from us, walked the same route. Older, bigger, and stronger than I, they pestered me every afternoon as we walked home. After Coretta's first day of class, as we started up the road toward home, they began their usual routine of obnoxious behavior. That afternoon, one of them pushed me in the back, causing me to stumble forward. Without warning, Coretta, half the boy's size and all of five years old, grabbed one of his legs and shouted, "Don't do that! She's my sister. Leave her alone." From that point on, they did.

Sensing early that our parents expected us to live up to the same high standards of achievement that they had set for themselves, Coretta studied with diligence. Although our mother and father never pressured us to obtain particular grades or scores, we knew they wanted and expected us to be good students. Yet, we were never made to feel that we had to achieve a standard set by some other child, and we were never compared with each other. We grew up in an atmosphere in which the standard for achievement was one's own potential rather than some other person's accomplishments. This minimized the spirit of competition between us as sisters and led instead to a spirit of cooperation. As a result, we never had to struggle with sibling rivalry, even later as adults.

When Coretta was in her last year at Crossroads School, the biggest event of the year was the county-wide Play Day held in Marion on the first Friday in May. The festivities included a parade down Main Street led by a band from Alabama State College in Montgomery. Black school children from throughout the county attended the event. The parade ended at the Marion Public School on Greensboro Highway. The first half of the day's program was held indoors and included skits, singing, and declamations. There were also exhibits. The second half of the program was held outdoors and included competitive as well as non-competitive sports.

For her part of the program, Coretta recited "Paul Revere's Ride" by Henry Wadsworth Longfellow.[1] Reciting the 130-line poem was an ambitious undertaking, especially for one as young as she. Her performance made a strong impression on both the adults and her fellow students. One of those, a young man named Bob Hatch,[2] introduced himself to Coretta after she had finished. He and Coretta spent the remainder of the day together. Before they parted late that afternoon, he asked if he could correspond with her during the coming summer. Bob Hatch was to become Coretta's first boyfriend, and their meeting on that festive occasion was the beginning of a courtship that lasted eight years.

8

Lincoln School

In September 1939, at the age of twelve, Coretta entered Lincoln School as a seventh grader. Already changes were beginning to take place in her behavior. Among other things, she had learned to control her temper. And she had begun to notice boys. The little girl was growing up.

For the Scott children, going to high school meant leaving home. By the time we entered Lincoln, the school no longer operated dormitories for students. Until I graduated in 1943, Coretta and I lived with families in Marion. The following year Mother drove a school bus, bringing students to Lincoln from northern Perry County. Consequently, Coretta lived at home during her last two years of high school.

℀

Lincoln had a colorful history dating back to the close of the Civil War when a wounded Union soldier remained in the area and began teaching black children to read and write. As the number of students grew, interest in establishing a school grew as well. In 1867, a group of former slaves incorporated Lincoln School of Marion. Needing financial assistance, the trustees contacted the American Missionary Association (AMA) and asked for help.

The AMA was an organization originally developed to support foreign missionaries. After the Civil War, it became heavily involved in working to improve conditions among newly emancipated slaves. It had a long history of working in Africa and was deeply committed to the best interests of both Africans and African Americans. Born of necessity, the AMA came into existence in response to an incident known as the *Amistad* Affair.

In the summer of 1839, a group of slaves bound for North America mutinied aboard the Cuban ship *Amistad*. After taking control of the ship, they sailed from Cuba thinking they were headed toward Africa. Two months later, they entered Long Island Sound. When they were discovered, they were taken ashore in Connecticut where they were arrested and charged with piracy.

As news of their arrival and the pending charges spread, concerned citizens stepped forward to help. To fund their legal defense, Simeon Jocelyn, Joshua Leavett, and Lewis Tappan formed an informal organization known as the Amistad Committee and began raising money. Through this committee and the efforts of many others, including John Quincy Adams, the Africans were eventually freed.[1]

The group had been captured from Sierra Leone and wanted to return there. To facilitate that trip, the committee agreed to contribute its remaining funds toward the cost of transporting the thirty-five surviving Africans back to Sierra Leone. After they were returned to Africa, the committee established the Mendi Mission and began working with Africans to combat the kidnapping of slaves in the Sierra Leone region.[2]

In the winter of 1846, many of the people who had been involved with the Amistad Committee, including Tappan, formally organized as the American Missionary Association for the purpose of addressing the issue of slavery.[3] Primarily supported by the Presbyterian and Congregational Christian churches, the organization represented every major religious denomination in the United States.[4]

As events in the United States moved toward civil war, the AMA turned its attention to the issues of slavery and the education of blacks. Eventually, it established over five hundred schools and colleges, among them Lincoln School in Marion, Alabama.[5]

Steeped in the centuries-old educational traditions of the New England Congregationalists, the first instructors in AMA schools were young idealists who taught with passion and conviction. At the same time, they held their students to the same high standards of personal conduct and scholastic achievement they expected of themselves. Based on the assumption that knowledge, morals, and their supporting habits could be taught, the educational policies of the AMA were simple. Whatever was good education for white children was also good for black children.[6] Along with knowledge and skill, a sense of mission and purpose was conveyed to students at Lincoln School. For those of us who attended, obtaining an education meant learning to think and to search for truth. Education was the means, the vehicle, by which we could pursue our dreams.

Beginning with the simple desire of one man to teach former slaves how to read and write, Lincoln School became one of the South's outstanding secondary schools.[7] As might be expected, the school met with opposition from the day it first offered classes. Erroneous notions about the nature and worth of blacks lingered long after the Civil War.[8]

For some, the name alone was enough to set their teeth on edge; the school was named after President Lincoln, a Yankee many in the South still regarded with disdain. Some found the name the embodiment of all they had opposed in the war. Many who still held to the old southern lifestyle were put off by the fact that all the teachers at Lincoln were white and most of them were from the North. Although the mixing of races offended local whites, it was one of the great advantages of the school. By placing education in a racially integrated context, the school opened our minds to new and previously unimagined possibilities. At the same time, it prepared us well in advance for the day when all education would be integrated. Not everyone in Perry County appreciated the effort. Whites who came south to teach blacks were not accepted by white southerners, who considered them intruders. Even in the 1940s, when Coretta and I were students at Lincoln, white faculty members from the school lived, worked, and worshipped in the black community, attending the Congregational Church located near the campus.

Aside from the problem of race relations, funding for the school was so scarce at times that keeping the school operating was a struggle. Then, in 1887, the segment of the school's program that trained African American teachers was transferred to Montgomery, where it later became Alabama State University. As a result, the state of Alabama withdrew its financial support from Lincoln. This and other factors pushed the school to the brink of financial ruin. Many feared it might close.

In response, the AMA sent a young woman named Mary Elizabeth Phillips to take charge of the school. Her mission was to save the dying school. The challenge was immense, but she was young, dynamic, and dedicated. She proved more than equal to the task.

Of Scottish descent, Miss Phillips was a native of Pittsburgh, Pennsylvania, and a graduate of Washington and Jefferson College. She had taught at Talladega College before coming to Marion. Finding little to inspire her except students who were eager to learn and parents who wanted their children to get an education, Miss Phillips' first year at Lincoln was one of great hardship. At the end of that year, the national office of the AMA informed Miss Phillips that the school would be closed.

In an all-out effort to save the school, Miss Phillips called a community-wide meeting, held at the Congregational Church.[9] After she told them the sad news, the black people of Marion refused to let their school go. Despite the impoverishment of most of the community, they pledged seven hundred dollars to help save the school. The teachers contributed five hundred dollars, and the students promised two hundred. The teachers even offered to return without salaries if the AMA would agree to keep the school open. When Miss Phillips informed the AMA of the fourteen hundred dollars that had been pledged, they agreed the school would remain open. From that low point on, the school grew rapidly.

In 1902, Miss Phillips raised money to construct Livingstone Hall and in 1908, Douglass Hall, a boy's dormitory, was added. The dormitory was built by the boys themselves with the supervision of a local black brick mason. Van Wagnen Hall was built in 1909 to house the elementary grades. In the spring of 1922, Miss Phillips, with the help of faculty, students, and friends, raised four thousand dollars. With matching funds from the AMA, the school constructed Woolworth Hall, which was used as a dormitory for teachers. And Ranney Hall was added as a girl's dormitory in 1925.

The design of the campus was neat and orderly. Its six redbrick buildings, symmetrically arranged on five acres, created an impressive scene deliberately planned to help mold the tastes and values of its students. Here black boys and girls were able to see with their own eyes that life could be beautiful. The simplicity and dignity of its architecture helped create an environment for students that complemented the classic education the school offered.

Although pleased with her accomplishments, Miss Phillips felt the school needed one more building to complete her vision. In her mind, a new auditorium would provide a location for indoor sports events and large public events, and would complete the campus design. Sadly, she did not live to see that plan come to fruition. During the winter of 1926–27, she became seriously ill. She died the following spring. However, the community did not forget her. In 1938, with the help of parents, students, and alumni, the school built the auditorium of Miss Phillips' dreams and named it in her honor as a memorial to her many years of sacrificial service.[10]

Lincoln School exposed Coretta to a new and different world, one that offered her not only encouragement to reach for the seemingly impossible, but the hope that she might actually attain it. When she arrived for classes, the campus looked much the same as it did when Miss Phillips left it, except for the addition of Phillips Memorial Auditorium. However, there had been one important change. With increased state support during the Depression, the cost of tuition had been reduced.[11]

By the time Coretta and I entered Lincoln in 1939, tuition had been eliminated. Students were charged only a fee of four dollars and fifty cents per year.

Though the elimination of tuition helped make education affordable, the school's educational objectives remained unchanged. Since the days of Mary Phillips, the purpose of Lincoln and the AMA had been that of educating black people and empowering them to fulfill their destiny. By providing education in a racially integrated context, students at Lincoln learned in ways students at all-white or all-black schools could not, which created in the students a sense of dissatisfaction with the status quo in the community around them. The racially integrated school environment made the racially hostile nature of Perry County all the more evident.

During the 1941–42 academic year, George White, a national officer of the AMA, visited Lincoln. There, he delivered an address on the purposes of the AMA's educational program. Concluding that speech, he said, "The AMA wants to produce good teachers, doctors, and lawyers, yes. But we are primarily concerned about turning out people whose lives will be a rebuke to the lines of caste. This is our larger purpose."[12] That speech found its answer in the life of my sister.

For Coretta, Lincoln School was an oasis in an intellectual desert, a place filled with ideas and stimulation for learning. Not only that, it was a place visited by many fascinating people engaged in a wide array of endeavors. One of those visitors was Dr. Buell G. Gallagher. At the time, he served as president of Talladega College. Later, he would become president of the City College of New York.[13]

Our campus also was a haven for black travelers for whom finding overnight accommodations in the area often proved difficult. Once while traveling for the Fellowship of Reconciliation, Bayard Rustin, quite young at the time, stopped over at Lincoln.[14] He held the students spellbound with a speech in which he related some of his experiences in opposing segregation.

At one point he said, "When I travel, I do not sit in the Jim Crow sections of trains and buses." Since he spoke with conviction, we believed his words but wondered how he got away with this kind of behavior in the South. There was a period of complete silence. Then Rustin said, "I know what you are thinking . . . You are wondering about the consequences of my conduct . . . There are scars on my body, as you can see . . . This is the price I am paying for my right to travel as a first-class citizen."[15] At that moment we saw a scar on his face that none of us had noticed before. The power of Rustin's speech on us was electrifying. Years later, during his involvement with the Montgomery Bus Boycott, Rustin visited Coretta and Martin in their home. Coretta reminded him that their lives had touched before at Lincoln.

The faculty members at Lincoln School were living examples of the kinds of people they hoped their students would become. The principal during Coretta's first four years at the school was Wilfred Gamble. He later became principal of two laboratory schools at Danbury State College in Connecticut and an assistant professor of education on the college staff. A native of Belfast, Northern Ireland, Mr. Gamble came to the United States when he was twenty-one years old. After completing high school, he graduated from Teachers College at Columbia University and obtained a master's degree in educational administration from there as well. In 1938, he accepted the position as principal at Lincoln, his first real position of responsibility in education. Untainted by experience, Mr. Gamble came to Lincoln filled with ideas and enthusiasm. Progressive in educational philosophy, he was a zealous advocate of student government and worked hard to create conditions that would give students a strong voice in determining their own affairs. Friendly but firm, he respected and admired the students. His wife, statuesque and charming, had a master's degree in speech and drama from Columbia University and taught speech and dramatics. As an undergraduate, she had spent a year in England studying at the University of the Southwest in Exeter and a summer at the University of London. As our speech teacher, she provided our first exposure to a more cosmopolitan style.

Lincoln had a strong faculty. We were instructed by teachers who were thoroughly prepared and knowledgeable in their respective fields and idealistically committed to their tasks. They had a clear sense that they were participating in a grand experiment, which, if successful, would have far-reaching implications.

Two people on Lincoln's faculty who contributed in no small measure to the course of Coretta's life were Frances and Cecil Thomas. They came to Lincoln in 1941, immediately following their wedding at Quaker Hill, in Richmond, Indiana. As idealistic young Quakers, they had been so impressed with reports of the work being done at Lincoln that they offered to work without salaries. Cecil taught social studies and was director of athletics, while Frances worked in the school office, taught private lessons in brass instruments, and was an assistant in physical education and recreational activities. Genuine outdoor people, they were the only adults in Marion who rode bicycles around town.

Seeing the dire need for wholesome organized recreational activities for black children in Marion, Cecil and Frances planned Friday night socials on the campus where they introduced our community to folk dancing with contagious enthusiasm. While Cecil called the dance moves, Frances played the music at the piano. Interspersed with games and social dancing, the evening's program usually ended with a lively and stately procession that we called the Grand March, led by the principal and his wife, Mr. and Mrs. Gamble. These social affairs gave students and faculty members an opportunity to play together after the completion of classes at the week's end.

During the years we were there, Lincoln had a strong music department. Built around several student chorus groups, the music program developed a reputation in the area for producing excellent concert events. The groups so impressed Cecil and Frances Thomas that they suggested we conduct a concert tour. By singing in churches and before civic groups, we could cover most of our expenses and have an opportunity to see other areas of the country. Most of us had never been beyond the borders of Alabama. With the help of the music instructors and other faculty members, the Thomases organized a chorus tour of Ohio and Indiana. During the spring of 1942, I traveled with that group, presenting programs at universities, colleges, churches, high schools, and club meetings in locations across both states.

One of our stops that spring was a concert at Antioch College in Yellow Springs, Ohio. That was my initial contact with Antioch. I loved the campus and the sense of openness and freedom we found there. A year later I was admitted to Antioch as a freshman and received a scholarship that paid tuition and room and board. Two years after I began at Antioch, Coretta followed in my footsteps.[16] The Thomases could not have known the effect that trip would have on us, but their interest in us set Coretta on the path to her destiny. Antioch was a key stepping stone in the maturation of her mind and spirit.

While Coretta was at Lincoln, Frances Thomas taught her to play the cornet. They continued to work together musically throughout their careers. The music for two selections, "My Feet Are Tired" and "No Crystal Stair," which Coretta performed much later in life, was composed by Frances Thomas.

One of Lincoln's most effective teachers was a black woman named Olive J. Williams. A native of Harrisburg, Pennsylvania, before arriving at Lincoln Miss Williams graduated from Howard University and studied music privately in New York City. She was a splendid musician and a strict choirmaster who was interested in the growth and development of all her students. She believed that appreciation of music and the arts formed the basis of all enrichment in our lives, yet she was concerned with more than music and had an easy rapport with students. Many on campus sought her counsel.

For six years Coretta took Miss Williams' classes in music appreciation. In addition, she studied voice and piano privately with Miss Williams and did choral performances under her direction. When Coretta was an eighth grader, Miss Williams introduced her students to flute-o-phones as a way of enabling them to grow in musical skill and understanding. Ten days before the students' annual recital, she assigned a particularly difficult piece to Coretta's class. Those who learned to play the piece accurately would be given the opportunity to play it at the recital. Coretta spent every spare minute practicing.

Three days later, each member of the class played the piece. Coretta was the only one who did so with technical perfection. Miss Williams then instructed her to memorize the piece. At the recital, Coretta appeared onstage wearing a light blue organdy dress trimmed with white ruffles. Composed and relaxed, she played an excellent rendition of "Arkansas Traveler." That year, she was honored as the most improved music student.

Miss Williams was a powerful role model for Coretta. She wanted to be like Miss Williams in every way, a lady who was not only a fine musician but a real person, one who did not subscribe to the narrow view of art only for art's sake. "I always knew I did not want to be the kind of person who knows nothing but music," Coretta often said. What she learned from Miss Williams showed her how to use music to establish harmonious relations with other human beings. The singers Miss Williams trained at Lincoln not only went on tour through Ohio and Indiana, they also made appearances in Alabama before white groups. Through that experience, Coretta saw the mollifying effect music had on racial tensions. She would use that idea later in life as she became an advocate for civil rights.

When Coretta returned to Lincoln as a junior in the fall of 1943, she faced new challenges. I had graduated and entered Antioch College. Bob Hatch, her boyfriend and classmate of the previous four years, had transferred to a high school in Montgomery. Increased funding from the state brought the application of stricter regulations. Segregation was the law in Alabama and meant all teachers at black schools were required to be black, which forced the removal of Lincoln's white instructors. This change would impact Coretta's life greatly, because many of her favorite teachers were white. The AMA still controlled the school, but their ability to direct Lincoln's programs was slipping away. Within a few years the county would own and operate the facility. Thankfully for Coretta, Miss Williams was back and would remain there throughout the next two years.

That same year, Reverend Earnest A. Smith, a graduate of Oberlin Theological Seminary, became Lincoln's first African American principal. With considerable experience in teaching and school administration, he worked hard to maintain Lincoln's best traditions. Scholarly, eloquent, and dynamic he was himself a product of private schools similar to Lincoln.

Coretta's last two years of high school were filled with many activities, including studying, performing, and teaching music. She became the leading soprano for the senior chorus, singing such arias as "Come Unto Him All Ye That Labor" and "I Know That My Redeemer Liveth" from Handel's *Messiah* in the Christmas program. In addition, she developed and directed a choir at her home church in North Perry County.[17]

In the spring of 1945, Coretta graduated from Lincoln as valedictorian of her class. She had spent six years studying under the careful and watchful eyes of some of the best teachers of that era. Not only did she master the information they presented, she absorbed the ethos and the agenda from which they taught. Driven by the notion that they could make the world better, our teachers imparted that same vision to Coretta. She received it gladly. Coretta might not have known with certainty what her final destiny would be, but by the end of her senior year, she knew she was destined to make a difference, and she thought that might be through music. Diploma in hand, she was ready to take the next step.

9

Antioch College

During her senior year in high school, Coretta applied for admission to Antioch College. After she was accepted, she applied to the Interracial Scholarship Fund for financial aid. The fund awarded her a scholarship that made it possible for her to attend. On the surface, Coretta's move to Antioch might have appeared a giant step. She was, after all, a young black girl from deeply segregated Alabama moving to Ohio to attend a liberal and academically challenging college. But for those who knew the kind of student Lincoln produced, the move did not seem at all out of place.

Antioch and Lincoln were similar in many respects. Both were progressive in nature and sought to maintain themselves as laboratories of inquiry, freedom, and democracy. Their differences were of degree rather than kind. Education at Antioch was a continuation of the education Coretta had already known. The attitudes that she had developed at Lincoln would be reinforced at Antioch and would form the basis of a social and educational philosophy that guided her for the remainder of her life. Antioch's program, which embodied the Greek ideal of education for the whole person—mind, body, and spirit—enabled Coretta to continue her quest to develop a well-integrated personality as a member of an integrated society.

Antioch College was founded in 1852 by the Christian Connection, a group that later became known as the Christian Church. Horace Mann, a nineteenth century pioneer in education, was elected its first president.[1] Mann came to Antioch from his position as secretary for the Massachusetts Board of Education where he led the effort to reform the state's education system. Changes that he introduced transformed the state's schools and spawned a national campaign to establish free and universal elementary school systems in every state. In conjunction with that, Mann had been instrumental in establishing Massachusetts' first public school for educating teachers.

Both Mann and Antioch were products of an intellectual and spiritual movement that developed in New England during the first half of the nineteenth century. The same movement that produced men like Emerson, Thoreau, Longfellow, and Whittier led to the establishment of the American Missionary Association and to the founding of the Christian Congregational Church.

In the years following the American Revolution, the country made great progress in securing its place as a nation among nations, but many domestic issues had yet to be resolved. The awakening that spawned Antioch College helped shape the country's discussion of that unfinished business, particularly as it related to education and race. Mann was at the forefront of that movement.

The founders of Antioch expected Mann to do for higher education what he already had done for primary and secondary education in Massachusetts. Antioch was to be coeducational and nonsectarian. Though not explicitly directed to do so, Mann took that policy one step further and admitted blacks.[2] Innovative and ahead of his time, Horace Mann in both his words and deeds inspired students for more than a century.[3] Succeeding generations continued to ponder his words to the graduating class of 1859, "Be ashamed to die until you have won some victory for humanity."[4]

Throughout its early history, Antioch faced recurring financial and institutional challenges. In the years following Mann's death, the school was reorganized on at least two occasions. In 1919, it was reorganized yet again, and Arthur E. Morgan, an engineer by training, became president. Morgan, who was deeply concerned about the direction of education in America, revamped the college's academic program. Students were not merely to be filled with information, but were to learn a way of thinking that would allow them to function in society as intellectual entrepreneurs.[5] Such terms as balance and symmetry became part of the Antioch creed; there was to be "education in life as well as books," and it was essential for students to develop "life aims and purposes."[6] Graduates would become agents of change, moving society toward greater and greater perfection. Morgan's efforts set the tone for the college throughout the first half of the twentieth century.

From its founding, educators at Antioch sought to keep the college's program on the cutting edge of American life and culture. To do that, Antioch was forced to continually reinvent and redefine itself. As America wrestled with the issues of race and civil rights, the college faced new challenges in its attempt to remain faithful to its original calling. One of its defining moments came just a few years before Coretta and I arrived there as students.

In 1941, Antioch College had no black students. For all its rhetoric and lofty ideals, the school had failed to incorporate its views of race and civil rights into its daily existence. No one could say for certain when blacks had last attended Antioch or why they had ceased to be a part of the student body.

From its beginning, Antioch had been guided by the notion that the context of education was as important as the content. The composition of the student body was part of that context and had a direct bearing on the nature of the educational experience. Exclusion of blacks deprived blacks from accessing Antioch's educational opportunities, but it also deprived white students of the opportunity to know, understand, and appreciate members of an historic American minority. At an institution where social awareness was considered essential to the education process, a student body without black students was particularly troubling. Antioch's doors had to be open in reality—not merely in theory—to all segments of society. The school needed to practice the principles it espoused.

To address that situation, members of the Antioch administration, faculty, and student body formed the Race Relations Committee and made a concerted effort to attract black students. When they learned that the expense of attending school might be a deterrent to potential students, the group set about raising money for a scholarship fund to underwrite the costs.[7] That fund became known as the Interracial Scholarship Fund.

During the fall of 1942, early in my senior year at Lincoln School, Miriam Eisenberg, chairman of the Race Relations Committee at Antioch, wrote to the principal at Lincoln and told him of Antioch's desire to attract black students. The Race Relations Committee, she informed him, had raised enough money to offer a few scholarships to outstanding students who qualified for admission. Eager to continue my education, I applied. Much to everyone's delight, I was awarded a scholarship.

In some respects, leaving home in the Deep South was daunting. Antioch was a white college in the North with high academic standards. It was a place where students were expected to accept responsibility for their lives as well as their education. My teachers at Lincoln thought I was capable of succeeding, and the Antioch admissions committee was sufficiently impressed with my academic credentials and my performance on the entrance examination to admit me. In spite of mixed feelings about venturing alone into the unknown, far away from home and family, I was excited by the challenge.

When I enrolled at Antioch in the summer of 1943, I was the only black student on campus. In the fall of that year, two other black girls enrolled. For two years we were the only black students at Antioch. Those two years were academically rewarding but socially challenging.

Although I blazed a trail ahead of her, Coretta had misgivings about following me to college.[8] Life at Antioch was not perfect. Dating was difficult, and there were students who did not share the college's broad vision. But Coretta and I had always been together, and I looked forward to having her with me again. Coretta wanted to continue her education and knew she could do that only by leaving home. Coming north and joining me at Antioch would afford her opportunities and privileges she could never find elsewhere. Those experiences were worth the effort—regardless of the hardships.

Despite the fact that my attending Antioch had some influence on Coretta's choice of college, she was not trailing in my shadow. As close as we had been while growing up, there had always been space in our togetherness. We confided in each other, but we never leaned on each other. Coretta was an independent, self-reliant girl. She expected to make her own way in life. As it turned out, we did not have much time to think about it. The day she arrived on campus I was busy taking final examinations. The following day, I left for Chicago where I had a co-op job.

Coretta spent her first semester on campus without me.

10

Becoming Coretta

When Coretta entered Antioch in the fall of 1945, World War II had ended. The college faced the difficult task of adjusting to peacetime life. A large veteran population brought its own special demands. All of that made college life different for Coretta than it had been for me. For one thing, men now outnumbered women on the campus three or four to one. Also, there were more blacks in the student body—six to be exact—at least two of whom were men.

In spite of the friendliness and informality of Antioch's students and faculty, the transition from high school to college gave Coretta a shock. Not only was she a long way from home, she was also in a different environment. Our home in Perry County was part of a close-knit community. People knew each other, sometimes too well, and our neighbors were predominantly African American. At Antioch, Coretta found herself among strangers who did not know her at all and who were predominantly white. Not only that, Antioch's emphasis on work and study placed additional burdens on all its students. Greater individual freedom brought with it greater responsibility. As a black student from the rural South, Coretta experienced more than the usual amount of freshman frustration.

In her life aims paper, written toward the end of her first year, Coretta discussed how she felt at Antioch. At first, "I was so inhibited . . . it seemed that I had retained nothing from my previous twelve years of school. I had to adjust . . . to a whole new economic, social, and cultural pattern. My previous study habits just would not suffice . . . I found myself baffled when asked to make comments in ordinary conversations."[1]

In the paper, Coretta attributed most of her difficulty to a loss of self-confidence, both socially and academically. Despite the excellent education she had received at Lincoln School, she felt unprepared for the classroom challenges she experienced. Antioch students were a highly select group. Competition was much keener than Coretta could possibly have imagined.

Although she had attended a good high school, competition at Antioch revealed the one area in which she was weakest. Lincoln School had prepared her with a well-rounded education that included exposure to classic works of art, music, theatre, and literature. Coretta knew the academic material better than anyone. She was socially comfortable, even in the most formal settings, and she could think her own thoughts, but her exposure to the breadth of current American experiences had been limited in Marion, Alabama, particularly within the black community. Many of the students at Antioch came from large metropolitan areas along the east coast. They had been immersed in the latest trends in American life. Those same trends took a long time reaching our community in Perry County. Though our parents and the faculty at Lincoln had worked hard to overcome those limitations, Coretta, like most blacks of her generation, could not escape the limiting influences of a racially segregated life.

By contrast, in several key areas Coretta was much better prepared than many of her peers. She was more self-sufficient than most college girls her age. That spirit of independence she had exhibited from childhood helped her mature into a young woman capable of negotiating daily life without need of constant direction from others. High school and our home life with our parents had taught her to make her own decisions and to accept responsibility for the consequences. The influence of our father and grandfathers taught her to see people as individuals rather than as stereotypes representative of an entire group.

Coretta came to college having already achieved the central goal of education. She had discovered that learning is a lifelong process. Coupled with that, at a very early age she had adopted a motto, one to which she remained committed throughout her life. That motto was simply, "To do my best and to make my best better."

In her first year of college, Coretta had clearly defined vocational aims. She wanted to pursue a career in music, but like her Lincoln mentor, Olive Williams, she was not interested in music merely for its own sake. She had a much larger view of life. Since childhood she had wanted to become a well-rounded individual, the kind of person that seemed so rare at the time, particularly in rural Alabama where she was reared.

No doubt, some thought her choice of Antioch a strange one for a person interested in a music career. At the time, the college did not offer a major in music. But Coretta was interested in more than merely a major field of study. Already, she was developing an agenda by which she would define her future career. Issues like racial and social injustice had captured her attention. Politics and the use of government to address those injustices were ideas that interested her, and though her ideas had not fully developed, she was moving in that direction. Even before she had graduated from Lincoln, she had seen the arts, particularly music, as a useful tool in bridging the great social divides of American life. She believed music was a means not just of conveying a message, but of reaching people with that message at a motivational level—touching their hearts in a way that moved them to action. When she chose Antioch, she could not articulate all of those ideas in clear, concise terms, but they were growing in her mind all the same. To make those ideas come alive, to give them force and meaning, she needed more than simply musical training; she needed social and political knowledge as well. Antioch was well suited to give her that, and despite a number of trying experiences, Coretta's first year ended well.

Unlike other universities, Antioch College required students to alternate between semesters of study and semesters of work in a routine designed to reinforce through practical experience what was encountered in the classroom. Job counselors helped students select employment that met the student's qualifications and provided opportunities for them to develop skills relevant to their field of interest.

That spring, as her first year came to an end, Coretta was offered a co-op job for the summer as a music counselor at a camp near Cleveland where she spent the summer teaching music to inner-city children. Sponsored by the nationally-known Karamu House,[2] the job encouraged Coretta's sense of personal initiative and helped her develop confidence in working with others. It also gave her a practical view of the different uses for music that captured her interest. Using music as more than entertainment, she was able to convey to the children a sense of the world beyond their own limited existence. Her experiences there also revealed weaknesses in her own abilities and inspired her to apply herself more seriously to the study of music and leadership. Though obtaining professional training in music at a conservatory was still her long-range objective, Coretta returned to campus that fall anxious to learn more about group dynamics.

In keeping with Coretta's interest, her second co-op job took her to the Friendly Inn Settlement House in Cleveland where she would focus on leadership and education techniques in a group environment.[3] Because of the nature of the group process and the amount of time required to develop rapport with group members, she was advised to combine two work semesters in order to allow her to spend a protracted period with the assigned group. As a result, during the academic year 1946–47, she remained at Friendly Inn for five consecutive months.

Working under experienced supervisors on a variety of tasks and occasionally filling in as staff leader, she learned to be flexible and resourceful. Along with that, she gained the confidence and poise that came from holding a position of authority. She assisted instructors and club leaders with activities for groups ranging in age from five years to almost ninety and faced many challenging experiences. One experience was that of taking members of the Golden Age Club, the eldest of whom was eighty-eight years old, to the Gratto Circus.

> It was not originally planned that I should take the group to the circus but because Miss Rosenbaum, who is the group leader and supervisor of the adult program, was ill the responsibility of escorting twelve Golden Agers to the circus was delegated to me. The more feeble members went by cab and the rest of us went by streetcar. I was just as excited as many of the children at the circus were because it was the first circus I had attended, although the Golden Agers didn't know that. I knew they were depending on me for protection (physical) and direction and I felt that I must do my utmost to strengthen their faith in me. No one got lost; no one was trampled down by the elephants; no one was seized by the circus tigers, and all were guided safely home. I was quite proud of this achievement and felt that this was one of my assignments which can be considered as one of my real contributions to the agency and the Golden Age Club because the circus meant so much to them.[4]

In the broad sweep of Coretta's life, escorting a group of the elderly to a circus might not sound like much, but at that moment it marked an important step. She was a young woman from the segregated South, living in Cleveland, Ohio, with responsibility thrust upon her for the care and control of a group of men and women four times her age, who had many times more her experience. For Coretta, it was a defining moment.

While working in Cleveland, Coretta became friends with Frances Lucas. She was Coretta's closest associate during her stay there. A graduate of Fisk University, Frances came to Friendly Inn to supplement her classroom knowledge with on-the-job training. From there, she went to the New School for Social Research in New York City where she prepared for a career in social casework. Fran and Coretta continued to correspond and visit, becoming lifelong friends.

During that same period in Cleveland, Coretta met a young man named Bob Madison. The two of them became friends and soon began dating. At the time, Bob was studying architecture at Western Reserve University. Talented, serious-minded, and ambitious, he was articulate and persuasive. Casual dating soon blossomed into courtship. Their romance was rather intense and continued after Coretta returned to the Antioch campus. When Bob came to Antioch for the spring dance, he and Coretta informed me that they had become engaged. I was surprised but not unduly disturbed by the announcement. I knew that not every engagement ended in marriage.

After the dance, Bob returned to Cleveland, and as the summer of 1947 wore on, time and distance took its toll. Alone with time to think Coretta began to debate the wisdom of her decision to get married. In her mind, she struggled with the effect marrying Bob might have on her education, her plans for a career in music, and the larger ideas to which she was rapidly becoming committed. At the same time, another Bob arrived at Antioch to pay her a visit: Bob Hatch.

Coretta and Bob Hatch had been friends since their elementary school days. At Lincoln School, they had been classmates in junior high and the first year of high school. Always together at social occasions, they were considered the perfect couple. They looked good together, and their compatible interests and temperaments made them the kind of young couple everyone hoped would eventually marry.

Then, at the beginning of their junior year, Bob's family moved. He was forced to transfer to a school in Montgomery ninety miles away. Nevertheless, they maintained a lively correspondence during the remainder of their high school years and saw each other on holidays and in the summer months when Bob's family returned to Marion. After graduating from high school, they corresponded regularly. When Coretta chose to attend Antioch in Ohio and Bob remained in Alabama, the distance between them only increased their sense of separation. In his letters, however, Bob often wrote about coming to Antioch for a visit. Coretta took those words to heart and looked forward to the day when she could show him the Antioch campus. In August of 1947, as Coretta struggled with her relationship with Bob Madison, Bob Hatch arrived.

That summer, Coretta was teaching three-year-olds in the Antioch Nursery School. Bob telephoned her at the school. He was visiting in a city not far from Yellow Springs and wanted to see her. Coretta was excited about his visit. At the same time, she was anxious. Time and experience had wrought many changes. She was no longer the girl from Lincoln School who left Marion with misgivings about the great wide world. She was different, and she wondered how much Bob had changed.

As promised, a few days later Bob Hatch arrived at Antioch. He and Coretta spent three fun-filled, exciting days together in the friendly and relaxed atmosphere of the Antioch campus and Yellow Springs. Coretta took immense delight in showing him some of the many things that enriched the students' lives. They walked in Glen Helen, stopping here and there to observe a rock formation, a sparkling spring, or a specimen of plant life. They attended a play at the Area Theatre, browsed through libraries, and stared from a distance at the gothic towers of Antioch's main building. Hiking and biking around Yellow Springs, they had time to rekindle their friendship, to talk, and to fill in the gaps.

Equally important, Coretta wanted Bob to meet some of the people at Antioch and in Yellow Springs who had come to mean so much to her. While he was there, Bob was the house guest of Mr. and Mrs. Elmer Lawson, a grand couple in Yellow Springs who first "adopted" me and later Coretta. We went in and out of the Lawson's home as if it had been the home of our own parents. We enjoyed and appreciated Mrs. Lawson's mothering. She knew instinctively when to offer advice and when to leave us alone. On the threshold of adulthood, we wanted freedom and privacy more than anything else. Mrs. Lawson had the rare ability to give us what we needed, and in the right proportions. The Lawson home became a pleasant retreat from the dormitory, giving us the advantages of both home and campus life.

The Lawsons also enjoyed playing host to our relatives and friends when they came to visit, so it was natural that Bob would stay with them. Bob's open and easy manner quickly won the Lawsons' admiration, and he appreciated the genuine interest they took in him.

After three days, Bob left. He and Coretta had talked about many things, but they had not discussed the future or what their relationship might hold. As Coretta and I talked, she found it strange that the topic had not come up during Bob's visit. A few weeks later he wrote that he was getting married to someone he had met at college. Coretta was upset but did not seem completely surprised. When I asked her why, she told me she had dreamed about Bob and in that dream he was married. Now, she faced the fact that her childhood dream of marrying Bob had been shattered.

Spring flowers became summer fruit, some of which did not ripen until the harvest season. By that fall Coretta's engagement to Bob Madison had been broken for reasons she never fully disclosed. Bob Hatch's visit had awakened in her a vibrancy she had not experienced with Bob Madison, and though she would not be Mrs. Hatch, she realized she could not become Mrs. Madison, either. The initiative to end the relationship was hers. Bob Madison took the news gallantly. His parting words to her that fall were simply, "I'll see you again, Coretta. You are not going out of my life forever."

The autumn of 1947 saw Coretta close her mind on two affairs of the heart, one of short duration, the other quite long. At the age of twenty, she had known something of the fun, frustration, and fulfillment of a long association with a member of the opposite sex and something of the ephemeral beauty of a winter and spring romance. On the surface, it seemed a personal passage of love sought and love lost, but in her heart there was more at work.

In many ways that summer and fall marked the moment when Coretta Scott truly left Marion and the Black Belt of Alabama. Bob Hatch was more than a childhood friend and more than a romantic dream. Her relationship with him was a deeply personal tie to a life that was rapidly slipping into the past. The time for that dream and that life had passed. Coretta had grown beyond a life viewed only through the prism of Marion, Lincoln, and our tight-knit community back home. She had her own destiny, and it lay somewhere ahead of her, not in her past. From that summer on, Coretta faced forward, fully embracing the future that was opening before her, and concentrated on the woman she was becoming.

11

Progressive

In the fall of 1947, I transferred to Ohio State University in Columbus. With me on the campus at Antioch, Coretta had had a difficult time becoming an individual in her own right. At Antioch I had been called "Scottie." Coretta was often asked, "Do you sing like Scottie?" And frequently she was referred to as Scottie's little sister and occasionally as "Little Scottie." For Coretta, my leaving made it easier for her to be seen as the unique individual that she was.

Antioch, like all white campuses in our time, had not faced up to the problem of mixed dating and its consequences. This was one major reason why blacks went elsewhere to school. Parents who had the financial means to send their children to a private college wanted their sons and daughters to have all the advantages a good college education afforded. That included full participation in campus social life. Consequently, children of affluent black families usually chose Fisk, Talladega, Hampton, or Howard where they knew they could meet prospective marriage partners and form lifelong friendships. In those rare instances in which a black student chose a white college, it was usually one of the prestigious eastern colleges or Oberlin. Oberlin offered degrees in music and theology and had a reputation, dating back to the days of slavery, of being liberal toward blacks. Except for two occasions when I went out with a white upperclassman, the only dates I had on campus were the times I invited a friend from off campus.

For me, college was all about books and ideas. The interminable discussions of race problems led me to the conclusion that mixed dating was frowned upon by Antioch students. Those discussions nearly always ended with the question, "How do you feel about intermarriage?" Many students who considered themselves liberal would say they felt blacks should have economic and political rights, but they did not think blacks and whites should marry, and if they did marry, they should not have children. In those days many people, black as well as white, were not willing to see the race problem in its totality. They talked about economic equality as something separate from social equality, saying they approved the former but did not feel blacks wanted the latter. Intellectually, Antioch students were more sophisticated and enlightened than the general population, but they, too, were products of a racist society, one that had robbed blacks of their dignity and sought ways to keep them subservient at every level. Coretta recognized those discussions for what they were and spoke about the underlying assumptions of her classmates in her senior paper where she observed, "[Antioch's] emotional and social maturity still lag far behind our intellectual acceptance of racial equality."[1]

The time came when I needed more than the academic phase of college life. Normal contacts and friendships with members of the opposite sex were an important part of growing up. Antioch had been a great experience, but I had been deprived of something fundamental, basic, and necessary to my overall development. Though I had fond memories of my years at Antioch and made friendships that would endure the remainder of my life, I transferred to the Ohio State University. Time would prove this a wise move.

During her first two years, Coretta had lacked a feeling of belonging at Antioch. Officially, she was a member of the college community, but psychologically she felt left out. As the new academic year began, she made a concerted effort to become more involved. Those efforts produced a remarkable result.

She had two major experiences that helped her to feel like a contributing member of the Antioch community. The first of those came in Antioch Area Theatre's production of Gilbert and Sullivan's operetta *Iolanthe*. Coretta had the role of the fairy, Celia. The second was the publication of an article, "Why I Came to College," in *Opportunity* magazine, the official organ of the National Urban League.[2] Those accomplishments gave her publicity and recognition on the local, campus, and national levels. Writing about the experiences three years later, Coretta said, "the little successes seemed to magnify themselves and the motivation which was supplied increased with each success."[3]

That following summer, Antioch was alive with political activity. One of the professors, Dr. Oliver S. Loud, became involved in the Ohio Progressive Party, part of the national Progressive Party formed to promote the presidential candidacy of Henry Wallace.[4] On June 19, 1948, at the state convention in Cleveland, Dr. Loud was elected chairman of the state party. Reflecting the stance of Henry Wallace, the

Progressive Party sought to end segregation, supported voting rights for blacks, and called for national health insurance. Because of Dr. Loud's involvement, a Young Progressives club was formed on campus. Coretta became an active member of the club.

As Coretta entered her fourth year, her adjustment at Antioch was so satisfactory that she considered that year her best. Her morale was at its highest, her quality of work superb. That same year, her growing reputation as a concert singer brought her invitations for appearances in surrounding communities. One opportunity of which she was most proud was her appearance in a program in Springfield, Ohio, where Mrs. Mary McLeod Bethune was the guest speaker.[5] In addition, Coretta sang with the Community Chorus of Springfield whose director was minister of music at Springfield's Second Baptist Church. To show their appreciation, the church presented her in a full recital.

The recital was held at the church in Springfield on Tuesday evening, November 9, 1948. Coretta was accompanied by Walt Rybeck, a fourth year white student who came to Antioch from Wheeling, West Virginia. The concert was publicized in the *Antioch Record,* the *Xenia Gazette,* the *Springfield News,* and a newspaper in Wheeling. About a hundred people attended—some from the college, others members of the church congregation. Modest as it was, that performance marked the beginning of Coretta's concert career. By popular demand, she repeated the concert the following Sunday evening at Kelly Hall on the Antioch campus.

Because Antioch had no major course of study in music, Coretta majored in elementary education. Still, music was in her heart, and she took advantage of every opportunity to develop her talent along musical lines, both as a performer and as a student of the subject. While continuing her study of piano and voice, she also took violin lessons and courses in music theory. She developed confidence and purpose as she performed and gained experience, which provided excellent preparation for the kind of professional work she eventually wanted to do.

Coretta's self-styled musical training at Antioch also included teaching the fundamentals of music to students at the Antioch Demonstration School, where she did two years of practice teaching. There, she taught the older classes to play the flute-o-phone, a simple pre-band instrument she had mastered at Lincoln School. Coretta was given freedom to experiment with new ideas and techniques and had fun in the process, too. Her supervising teachers commended her work, and parents complimented her on the job she had done with music in the school.

While she continued to develop as a musician and teacher, Coretta also cultivated an interest in social and economic justice through the Young Progressives club. In conjunction with that, she appeared on a program with Paul Robeson at the Majestic Hotel in Cleveland, which was sponsored by the Progressive Party of Ohio.[6] The occasion was a March 10, 1950, reception held in Robeson's honor. Accompanied by Larry Brown, Robeson's pianist, Coretta sang "Vedrai Carino" from *Don Giovanni,* "Bird Courtships," and "Let Us Break Bread Together." Afterward, Robeson congratulated Coretta and commented favorably on her voice, encouraging her to continue to study.

The Progressive Party was racially inclusive and allowed Coretta to see blacks and whites working together in an attempt to achieve common political goals. Her involvement also exposed her to the national debate regarding racial equality, economic justice, and international peace—issues she would spend her life promoting. The Party ultimately floundered, but for Coretta that initial brush with politics marked a significant step forward in understanding the calling and mission of her life. That day in Cleveland singing with Paul Robeson would not be the last time she combined her interests in music and politics.

Back at Antioch, the experience in Cleveland and encouragement from Robeson gave Coretta renewed confidence for a concert she was scheduled to give in Harrisburg, Pennsylvania, three weeks later. Held at the Capitol Street Presbyterian Church, the concert had been made possible through the efforts of Miss Olive J. Williams, Coretta's music teacher at Lincoln School. To Coretta's delight, Miss Williams accompanied her in a stellar performance.

During the summer of the same year, Coretta returned to Alabama where she was presented in concert at Lincoln School by the Marion Baptist Academy PTA. The concert was publicized among blacks and whites and was the first time in the history of Perry County that a local black girl received such recognition. The leading white merchants accepted placards announcing the program, which they displayed in their store windows. The *Marion Times Standard* carried a front-page article about the concert.[7]

Mrs. T. A. Woods, a white piano teacher from Marion, accompanied Coretta. The mixed audience responded warmly to each selection. Coretta was in good voice and commanded respect from members of the audience, both white and black. She was a person of talent and accomplishment, and they were proud of her as a hometown girl, a sentiment they did not hesitate to show. Writing about it later, Coretta said, "With sincere congratulations and lavish words of praise coming from southerners, for the first time in my life in the South I felt like a real person . . . I felt an inner security and confidence which I had never felt before. It is amazing how this one . . . experience in good race relations in my home town has influenced my whole outlook on the South."[8]

Although Coretta was the "token" black in a white college, she found Antioch to be "the best possible experience for me at the time because my training at Antioch— all of it—helped to prepare me for the kind of life I was destined to lead."[9] During the years that Coretta was at Antioch, she saw the community's attitude change from racial divisiveness toward an acceptance of blacks as equals.

Three years after blacks began attending, mixed dating became a reality. Coretta developed a relationship with a white male student that lasted several years. The relationship ended when their friendship turned to courtship. Though he enjoyed Coretta's company, he did not have the strength to follow that courtship to marriage. That experience made real for her the nature of the issues she faced as a black woman in a society dominated by whites.

12

Graduation

At Antioch, education majors were required to complete two years of practice teaching, one at the campus demonstration school and the other through the Yellow Springs public school system. Coretta completed the first year at the demonstration school without incident.

In 1950, during Coretta's last year of college, schools in the Yellow Springs school system were white. Coretta's assignment to an all-white school would raise questions of race. Ohio was not racially segregated by law, but it was by practice. Sending her to an all-white school would cross that unwritten but very obvious color line.

In an attempt to forestall trouble over her student teaching assignment, Coretta met several times with her supervisor to discuss her assignment and the difficulty she faced. Those discussions were fair, frank, and honest, but she could sense her supervisor was uncomfortable with the situation and was not interested in addressing the racial issues head-on. If the choice came down to a confrontation with the school system, Coretta was convinced the supervisor would opt for the least disruptive solution.

When parents of students in the Yellow Springs school system learned that Coretta could be assigned to teach their children, they protested. Faced with opposition, the Yellow Springs school board refused to allow her to teach. Coretta's supervisor offered her two options. She could go to Xenia, Ohio, nine miles away, and do her second year of student teaching there in an all-black school. Or she could return to Antioch's demonstration school.

Although Coretta had been wary of the assignment process, she was not prepared for the college's decision. She knew the administration faced a tough situation, but she did not think they would make their determination based solely on race. Not at Antioch. "Well," Coretta thought, "it has happened here. The same thing I left Alabama to get away from."[1]

In the brief interim between the decision and the date on which her practice teaching session was to begin, Coretta attempted to enlist the support of her fellow students to pressure the college administration to change its position. Coretta described what happened next.

> I did everything I could, but my classmates would not support me. "If we protest," they argued, "all our practice teaching facilities may be taken away and none of us will get our degrees." Most of the students would not even discuss the subject with me. As a last resort I decided to go directly to the president of the college and discuss this matter—its implications and ramifications—with him. Aside from Antioch's responsibility to me as an individual and the precedent which my case would establish for Negro students, I felt the College had an image to live up to. A school that professed to be a laboratory in democracy could not brush aside such flagrant discrimination so easily.[2]

When Coretta entered Antioch College, Algo Henderson was president, a post he had held since 1936. At the time he took the job, he was only thirty-nine years old. His youthful energy and commitment to the historic mission of the school had led to the establishment of the Interracial Scholarship Fund that allowed Coretta and me to attend. However, in 1948, he left the college to take a position with the state of New York. His successor, Douglas McGregor, was quite a different man.

McGregor had been a professor at MIT where he developed several new management theories. One of those theories suggested employees were more productive in a cooperative, participatory work environment as opposed to one that was autocratic and authoritative. Ahead of its time, his team concept was a controversial departure from the top-down orientation of American business. Serving as president of Antioch gave him an opportunity to put those theories to a practical test.[3] McGregor was a serious-minded man, but he was out of step with the Antioch spirit and the historic traditions of the school.

When Coretta met with McGregor, she stated her case boldly but respectfully. If the college administration would support her, she could teach where her classmates would be teaching and where Antioch student teachers had always taught—in the public schools of Yellow Springs. Forcing her, merely because she was black, to teach at an all-black school was an affront to her and to the tradition of the school. The matter might be resolved merely by the college insisting that she be accepted along with the other student teachers. At least an attempt was required, and she did not feel that this had been done.

McGregor listened attentively but made little constructive comment. Finally, Coretta pressed the point.

"What do you intend to do? What do you think the college can do to help me?"

"Nothing, Coretta," McGregor replied. "There's nothing we can do."

Coretta was shattered. In the days leading up to their meeting, she had refused to believe that she could become the victim of racism at one of the most liberal white colleges in the country. Now, hearing it from the president's lips, she was stunned. As she walked from his office, she felt like crying.

For Coretta, that day was a day of reckoning, a moment of discovery and decision. She knew who she was, and she knew her life had purpose and meaning. Still, the situation she faced and the college's refusal to support her was hard to take. She did her best to learn from it and to put the experience in its proper perspective. "I am a Negro, and I am going to be a Negro for the rest of my life, and I have to face these problems. So I'm not going to let this one get me down. I'll have to accept a compromise now, but I don't have to accept it as being right." Reluctantly, she did just that and completed the necessary requirements for her degree at the Antioch school, refusing to teach in Xenia's segregated black school.

The student teaching experience aside, Coretta's last year at Antioch was one in which she felt more secure as a person and more certain of her goals than at any previous time in her life. She served successfully as a dormitory counselor for a group of freshmen girls and was a real big sister to our brother Obie Leonard, who was attending Central State College, just a few miles away.

Later in life, Coretta spoke with clarity and conviction about the faculty influences at Antioch, naming two people in particular who gave her the affection and understanding she needed. Those two were Walter F. Anderson, chairman of the Music Department,[4] and Mrs. Jessie Treichler, Coretta's faculty adviser.[5]

A friend to all students, Mrs. Treichler was a rare combination of idealist and realist, dreamer and performer. Even when thoroughly committed to a cause, she still got things done effectively. With the honesty of an artist and the love of a friend, she had a way of helping students discover truths about themselves and their personality that were liberating and empowering. Mrs. Treichler remembered Coretta and spoke of her with fondness.

One day she came into my office and said that Julius Kiano had asked her for a date. I said, "Well, of course you've accepted, haven't you?"

"No," Coretta replied.

"Why ever not? Julius is going to be famous someday—the Gandhi of Africa, maybe.

"I know," Coretta said. "But when I go out on a date, I want to go on a date—I don't want to go out with a cause."[6]

That was Coretta, clear, concise, and incisive. She had been that way since childhood and would remain so throughout her life. Later, she expressed such opinions only to a few close family members and a handful of well-chosen friends. But in 1950, as a college senior, she was not worried about what others thought.

Antioch's program of work and study normally required five years to complete. Coretta was officially enrolled there six years. As the 1950–51 academic year drew to a close, she neared the end of one phase of her life, a phase that would later prove critically important and one from which she would draw great strength and direction. Yet she was already anticipating a new beginning and a time when she could devote her energy and efforts exclusively to the study of music. Despite having no money, she was certain she wanted to continue in school and do it without asking our parents for help. They had borne the expense of sending her to Lincoln School and helped her with the costs of attending Antioch not covered by her scholarship. She had relied on them long enough. It was time to pursue her dream on her own.

During her senior year, Coretta applied to some of the best music schools in the country. Gradually, she narrowed her options to two of the most prominent—Juilliard School of Music in New York and the New England Conservatory in Boston. Juilliard had been her first preference but the slower pace of life in Boston suited her better. Boston's reputation as a cultural center was a consideration as well, and in the end, she chose the New England Conservatory of Music. Perhaps, too, she remembered lines from a poem she had recited while still a child, words that not only described events in Boston long ago, but that would also become a refrain for her life.

A cry of defiance and not of fear
A voice in the darkness, a knock at the door,
And a word that shall echo forever more![7]

With the choice of schools settled, Coretta's next task was raising money to defray the expense of that further training. She applied to several foundations for scholarships and aid, one of which was the Jessie Smith Noyes Foundation. Established by real estate developer Charles Noyes and named in honor of his wife, from 1947 through 1959 the Noyes Foundation offered scholarships to students attending accredited colleges and professional schools. Half of those scholarships were reserved for minority students. Coretta was confident things would work out, but as graduation came and went, she had not heard from any of the foundations to which she had applied. Undeterred, she moved forward with her dream of pursuing a career in music and made plans to travel east.

For Coretta, the years at Antioch had been a very meaningful experience in personal development. What she learned there and the things to which she had been exposed equipped her with some special qualities that, as time would show, proved to be excellent preparation for the life that lay ahead.

13

Boston

Coretta spent the summer of 1951 in New York where she worked at the Riverside Branch of the New York Public Library. Those few months offered her a brief interlude in which to catch her breath, work, study, and make additional contacts before going on to Boston. She was not interested in becoming a permanent resident of New York, but it was the center of the music industry. Anyone aspiring to a career in that business sooner or later went to New York.

While in New York, Coretta studied voice with Ora Witte, who gave her extra lessons free of charge. During those three months, Coretta also performed on several occasions. One of those events included a Sunday appearance at Harlem's Abyssinian Baptist Church where she sang at a service where Congressman Adam Clayton Powell Jr. preached.[1]

Coretta enjoyed visiting in New York and she made valuable contacts there, but as the summer wore on, she still did not know how she would finance her music education in Boston. She was prepared to work, but musical training was expensive and she did not expect to be able to earn enough to pay her way through the conservatory. As she wrestled with the problem of her finances, she remembered that before she left Antioch, her adviser, Jessie Treichler, had given Coretta the names of several people in New York who Mrs. Treichler thought might be of help. One of those people was legendary talent scout and recording producer John Hammond Jr.

With a career that spanned most of the twentieth century, Hammond had launched or assisted the careers of numerous musicians from Benny Goodman to Stevie Ray Vaughan. In the summer of 1951, he was involved with the work of Hazel Scott and

Lena Horne, among others.[2] Hammond's wife was a graduate of Antioch. As Coretta thought about her financial situation, she decided to give Hammond a call. He graciously agreed to meet her and even agreed to listen to her sing.

The visit began with Coretta telling Hammond about her background at Antioch, her concert experiences, and her plans for further training. When he asked about her plans for the future, she told him she wanted a career as a concert singer. He listened attentively, then asked her to sing.

After Coretta had completed several songs, Hammond complimented her voice and style, then asked whether she would consider a career in popular music. The market for popular music was quite large compared to the classics, and remuneration in that field was high. Hazel Scott was earning $75,000 a year, which was quite a sum at the time. Coretta's chances for success, he thought, were far better in popular music than in the classics.

I am not certain Coretta understood the extent to which Hammond could have assisted her in a career in popular music, but her mind was made up about the direction she intended to take. She was not interested in money or in music alone, and she was not approaching a music career with the goal of merely entertaining. She had a sense of calling and purpose that she meant to fulfill.

Coretta listened politely, then told Hammond that before she launched a career she wanted to get the best musical education possible, which was the reason she wanted to study at a conservatory. Although many popular singers were highly trained, she did not think that conservatory training was really necessary for people who wanted to sing popular music, and she was not willing to change her goal. She was ready to take her chances. Their conversation ended pleasantly as Coretta thanked him for seeing her and he wished her well.

As Coretta left Hammond's office, she was disappointed and melancholy. The meeting had not turned out the way she had wanted. She was looking for help in achieving her goal, not in achieving someone else's goal for her. Sadly enough, she was no closer to solving her financial dilemma.

By the end of July, Coretta still had not received a response to her financial aid applications. With summer rapidly drawing to a close, she left her temporary job in New York and went home to Alabama during the month of August to spend time with our parents. She was convinced the New England Conservatory was the place for the next step in her musical education and continued to believe the money to make it happen would turn up soon, though she was less certain of how that would happen.

At home in Alabama, Coretta stubbornly refused to ask our parents for any financial support. By this time Dad's business was a success. He was fully capable of helping her, but that was not part of her plan.

A few days before she was to leave, Dad took her aside for a talk. "I wouldn't go up there without any money," he said. Like any parent might, he worried about what would happen to her. "What are you going to do if you don't get a scholarship?"

"I'm still waiting to hear from one foundation," Coretta replied. "I hope they will give me a favorable response. But if they don't, I'm still going to Boston. I'll find a job once I'm there. A way will open for me to continue my studies in music. I know it."

On the day Coretta departed for Boston, Dad gave her train fare and some spending money. I left home the same day to return to a teaching position in Talladega, Alabama. As Coretta and I said our good-byes, I whispered a prayer for her. She was sustained at that moment only by her own childlike faith. Standing there in the yard at our parents' home in Perry County, the future for Coretta looked very uncertain, but somehow I felt she would make it.

When Coretta reached New York, she had to change trains. There in the station, she telephoned the Noyes Foundation to see if they had responded to her application. She was nervous as she approached the pay phone. Suppose their decision was negative, she thought, as she hesitated before inserting her dime in the pay telephone. She took a coin from her purse and slid it into the slot on the phone, then slowly dialed the number. Finally, after getting the right person on the line, she was informed that a letter already had been mailed to her announcing she had been granted a scholarship of six hundred fifty dollars. Coretta was overjoyed. With fresh courage, she confidently boarded the connecting train to Boston.

Six hundred fifty dollars does not sound like much now, but in 1951, it was enough to cover tuition at the conservatory. With that scholarship, Coretta would be able to register as a full-time student. However, she still needed money for additional fees and living expenses. She had obtained a room in advance with Mrs. Bartol, a contributor to Antioch's Interracial Scholarship Fund who lived on Boston's Beacon Hill. That meant Coretta had a place to go upon arrival in the city, but she would need a part-time job to pay for it.

As her train jogged northward, Coretta thought about Boston and the challenges that lay ahead. She had found a way to thrive at Antioch, and she was certain she would thrive in Boston, too. The challenges would not be the same, but she would apply the things she had learned—dogged determination, hard work, and faithfulness to her dream and goals. She looked forward to the fulfillment that would come from being immersed in the thing she loved. The sacrifices would be small compared with the satisfactions. Boston offered her an opportunity to pursue her first love. Doing so would lead her to the love of her life.

❦

Coretta arrived in Boston in early September 1951. It was her first trip that far north. As she arrived in the city, she noted its distinctive character. Founded in 1630, it was one of the oldest cities in the nation. As she walked along the streets, she found herself staring at buildings and sites she had read about in books. Fascination and trepidation met her with every step.

The house on Beacon Hill sat along a narrow, winding street. Not far away was a park with lush green grass. Towering trees provided shade and in the fall turned the ground red and brown and yellow with fallen leaves. A four-story Georgian structure, the house had a center entrance that was flanked on both sides with windows arranged in neat, orderly rows. Windows, equidistant from each other in a perfectly symmetrical arrangement, looked out from the three floors above as well.

Inside, a stairway rose along the wall to the right. Steep and narrow, it ran from the ground floor all the way to the top. Coretta's room was on that top floor. Originally the attic, the space had been partitioned to allow for multiple boarders. Two other students shared the floor with her.

The New England Conservatory of Music was conveniently located a few blocks from the house. Founded in 1867, the same year as Lincoln School, it was one of the oldest and most venerated schools of its kind in the United States. At the conservatory, Coretta would encounter people for whom music was the noblest of professions. There she would learn to nurture, develop, and discipline her talent. And she would learn that doing so required a total commitment. Throughout her years there, she would enjoy freedom from all the things that hindered her from achieving her goal, her objective, her dream. Finding the discipline to give music the larger place in her life would force Coretta to face difficult choices about marriage, family, and love. Behind all the glamour and prestige, the real business of the conservatory was work with a purpose—the most intensive kind of work. Coretta had come a long way from Lincoln School—first to Antioch and then to the New England Conservatory—but she would soon find she had only reached the beginning of her journey.

Boston's long history of vigorous intellectual life dated back to its founding as one of the first American colonies. Once known as the Athens of America, it offered a rich store of historical, cultural, and educational landmarks. Along its Freedom Trail, there was Boston Common, the Paul Revere House, the Old South Meeting-house, and the Bunker Hill Monument. A proud city, Boston was a place where family and culture counted, and where learning and the arts had been supported by some of the nation's wealthiest people. Not merely patrons of the arts, prominent citizens of the city, including the early abolitionists, had a history of supporting other liberal causes as well.

In Boston during the early 1950s, when Coretta was a student there, one could sense something of the lingering spirit of the creative and heroic men and women who had helped shape America's finest traditions. It was against this backdrop that Coretta's student days at the conservatory unfolded.

Rather than hide her financial condition, Coretta explained her situation to Mrs. Bartol. Sympathetic and helpful, she permitted Coretta to do some cleaning in the house in exchange for her room and breakfasts, and Mrs. Bartol refused to accept pay for the first six weeks. At the same time, the conservatory gave Coretta a one-hundred-dollar scholarship. A few weeks later, she obtained a part-time job as a file clerk with a mail order firm, a job secured for her by the Urban League. All those pieces together covered her basic expenses but getting them in place took time. In the meantime, Coretta got hungry. She had breakfast at the house on Beacon Hill, but lunch and dinner were a problem.

After a week in the city, Coretta's money was almost gone. She had budgeted carefully and eaten the lightest meals possible. Even so, the spending money Dad had given her did not last long. By the Sunday after she arrived, she was down to less than a dollar.

All day long she held out, trying to distract her mind from the growing sense of emptiness in her stomach. Finally, late in the afternoon, she went to a neighborhood grocery and bought a package of Graham crackers, a jar of peanut butter, and a few pieces of fruit. A handful of crackers with peanut butter and a piece of fruit tasted good, but it did not fill her stomach. In the early evening she grew increasingly uncomfortable. In desperation, she looked through her address book for the names and telephone numbers of people she had been told would be good contacts when she arrived in Boston. She decided to telephone Bertha Wormley.

A perceptive person, Mrs. Wormley sensed Coretta's need. Before their telephone conversation ended, Mrs. Wormley asked Coretta to stop by her office at the State House the following day. When Coretta arrived there, Mrs. Wormley gave her an envelope and assured her, "You'll make it. Of course, you'll make it."

As she rode to school on the subway, Coretta opened the envelope and found fifteen crisp dollar bills. From that day onward, Mrs. Wormley kept an eye on Coretta, doing those little things—a note, a word, a meal offered at just the right moment—that make the difference between success and failure, particularly in difficult times.

The irony of her situation was not lost on Coretta. She lived in a residence where all the other occupants were white, in an old, exclusive section of Boston, surrounded by descendants of the city's founding families, yet she was black, hungry, and all alone. While she resided at one of the most fashionable addresses in town, in an area inhabited by people who had arrived socially, she felt totally isolated. The weekends especially were lonesome for her at first because they offered no diversion from her weekday routine of study, work, and practice.

Once during this period, on a cool autumn Sunday afternoon when Coretta felt she could no longer endure being confined in the four walls of her small room, she walked out of the house and down the hill to Tremont Street. A few blocks later she came to a stop in front of the Tremont Temple, an African American church, where a service was in progress. She stood there on the sidewalk and listened to the sound of singing coming from inside. The hymn was familiar and a sense of nostalgia swept over her, bringing with it thoughts of home and all the things she sought to leave behind. As she stared into space, lost in the moment, the music became less audible as her mind focused on her condition and the deep yearning inside for familiar scenes and faces. Then, as the music from the church came to an end, her mind slowly came back to the present. As she did, she became aware of a man standing a few feet away. Not just a man but a familiar face, someone she knew. Suddenly, she realized the man in front of her was Bob Madison.

Just as stunned as she was, Bob blurted out, "Coretta, what on earth are you doing here?" He quickly introduced his wife, Leatrice, and the three of them talked briefly about how they came to be in Boston. He was a graduate student at Harvard. After they had chatted a while, the Madisons, who were driving, dropped Coretta by her residence and promised to invite her to dinner some time. As they drove away and Coretta turned to go inside, she thought about how heartwarming it was to meet an old friend on the lonely streets of a large city.

During those first months in Boston, Coretta struggled to get by. However, being a music student, she wanted a piano at home as a way to practice. She located one in fair condition that she could get for the cost of moving it. Mrs. Bartol agreed to let her bring the piano into the house. There was room for it downstairs, and no one minded the prospect of hearing her play. Only one obstacle remained—the cost of moving the piano—and she only had a few days to find the funds. The owner of the piano needed to move it out of her house quickly. Coretta checked around and found she could have the piano moved for twenty-five dollars. It was a reasonable price, but it was a sum that Coretta did not have.

Days passed, and Coretta still did not have the money to move the piano. Once again, her faith began to waver. When she had located the piano, she had been certain the money would come to allow her to move it. In an act of faith, she contacted the moving company and arranged to have it delivered. Now, with the day of delivery upon her and still without the money, she was crestfallen. When she arrived home from school that afternoon, she entered the house feeling disappointed and dejected. As she started up the stairs, Mrs. Bartol called to her from around the corner.

"Coretta, you have a letter." She handed Coretta the envelope and smiled. "Looks like it's from your sister."

Coretta took the letter upstairs and opened it in her room. Tears filled her eyes as she saw, tucked between the folds of my note, a check for twenty-five dollars.

I had not known about the piano or her need for that specific amount, but I knew my sister was in Boston facing dire financial circumstances. When we had parted company at our parents' home that summer, I knew as I had always known that God had a purpose and calling for Coretta. Something important, something bigger than either of us could understand at that moment, would come from her life. God had put her on my mind for a purpose, and I was certain it had to do with her finances. I decided to help her reach her destiny. After that experience, I made a commitment that every payday after that, for the duration of her time in Boston, I would send her a check.

Coretta obtained the piano and wrote that same day to tell me about it. Neither of us called it a coincidence. We knew it was God's timing. He was training her voice to sing and equipping her spirit to know that He would always be one step ahead of her, opening the next door just as she arrived. It was a lesson essential for the next stage of her life, one that was nearer than either of us realized.

After three months at the conservatory, someone suggested Coretta might be eligible for out-of-state tuition assistance from her home state. Because the kind of professional program she was pursuing was not available to African Americans in Alabama—segregation laws prohibited her from attending state public universities that offered comparable training in her field—the state might be able to assist her in obtaining that training elsewhere. Coretta was skeptical that the suggestion would work, but she applied to the state of Alabama for help anyway.

To her profound amazement, Coretta's application was approved. At the time, southern states argued that their segregated education system offered "separate but equal" education for both blacks and whites. As a way of bolstering that argument, the state implemented a policy to compensate blacks for those programs offered to whites in white schools that were not offered to blacks in black schools. That policy applied to Coretta's situation, and though she disagreed with Alabama's segregation policy, she was thankful for the financial assistance. As Scripture reminds us, what others intend for evil, God can use for good.

The money came in an amount calculated to cover the difference between the cost of a comparable program at The University of Alabama and the cost at the New England Conservatory. At the time, fees at The University of Alabama were very low compared to those at the conservatory, which meant the state of Alabama paid a large portion of the cost of Coretta's course of study. The state also paid the cost of her room and board and reimbursed her for transportation expenses in getting to and from Boston. Having the state aid meant she could give up her job at the mail order house, concentrate fully on her study program, and eat regular meals.

14

Martin

Although she was not completely satisfied with her life in Boston, Coretta was in good spirits at the start of the second semester. The knowledge that she could make it financially and the satisfaction of showing promise as a young singer allayed her anxieties in two extremely important areas. On the surface she had every reason to be happy. She was doing the thing she had worked toward since high school. Even so, Coretta still felt isolated. She had no personal attachments, and this was not good even for a young woman bent on a concert career. All her life, Coretta had been a social person. She was always surrounded by friends. Even in elementary school, she had had a boyfriend. She needed someone to be concerned about who also would have her welfare at heart. Until the second semester, her dating life in Boston had been casual. She had not met anyone about whom she had cared enough to develop a real friendship. Across town, Martin Luther King Jr., a young doctoral student at Boston University, faced a similar dilemma.

Born and reared in Georgia, Martin enjoyed soul food, home-cooked meals in a style similar to those served in the South. Because of that, he usually ate his evening meals at the Western Lunch Box on Massachusetts Avenue, a café that specialized in that kind of food. While he ate, he enjoyed the camaraderie of many other black students. One evening he was joined at dinner by Mary Powell, a friend from Atlanta who was a student at the conservatory. That night, he asked Mary if she knew any nice girls. "I have met about everything Boston has to offer, and I'm about to get cynical."

Mary named two girls, Coretta and another student at the conservatory. Martin already had met the other girl and had been unimpressed. This left Coretta, about whom he was eager to hear more. Mary's description of her aroused his curiosity, especially when Mary suggested she bore a striking resemblance to a woman in Atlanta whom they both knew. When Martin appeared intrigued, Mary cautioned that while Coretta was a very fine and talented young woman, she was not religious. Mary, a devout Catholic, knew that Coretta had not been attending church.

Shrugging his shoulders, Martin replied, "That's all right. She doesn't have to believe in a literal interpretation of the Bible." Before they left the café that evening, Mary gave him Coretta's telephone number.

In the meantime, Mary spoke to Coretta about the young minister from Atlanta whom she thought Coretta would enjoy meeting. When Coretta failed to show much interest, Mary went on to say that he had a very promising future and that Dr. Benjamin Mays,[1] who was president of Atlanta's Morehouse College, was one of his staunchest supporters. Coretta's plans at that time did not include marriage to a minister, at least not the kind she had known back home, most of whom were conservative, overly pious stereotypes. Mary persisted, and after a while, Coretta relented. She told Mary she would be willing to talk to Martin on the telephone.

Martin called the following Thursday evening. After introducing himself, he went on to talk for almost fifteen minutes with barely a pause. He was effusive and over the top, telling Coretta how much he liked the image of her given him by Mary Powell. As he continued, his self-confidence seemed to ooze through the phone line, telling her, "I am like Napoleon at Waterloo before your charms. I am on my knees." Coretta was alternately amused and taken aback by his straightforward delivery of lines the likes of which she had never heard before. However, those "lines" proved effective enough, and Coretta agreed to meet him for lunch the following day.

Friday at noon, Martin drove from Boston University to the conservatory where Coretta waited for him in front of Jordan Hall. As he came from the car to greet her, she looked him over. Her first impression was that he seemed a little short.

When they arrived at the restaurant, Coretta removed her coat and kerchief. Martin gave her that look typical of most men, taking in all of her in one lingering glance. When he saw that she noticed, he gave her an embarrassed smile and said, "You have some great hair." Coretta let him recover, and soon they were talking freely.

While they ate, Martin began an intellectual discourse about class relations in modern society. When Coretta made what she later described as a few half-way intelligent responses, Martin's eyes lit up. "Oh," he replied, "so you can do something else besides sing. You have a good mind, also."

On the drive back to the conservatory, Martin smiled across the seat at Coretta. "I can tell you have everything I want in a wife. There are only four things, and you have all of them. Beauty, personality, character, and intelligence." Again taken aback by his brash nature, Coretta was at a loss for words. Already she felt there was something unusual about him, and although it was too soon to take his words seriously, she didn't take him lightly, either.

As Coretta stepped from the car to the sidewalk, Martin was emphatic. "I want to see you again. When can I see you?" Coretta suggested that he call her that evening and she would decide then.

On Saturday night, Martin escorted Coretta to a party in Watertown. On their way, they stopped off at Conservatory House, the dormitory where Mary Powell lived. Referring to Coretta, he beamed and told Mary, "I owe you a thousand dollars."

When they arrived at the party, every girl in the place seemed to know Martin. They all gathered around him, ignoring Coretta and making a fuss over him. "He played back with them to impress me," Coretta recalled. "And I was impressed. It always helps to know that the man you might be interested in is in demand."

Two weeks after meeting Coretta, Martin wrote his mother and told her that he had met his wife. Like Pygmalion, Martin had fallen in love with an image and an ideal. Later, he found she was more than image, beauty, and integrity—and more than a match for his intellect.

In the week following the Watertown party, Martin called Coretta every other day. Not long after that, he called her daily. He and Coretta began seeing each other twice a week and then almost every day. They attended movies and concerts together, ate together, and sometimes just sat and studied together. "The more I saw him," Coretta said, "the better I liked him. There is something about him that grows on you." She found him challenging and intriguing.

He was one of the best dancers in Boston, popular, with a great line, yet he had such a serious side to most of his conversations. He talked so often about what he planned to do with his life, or what he hoped to contribute to the race and to humanity at large that I sometimes found myself asking, "Where did he develop such a social conscience? He didn't go to Antioch."

Though middle-class in outward appearance, he often expressed his concern for the plight of the masses, saying how much he abhorred the evils of our economic system. But, for reasons which he would explain, he would say he could never be a Communist either. It didn't take long for me to see that Martin had social and political views similar to my own, and that here was a young man who knew where he wanted to go and how he intended to get there.[2]

Early in their courtship Coretta wrote me an enthusiastic letter about Martin, the tone of which let me know she liked him a lot. When I went to Boston in the summer, some months after they had met, I had the opportunity to judge Martin for myself. Like Coretta, the more I saw of him, the more impressed I became. On double dates to see the Boston Pops Orchestra, driving to the suburbs for delectable fried clams, and on Sunday afternoon strolls across the Common, we had a delightful summer of fun and romance.

Once we were face-to-face, Coretta and I could talk about her relationship with Martin, and I could see how much he meant to her. Very soon it became clear that this romance was real, despite the strong conflict Coretta felt between marriage and her career. She had been brought up to believe that one should obtain an education and then do something with it. Having envisioned a concert career for herself, she had not planned to marry until her career had been launched and established. Coretta could not envision a minister's wife pursuing a separate career for herself. Besides, Martin already had described what he wanted in a wife—someone to come home to. Yet, because Martin possessed so many of the qualities she liked in a man, Coretta found herself becoming more involved with every passing moment.

When it appeared to me that Coretta was slowly but surely committing herself to the love of a man more than to her love of music, I asked her, "What is it about this man that makes him so appealing to you?"

After several superficial answers, Coretta finally said, "I suppose it's because Martin reminds me so much of our father."

This is it, I thought. This man is the one.

Martin's father, Martin Luther King Sr., known to many as Daddy King, followed a practice of visiting his children who were living away from home at least once a year. When he arrived in Boston in the fall of 1952, Coretta and Martin had been dating steadily for about ten months. Daddy King admonished her, "Unless you know my son better than I do, don't take him seriously. He's gone out with some of the finest girls—beautiful girls, intelligent, from fine families. We love people and we want to be nice to everyone, but we don't know how to act. He gets us involved, then he just seems to lose interest. Those girls had a lot to offer." Speaking politely but with steeled composure, Coretta replied, "I have a lot to offer, too."[3]

After observing Coretta and Martin together and sensing the kind of relationship that was developing between them, Daddy King and his wife, Mama King, decided it was time they met some other members of Coretta's family. That fall, I was in New York working on a master's degree at Columbia University. The Kings obtained my telephone number from Coretta and contacted me on their return trip to Atlanta. Telephoning from the Hotel New Yorker, Daddy King invited me to have lunch with him and his wife the following day. I gladly consented.

At lunch, the Kings were warm and gracious, but Daddy King quickly directed the conversation to the subject that was uppermost in his mind—my sister's relationship with his son. He felt they were contemplating marriage and wanted to know whether I felt Coretta was strong enough to be the kind of wife Martin was going to need. He kept saying, "My son is going to need a very strong woman behind him."

On this question, I knew I could speak honestly and proudly, without any hesitation. I assured the Kings that Coretta was one of the strongest people I knew and that she had an iron will and inexhaustible physical stamina. I spoke candidly. In my opinion, Coretta had no need to bargain for a husband.[4]

A few months later, on Valentine's Day 1953, Coretta and Martin announced their engagement. The announcement was published in the *Atlanta Daily World*. Their wedding was set for June. But Coretta's conflicting desires had not been resolved. She continued to wonder whether her investment in musical training would be wasted if she were to get married now. Moreover, she questioned whether she would make a good minister's wife. Martin knew he wanted to pastor a church. Typically, pastors needed and wanted the assistance of their wives as copartners in their work. Maybe if she married a man in a different profession, Coretta thought, it would be easier for her to have a concert career. Besides, her friends in Boston, especially those at the conservatory, talked against the marriage. They did not feel Martin King would ever amount to much. Sacrificing her musical gift for him, they argued, would be a terrible mistake.

Just before Easter vacation that spring, I received a letter from Coretta in which she once again expressed doubts about the wisdom of her decision to marry Martin. Her conflict again centered on the prospect of giving up a singing career, a dream for which she had worked so hard, and upon the larger issue of "doing something" with her life. Since high school, she had been guided by a sense of purpose and calling. Many things in her life—friendships, courses of study, co-op jobs, other serious relationships—all had been weighed, judged, and evaluated based on the notion of "doing something." Many of the previous options she had been given had seemed limiting and confining for the larger purpose she sensed for her life. If she married a minister and settled down as a pastor's wife, she would be expected to involve herself in the lives of the congregation. Could that life sustain her? Would it be adequate to achieve her as yet amorphous notion of her calling?

Frankly, at the time, I was somewhat surprised and a little impatient with Coretta's continual vacillation and ambivalence. She had come to this point with other men in her life, but that was several years earlier. Now, things were different. In answering her letter I wrote, "Don't be foolish, girl. If you love Martin, marry him. He will not be an ordinary preacher. As his wife, you will have many opportunities to sing." Even at that time, I could see no reason why her marriage to him would deprive her of some, if not all, of her dream of reaching large audiences with her music. I did not see this as a choice between Martin and career. She could have both. More important, I felt that she and Martin were spiritually attuned to each other. To me that was the real basis for marriage.

Before she received my letter, Coretta meditated for the last time about her decision, phrasing her dilemma in the form of two questions: "Do I love him enough to make any sacrifice?" and, "Can I give him up and not miss him?" The answers to those questions came from within. She did indeed love him enough to make any sacrifice, and no, she could not give him up without a sense of loss. When my letter arrived, it served only to reassure her of something she already knew.

15

Marriage

At six o'clock in the evening on June 18, 1953, Coretta and Martin pledged them-selves to one another in a simple but dignified wedding ceremony on the lawn of our parents' home near Marion, Alabama. Martin's father officiated, and his brother A.D. was best man. I was Coretta's maid of honor.

In attendance at the wedding were neighbors, relatives, and friends from as far away as Birmingham and Atlanta. Two prominent white citizens from the commu-nity joined us for the ceremony. With music drifting across the lawn and the scent of fresh flowers wafting through the air, that warm summer evening became a beau-tiful moment in the lives of two anxious young people. As I stood beside Coretta, I could not help but sense her joyous anticipation and sorrowful reflection—excited about beginning something new yet sad to let go of the dream which she had gripped so tightly for many years.

For the remainder of the summer, Coretta and Martin lived with Martin's parents in Atlanta. Coretta worked at Citizens Trust Bank, not far from their home. Martin assisted his father as co-pastor of Ebenezer Baptist Church. Living in the house with her in-laws brought Coretta a fresh set of challenges, but she and Martin learned to cope and even flourish.

In the fall, Coretta and Martin returned to Boston to continue their schooling. She had work to complete in order to receive her degree in music. He was not quite finished with his doctoral program. They rented a four-room apartment on North Hampton Street for thirty-five dollars a month and settled into life as married stu-dents. The apartment was located within walking distance of the conservatory.

Coretta dashed about, hurrying to complete her program in voice. Martin did most of his studying at home. Playing the role of a good husband, he kept the house, even cooking dinner once a week, and did his best to make life comfortable for them both.

The academic year of 1953–54 was hectic for them, but their hard work paid off. Coretta completed her studies and graduated in June with a distinguished record of achievement. While there, she studied voice with former Metropolitan Opera star Marie Sundelius. As a member of the New England Conservatory Chorus, Coretta performed with the famed Boston Symphony Orchestra. She sang regularly with the historic Old South Church Choir and premiered at the New England Conservatory of Music presentation of *Motives de Son,* a series of songs by Cuban composer Amadeo Roldan. In addition, she made numerous solo appearances before church and community groups and appeared on the radio.

Martin continued work toward completing the course requirements for his doctoral degree. At the same time, he considered the options for his future. By the time Coretta graduated, he would have only his dissertation left to complete. Work on that did not require his presence in Boston. He could write from any location. As fall gave way to winter, he began exploring pastoral options. Martin consistently had expressed an interest in a career as pastor of a church, and he was particularly interested in returning to the South. Still, he did not ignore other possibilities and considered churches in other locations. He delivered sermons to congregations in and around Boston, spoke to a church in Detroit and to one in Chattanooga, Tennessee. Then he heard about an opening at Dexter Avenue Baptist Church in Montgomery.

Dexter was an interesting church. A downtown congregation, its members were accustomed to eloquent and erudite sermons. Located only a few blocks from the state capitol building, it sat in the center of bustling civic activity. The former pastor, Vernon Johns, had only recently been dismissed. Martin was intrigued.

Coretta preferred to stay in the North, where race relations were not so strained. Though blacks and whites were still at odds, in most northern states segregation was not the law. In contrast, Montgomery was only fifty miles from her hometown. She knew the region well—too well. She had grown to like and appreciate the freedom of the less rigidly segregated North, and she was certain a career in singing would be much easier there. But Martin would not be dissuaded.

In late winter he traveled to Montgomery and delivered a sermon. In the spring, the church formally offered him the position of pastor, which Martin accepted. He and Coretta were to arrive there in September.

While in Boston, Coretta and Martin had plumbed the depths of that city's rich social and cultural heritage. What they saw and did, however, was only a part of their preparation for the days ahead. Of greater significance was the spiritual strength they acquired—Coretta through her struggle to overcome obstacles and complete her degree, Martin through the expansion of his understanding of fundamental theological concepts, his increased awareness of a deeply troubled American culture, and his growing familiarity with seminal ideas of nonviolent response. They were a young couple filled with fervor and zeal for service but were old enough to have gained thorough preparation for the monumental tasks that lay ahead as they moved from the cradle of American liberty to the cradle of the Confederacy.

IV BLOSSOM

The desert shall rejoice and blossom as the rose.
—Isaiah 35:1

16

Montgomery

Dexter Avenue Baptist Church provided an excellent forum for an ambitious young minister interested in making full use of his training and talents. Montgomery was not only the capital of Alabama, but also a college town. Dexter's congregation was composed largely of faculty and staff members from Alabama State College. Full of serious-minded members, the congregation was often at the forefront of events in the black community. Those advantages, however, came at a price. Dexter had a reputation as a difficult church to pastor.

Although she had misgivings at first, Coretta came to see Dexter as the kind of challenge for which Martin had been searching. Montgomery was not as cosmopolitan as she would have liked, but as she wrestled with that fact, she realized they had an obligation to return to the South. Blacks in the South needed educated leadership. She and Martin had received the finest education available to blacks. Already, they sensed the restless discontentment that was slowly gaining momentum and pushing events in the direction of something new. Change was coming, and they wanted to be there when it happened. Even Coretta, for all her misgivings about abandoning her dream of a concert career, could not deny the unmistakable prompting of the Holy Spirit urging them toward the work in Montgomery. As Martin would later describe it,

> [S]he had breathed the free air of unsegregated colleges, and stayed as a welcome guest in white homes. Now in preparation for our long-term return to the South, she visited the Negro section of town where we would be living without choice. She saw the Negroes crowded into the backs of segregated buses and knew

that she would be riding there too. But on the same visit she was introduced to the church and cordially received by its fine congregation. And with her sense of optimism and balance, which were to be my constant support in the days to come, she placed her faith on the side of the opportunities and the challenges for Christian service that were offered by Dexter and the Montgomery community.[1]

On September 1, 1954, Martin became Dexter's full-time pastor. He and Coretta moved into the church parsonage on South Jackson Street shortly thereafter. The house, a white frame structure with a deep, comfortable porch, was rather old-fashioned but adequate. Inside, the parsonage was configured to suit the needs of a minister's family. The living room, which ran the full width of the house, provided adequate space for entertaining. Beyond it was an eat-in kitchen that was cozy enough for the family and yet capable of servicing large gatherings. Fully furnished, the house was well-appointed though not luxurious.

Coretta devoted the first few months in Montgomery to getting settled and organized. She brought with her a grand piano, a television, and several pieces of art, including a collection of African masks, West Indian gourds, and a number of paintings. With her touch, the house took on an air of unpretentious sophistication.

At the church, Coretta went about learning her role as a minister's wife. Poised and confident, she was at her charming best. Alabama had a male-dominated society, even among blacks, but the men of Dexter soon learned to admire and respect her. A capable homemaker, she quickly convinced the older women that she was not merely young and attractive. As the first few months went by, they learned she could handle herself quite well. Already they could see she was as strong as her husband, if not stronger. The youngsters liked her, too. Her youthful appearance and the fact that she took a friendly interest in them easily won them over.

As might be expected, Coretta gravitated toward the church's music program, becoming a regular member of the choir, but that was not all she did. She also taught Sunday school, worked with the Baptist Training Union, and participated in the Missionary Society. She might have come to Montgomery with reluctance, but once she arrived, she dove into her role as minister's wife with enthusiasm. Only after she had her home and position in the church established did she begin to consider the options for a broader musical career.

In November 1954, three months after arriving at Dexter, Coretta appeared in concert at Shiloh Baptist Church in Brunswick, Georgia. She was accompanied by Mildred Greenwood Hall, a faculty member at Alabama State College. Four months later, on March 6, 1955, she made her Montgomery debut at First Baptist Church, where the Reverend Ralph D. Abernathy was pastor. More than a thousand people attended the concert.

E. P. Wallace wrote about the event, "Mrs. Coretta Scott King, talented soprano, captivated her concert audience at First Baptist Church recently. The charming singer combined youthfulness, informality, and a magnificent voice in this varied concert. Mrs. King had complete control of the audience from the very first moment she appeared on the stage. Perhaps among her listeners were talented artists, occasional concert goers, and casual music lovers, yet their decisions were unanimous, 'It was wonderful.'"[2]

Soon after the Montgomery concert, the Wilcox County Teachers Association presented Coretta at Camden Academy, in Camden, Alabama. With an excellent voice and a gift for entertaining, Coretta found her music career blossoming in ways more meaningful than she had anticipated. These were not the concert stages of New York or other large cities, but the audiences in the small towns and communities where she sang were warm, receptive, and enthusiastic. Not only that, she had the deep satisfaction of introducing them to an aspect of cultural enrichment many might never experience otherwise.

While Coretta went about fulfilling her role in the church and finding her niche in the Montgomery community, Martin worked diligently to formulate and develop a meaningful program for the Dexter congregation. One of his first concerns was that of changing Dexter's reputation in the Montgomery community as the "Big Folks" church, a derisive reference to the perception that Dexter's members thought they occupied a more important position in local society. Martin felt the church should be a place where people of all classes could realize their oneness under God.

In recommending a program, Martin set out to organize the church's activities around a concept that would later be described as the Beloved Community. For him, a fully functioning church should not only address the spiritual needs of the congregation, but should also demonstrate for the world the redeemed Body of Christ in the fullest manifestation possible. This meant making the Gospel the point of integration for every aspect of life: spiritual, physical, cultural, and political. The program he proposed in his first year reflected that perspective and included initiatives for religious education, care for the sick, scholarships for high school students, use of the arts in worship, and a committee to address social and political issues.[3]

Because of the innovations suggested by this program, Martin was dubious about its chances for acceptance. He offered it with the zeal of a first-time pastor but viewed its prospects with the wary eye of one who was not unwise to the vagaries of pastoral ministry. Much to his surprise, his program was heartily approved by the church leadership. With their backing, it received the immediate support of the membership. Committees were formed to address each of his concerns, and they went to work almost immediately. Within a few months the wisdom and foresight of Martin's program became obvious as the congregation began to grow. With the increased attendance came a renewed interest in proclaiming the Gospel not only as a witness to the black community, but to the entire Montgomery community as well.

Active before Martin became pastor at Dexter, the Social and Political Action Committee received new energy from his presence. Under his direction, it became an integral part of the life of the church. Its work was of primary importance in setting the stage for the many events that would soon follow. "By the first of November it was publishing a bi-weekly newsletter . . . which was distributed to every member of the church and proved to be of great value in placing major social and political issues before the church members. Under the committee's auspices a voting clinic had trained almost every unregistered member of the congregation in the pitfalls of discriminatory registration procedures."[4]

Martin's pastoral support elevated the committee's work to the attention of the entire congregation and helped involve more members in the effort. As a result of the committee's renewed efforts, Dexter led all Montgomery churches in contributions to the National Association for the Advancement of Colored People (NAACP).

For several months after he moved to Montgomery, Martin divided his attention between completing his doctoral dissertation and his duties as pastor. However, his deep conviction that a "religion true to its nature must also be concerned about man's social conditions" soon compelled him to take a more active role in the community.[5] As he grew more comfortable in his role as pastor, he grew increasingly restive toward the seemingly intractable issues of race and social justice. Not long after his arrival in Montgomery, he joined the local chapter of the NAACP and was named to the executive committee. Rosa Parks was secretary of the chapter when Martin joined. They worked together on many issues even before the bus boycott.

At about the same time, Martin attended meetings of an organization known as the Alabama Human Relations Council. An interracial group, the council sought ways to address Montgomery's growing racial tensions. Though well-intentioned, the group proved largely ineffective.

Involvement in the issues facing Dexter and blacks living in Montgomery gave new life and urgency to many of the ideas Martin had begun to consider at Boston University. Ideas that were theoretical in the classroom now took on new meaning in the practical world of a deeply segregated southern city. During that first year at Dexter, those ideas coalesced into a loosely defined philosophy of the role of religion in society and the relationship it bore to civic affairs. Martin later elaborated his views on the subject. "It [religion] seeks not only to integrate men with God but to integrate men with men and each man with himself. This means, at bottom, that the Christian gospel is a two-way road. On the one hand it seeks to change the souls of men, and thereby unite them with God; on the other hand it seeks to change the environmental conditions of men so that the soul will have a chance after it is changed. Any religion that professes to be concerned with the souls of men and is not concerned with the slums that damn them, the economic conditions that strangle them, and the social conditions that cripple them is a dry-as-dust religion."[6]

Echoing the words of Martin Luther, his sixteenth century namesake, Martin used the power of words and symbols to draw vivid images for his listeners. Burned indelibly on the minds of his congregation, those images brought the message of the Gospel to bear on their personal circumstances, casting everyday events against a historic backdrop. Just as Martin Luther's words provided the foundation for a new beginning in Europe, so too, Martin Luther King Jr. framed the debate in Montgomery, motivated his congregation to action, and moved to the forefront of a new beginning in the South.[7]

As a busy young couple genuinely concerned about the challenges of Christian ministry, Coretta and Martin saw the seasons of that first year turn rapidly. For each, it had been a rewarding year. In June 1955, Martin received a PhD in systematic theology from Boston University. Coretta had established her own identity in the congregation and had taken the first tentative steps toward a career as a concert singer. Now they looked forward to beginning a family.

A little more than a year after coming to Montgomery, their first child was born on November 17, 1955. At Coretta's insistence, they named her Yolanda Denise. Martin was not altogether pleased by the choice of names, but he was overjoyed at the arrival of his daughter. Nicknamed Yoki, she quickly became the object of the church's attention.

At Thanksgiving of that year, Coretta and Martin had much for which to be thankful—an excellent beginning to a new career, a new and expanding family, and a growing position of leadership and influence in the community. That first year at Dexter would be the most tranquil months they would see for a long time.

The joy of Thanksgiving gave way to the happy anticipation of Christmas. Shoppers turned their attention to a season of gifts and plans for entertaining family and friends. Parties both large and small filled almost everyone's schedule and with them the need for appropriate attire. Around town, clothing stores and seamstresses did a brisk business.

On Thursday afternoon, December 1, 1955, Rosa Parks left her job at a downtown department store and walked up the street to the bus stop. When the bus arrived, she stepped onboard, paid the fare, and took a seat.

Across town, Coretta and Martin went about their daily routine. Martin tended to his duties at the church. Coretta kept house and looked after Yolanda. Life for them was peaceful. But within hours, the world as they had previously known it would come to an end.

17

The Bus

On the surface, the social and economic problems facing blacks in Montgomery were typical of those in other southern cities of comparable size and wealth.[1] Most blacks in the city worked at menial jobs for low wages; the region had little industry outside the business of state government. While providing an income, those jobs were a trap that offered little in the way of potential advancement and stifled real opportunity. Education, housing, hospital care, recreation, and cultural life were strictly segregated. Always forced to enter public buildings by separate doorways and sit in separate areas, blacks were excluded from some events and locations altogether. At the time, it was easier for most blacks to travel to New York to hear the Metropolitan Opera than to hear it on tour in southern cities.

Blacks were also excluded from the political process. Through the imposition of poll taxes and other abusive practices, blacks were effectively precluded from voting. When they did, they voted in such small numbers that their votes were of little effect in asserting their opinions on the choice of leadership. There were no black elected officials in city or state government to champion the black community's cause.

Imperceptible to whites, racial tensions were already simmering long before any of the historic public events occurred. Growing unrest centered on southern policies of segregation and the abuse those policies engendered. Between 1954 and 1956, a succession of events worked to bring those tensions to the surface.

On December 9, 1952, the United States Supreme Court heard oral argument on the appeal of a group of cases that were known as *Brown v. Board of Education*.[2] The cases originated in the states of Kansas, South Carolina, Virginia, and Delaware as challenges to local school board policies enforcing state segregation laws in public schools. Under the Court's previous holding in *Plessy v. Ferguson,*[3] school boards in many states had maintained a "separate but equal" school system—one system for whites and another for blacks. In *Brown,* African American plaintiffs filed lawsuits in their respective states challenging that practice.

They alleged that the school systems were not equal, could not be made equal, and that segregation of the school system denied blacks equal protection as guaranteed by the Fourteenth Amendment of the US Constitution.

At trial, the courts had all ruled against the plaintiffs and upheld the school board practices. The plaintiffs appealed.

Led by Chief Justice Fred Vinson, the Supreme Court heard oral argument but was unable to reach a decision. The Court granted a motion for reargument, but before the case could be heard, Vinson died. Earl Warren was appointed to replace him. Blacks and whites across the nation watched and waited with great anticipation. Some saw the reargument as a positive sign for the plaintiffs, others as good news for the defendants.

Finally, on May 17, 1954, the court issued a unanimous decision finding segregation in public schools inherently unconstitutional. A subsequent ruling in the case turned the matter of integration over to federal district courts for implementation. The ruling was a monumental victory for the NAACP—one that energized blacks throughout the country—but its effects were long in becoming reality. While blacks hailed it as the greatest victory in the courts since Reconstruction, southern whites reacted with a vengeance.

In state courts and in state legislatures, whites used every means possible to delay implementation of the Supreme Court's ruling. Numerous individual court actions were required, almost on a district-by-district basis, to force school boards to act. In cities and communities across the South, citizen's councils sprang up under the guise of preserving "southern heritage" and "states' rights." In philosophy, they were little more than auxiliaries of the Ku Klux Klan.

On August 28, 1955, Emmett Till, a fourteen-year-old boy from Chicago who was visiting relatives near Money, Mississippi, was kidnapped. He was beaten and shot, and his body was dumped into the Tallahatchie River. Two white men were accused of the murder but were quickly acquitted by an all-white jury. Their heinous act received wide publicity and ignited an angry response from blacks everywhere. Emotions ran high as civil rights groups across the nation and around the world focused on the trial and subsequent acquittal.

In March 1955, sandwiched between the Supreme Court's historic ruling in *Brown* and the ruthless murder of young Emmett Till, fifteen-year-old Claudette Colvin boarded a Montgomery city bus on her way home from Booker T. Washington High School. When she refused to give up her seat to a white passenger, she was arrested, handcuffed, and jailed.

News of Colvin's arrest spread quickly through the Montgomery black community. E. D. Nixon, the local NAACP president, had been searching for a case that could be used to test Montgomery's ordinances that required segregation of the city bus line. Many at Dexter and others around the city talked of boycotting the bus service. A citizens committee, of which Martin was a member, met with representatives of the city commission and the bus company and demanded concessions to rectify seating arrangements and to address the discourteous manner in which black passengers were treated aboard the buses. City officials were willing to cooperate, but bus officials refused. Discontentment, already at a heightened state, was pushed to the verge of public protest. As events unfolded, Nixon and others decided that Colvin might not offer the best test of Montgomery's segregation laws.[4] In the end, leaders of the black community called off a boycott of the bus lines and held off filing a lawsuit on Colvin's behalf.

Under other circumstances, the determination of seating arrangements on city buses might have been viewed as one of the more mundane decisions of city government. But in 1955, the seating policy and practice on Montgomery city buses and others throughout the South was of paramount importance. Inhumane treatment of blacks—rooted and grounded in laws and policies meant to enforce segregation and to continue the plantation culture, lifestyle, and worldview that had so dominated the South—reached all the way to the determination of which seats blacks were permitted to occupy on the city bus. Having forced the hand of oppression so deeply into the lives of African Americans as to determine even where they would sit, white domination stood on the brink of depriving blacks of all civil rights and liberties. As L. D. Reddick observed, "the race relations pattern of the bus service was so old-fashioned that it just could not have persisted much longer under any circumstances. It was crude and inefficient, violating the cardinal maxim of good business that 'the customer is always right.' There were few places in the world of the twentieth century business where the principal customers were so rudely mistreated as were the Negro riders of Montgomery. They made up 70 percent of the trade."[5]

With no black drivers and white drivers who all too often expressed contempt for black passengers—referring to them as niggers, black cows, and black apes—black people were subjected not only to discrimination but to outright abuse. One obnoxious practice was that of having blacks pay their fare at the front door, then get off and reboard the bus at the rear or side door. Sometimes a bus driver would drive the bus away before paying black passengers had time to reach the rear door, leaving them standing in the street.

The first four seats of all buses were reserved for whites only. Blacks could not sit in those seats regardless of whether the bus was full or empty. Even if the bus was full and no white passengers were on board, blacks still could not occupy those seats. Often they stood over empty seats on those first four rows the entire length of the ride. Moreover, if white passengers were already occupying all seats reserved for them and additional whites boarded the bus, blacks sitting in the unreserved section immediately behind the whites were expected to stand so that the whites could be seated. Blacks who refused to vacate their seats were either removed from the bus or arrested.

When Rosa Parks, a small-framed, soft-spoken woman, boarded the bus that Thursday afternoon in December 1955, she paid the required fare and took a seat on a row just behind the area reserved for whites. Three stops into her trip all the seats reserved for whites were filled. When a white passenger was left without a seat, the driver told Mrs. Parks and others seated near her to give their seats to the white passenger.[6] Mrs. Parks refused to move. Minutes later, police arrived and arrested her.

Mrs. Parks had ridden that bus many times. When asked why she chose that particular day to refuse to stand, she said, "I was tired, but I was usually tired at the end of the day, and I was not feeling well, but then there had been many days when I had not felt well. I had felt for a long time, that if I was ever told to get up so a white person could sit, that I would refuse to do so."[7]

The protest that followed arose from the miserable, agonizing pain that had accumulated after years of inhuman treatment, of absorbing brutalities imposed from without, of being paralyzed by a sense that there was no recourse until no one could take it anymore. Coupled with the notion that tolerance of humiliation had reached its limit was the inescapable realization that the time had arrived, the divine moment had come. The momentum of the era had reached a tipping point. Scripture says, "There is a time for everything, and a season for every activity under heaven"[8] The African American's moment in history had arrived.[9]

18

Boycott

Although the events of December 1955 had not been planned in advance, they were not unanticipated, either. Despite the usual factionalism that had characterized blacks and their organizations, a strong branch of the NAACP and other like-minded groups—namely the Progressive Democrats, the Citizens Committee, and the Women's Political Council—were well-established in Montgomery. These organizations had strong, dedicated leadership and common goals, and they had been hard at work, creating an awareness of the need for united civic action.

The Reverend Vernon Johns, who preceded Martin at Dexter Avenue Baptist Church, had never missed an opportunity—in the pulpit, on the street corner, or while riding a city bus—to lash out against the conditions foisted upon blacks and the complacency of black people in accepting it. His insistence on speaking out against the treatment of blacks at the hands of whites and about the need for blacks to respond had been a major reason for his dismissal as pastor of Dexter.

E. D. Nixon, who worked as a Pullman porter, had devoted himself for more than thirty years to the task of shaking blacks free from their apathy. He had served as state president of the NAACP and in 1955 was president of the local NAACP in Montgomery. In that capacity, he had encouraged hundreds of blacks to register to vote.

In his analysis of the Montgomery protest, Martin wrote of the work of Johns and Nixon, "These were the fearless men who created the atmosphere for the social revolution that was slowly developing in the Cradle of the Confederacy."[1]

Still a newcomer to Montgomery, Martin was at first reluctant to take the lead in coordinating the black community's response to Mrs. Parks's arrest. Yet he was uniquely positioned for that role. He had been in Montgomery just long enough to establish himself as a nonpartisan leader. At the same time, he was familiar enough with the history of events to understand the roles and interests of the parties involved.

While attending college and graduate school, Martin had steeped himself in the writings and ideas of men like Henry David Thoreau and Mohandas K. Gandhi. When Martin read Thoreau's essay "Civil Disobedience" as a student at Morehouse College, he was so moved and fascinated by the idea of refusing to cooperate with an evil system that he reread the work several times. Thoreau's ideas were powerful and persuasive. Not only that, Thoreau practiced what he preached, even going to jail once for refusing to pay a poll tax. On the question of slavery, Thoreau had written, "I know this well, that if one thousand, if one hundred, if ten men whom I could name—if ten honest men only—ay, if one HONEST man, in this state of Massachusetts, ceasing to hold slaves, were actually to withdraw from the co-partnership, and be locked up in the county jail therefore, it would be the abolition of slavery in America."[2]

Further along in the essay, Thoreau stated, "A minority is powerless while it conforms to the majority; it is not even a minority then; but it is irresistible when it clogs by its whole weight."[3]

In reflecting upon the content of Thoreau's essay and the writings of Gandhi, who had used the nonviolent approach in India to help his people gain their independence from the British,[4] Martin came to see nonviolence as a potent weapon for effecting change in the South. As a practical and realistic approach, it seemed to provide the answer to the African American's need for a workable methodology. Outnumbered and relegated to a menial position in society, blacks had known that they could not outwit their oppressors by use of direct force and aggression.

Martin's philosophical orientation, his firsthand knowledge of the situation facing blacks, and his sound judgment made him the right man for the times. A resistance movement operating from the position of love, forgiveness, and passive resistance had an appeal and a mystery about it that confounded and confused the white opposition. It was a phenomenon they simply did not understand.

On Friday morning, December 2, 1955, Jo Ann Robinson, on behalf of the Women's Political Council, suggested that a one-day boycott of city bus lines was necessary as a way of responding to Mrs. Parks's arrest. E. D. Nixon agreed. The boycott would begin the following Monday, the same day Mrs. Parks was scheduled for trial. Boycotting the bus lines that day would send a clear message of protest. After discussing it at some length, Mrs. Robinson prepared leaflets urging all blacks to avoid using the city bus service the following Monday. Two thousand leaflets were distributed.

Nixon also began organizing local pastors. For the boycott to be successful, it would require the broadest response possible. He called Ralph Abernathy first. Ralph, an outspoken and persuasive pastor, was Martin's best friend. When Nixon suggested a meeting was necessary, Ralph agreed and suggested Dexter Avenue Baptist Church as a good location. Nixon then called Martin who made the church available.

That night, leadership from the black churches in Montgomery met in a large meeting room below the sanctuary. After a lengthy discussion, the group endorsed the Monday, December 5, boycott. Pastors who attended the meeting agreed to publicize the boycott from their pulpits on Sunday morning. A community-wide mass meeting was scheduled for Monday night at the Hope Street Baptist Church to assess the results of their efforts.

Nixon and others present that evening were serious about the boycott but uncertain about the outcome of such a demonstration. Time was short, and the leaflets could not reach more than 10 percent of the black population. Announcing it in church that Sunday would help, but not everyone attended Sunday services. Many wondered if the result would be worth the effort. Yet already, events were conspiring to spread the news.

That afternoon, a white woman found one of the leaflets in her kitchen. It had been left there inadvertently by her housekeeper, a black woman. Incensed, the white woman telephoned the newspaper to report the pending boycott. When the *Montgomery Advertiser* ran a front-page story in the Sunday edition, it gave the protesting group publicity they never could have purchased.

Then, in a desperate attempt to undermine the protest, Clyde Sellers, the Montgomery police commissioner and a member of the White Citizens Council, went on television and promised to protect any blacks who rode the buses. When Sellers put motorcycle policemen behind every bus, the blacks who were neutral stayed away from the bus lines, fearing there would be trouble.

Coretta and Martin rose earlier than usual on Monday, anxious to see what would happen. There was a bus stop located a few feet in front of their house. Coretta stood at the window and watched as the first bus drove up. When it slowed in front of their house, she called to her husband, "Martin, come quickly!" As he ran into the living room, Coretta exclaimed, "It's empty!"

The first bus was completely empty, and in fifteen minutes a second bus came by. It, too, was empty. Later, a third bus passed with only two passengers. Both of them were white. "I jumped in my car and for almost an hour I cruised down every major street and examined every passing bus. During this hour, at the peak of the morning traffic, I saw no more than eight Negroes riding the buses. By this time I was jubilant. Instead of the 60 per cent [sic] cooperation we had hoped for, it was becoming apparent that we had reached almost 100 per cent. A miracle had taken place. The once dormant and quiescent Negro community was now fully awake."[5]

It was a spectacle the likes of which no African American in Montgomery, or anywhere else for that matter, had seen before. College students walked and thumbed rides. Working people took cabs, rode in private cars, rode mules, or walked. Resorting to any possible means of transport, black citizens employed more than one horse-drawn buggy on the streets of Montgomery that day.

Monday began as a tense and serious morning. By noon, when nothing tragic had happened, the tension gave way to a sense of cautious relief. Throughout the day, buses remained empty as they drove through the black sections of the city, trailed by policemen on motorcycles. Toward the end of the day, youngsters could be seen pointing to the buses and laughing, "No riders today?"

That same day, Mrs. Rosa Parks was tried in municipal court for disobeying Montgomery's segregation ordinance. Found guilty, she was fined ten dollars and the costs of court. Unlike previous cases of this kind, Mrs. Parks appealed her conviction in an attempt to test the validity of the segregation law. As a leader of the black community, she also wanted to rouse blacks in Montgomery to positive action.

Throughout the day, Martin and the other ministers continued to discuss the situation. By lunchtime, they knew the outcome of Mrs. Parks's case. That afternoon, they met to plan the evening's mass meeting and to discuss a further response to the city. As they talked, many were persuaded that the protest should continue and that it needed an identity apart from existing organizations. Ralph suggested they name their organization the Montgomery Improvement Association (MIA). Martin was elected president without opposition. Rufus Lewis was named vice president. E. D. Nixon was treasurer. As the planning session ended, Martin found himself the spokesman for the emerging protest.

Martin did not seek the role of leadership. He did not campaign for it or invite others to campaign on his behalf. "[L]eadership sought him. He did not choose nonviolence; nonviolence chose him, imposing itself on him, as it were, as an interior demand of the situation . . . 'Tracked down' and 'chosen' by the times, King transcended the occasion, changing the times and transforming a diffuse uprising into a mass movement with passion and purpose."[6]

And he was not alone. At the same time Martin and the others were elected to office, an executive committee was appointed, which was composed of Montgomery's finest black men. With them also was the association's general membership that included people from all areas and denominations and from occupations as diverse as schoolteachers, businessmen, laborers, and lawyers.

With little time to spare, Martin rushed home from the meeting to tell Coretta about the day's developments. He had less than an hour to eat and prepare a message for the citywide mass meeting that evening. Coretta was surprised that he had been chosen to lead the organization that would guide and direct the protest, but she was proud to see others recognize his abilities. In spite of the fact that Martin was young and relatively new to the city, responsibility had fallen to him. He had no alternative but to accept it. She was aware of the dangers the entire family now faced, but in her usual unperturbed manner, she assured him that he had her full support. After eating, he went to his study and jotted down a few notes. With no time to prepare a detailed text, he would have to speak from his heart, drawing on the events of the day and the deep well of understanding he had spent most of his life preparing.

The meeting that night was held at Holt Street Baptist Church. As Martin drove across town, he wondered who would attend and how they would respond. While he was still a few blocks from the church, traffic came to a stop. Cars were parked along the curb and on the side streets in every direction. Sidewalks were filled with people, all of them headed toward the church. Martin parked his car several blocks away and hurried toward a side entrance. Already, an overflow crowd had gathered near the front doors.

By the time Martin rose to address the group, thousands of people had gathered in and around the church. Packed into the sanctuary and clustered out front near loudspeakers, they listened attentively as Martin took them on a tour of the events that had transpired since Mrs. Parks's arrest. Setting those events in context, he recounted for them the many insults and injuries they had received solely because they were black. He reminded them of language in the US Constitution and the mandate that those constitutional protections should be afforded to all. And he reminded them that their cause was the cause of the Gospel, the cause of Christ. For perhaps the first time, he explained at length the necessity of nonviolence and urged all to conduct themselves in a manner befitting those of the Christian faith.

As he reached the conclusion, he urged those gathered to continue their protest until an acceptable result had been attained. "If you will protest courageously, and yet with dignity and Christian love, when the history books are written in future generations, the historians will have to pause and say, 'There lived a great people—

a black people—who injected new meaning and dignity into the veins of civilization.' This is our challenge and our overwhelming responsibility."[7]

When Martin was finished, Ralph read a proposed resolution calling on blacks to avoid riding the buses until courteous treatment by bus operators was guaranteed, passengers were seated on a first-come, first-served basis—with blacks seated from the rear of the bus toward the front while whites seated from the front toward the back—and black bus drivers were employed on predominantly black routes. Those gathered that evening gave their overwhelming support. The protest would continue until the city met their demands.

With a two-week-old baby to tend and events around her speeding forward at a rapid pace, Coretta was swept into a whirlpool of activity. Their home, already a church parsonage, became the boycott's center of activity—at times so much so their newborn baby was prevented from sleeping. Formal and informal leadership meetings were held in their living room. Many of those meetings occurred at odd hours of both day and night. Friendly callers telephoned with the latest news or to receive an update. Hostile callers phoned with threats, false accusations, or to hang up and call again. There were visitors at the front door with questions about alternative transportation, reporters from all over the country clamoring for interviews, friends "just checking in," and as many more at the back door. In the span of a few hours, Coretta saw her home converted from a peaceful retreat to an international rallying point as people from all parts of America and several foreign countries came to see for themselves the things that were happening in Montgomery.

Like many blacks, we had grown up in a culture beset with fear. Our father was the subject of almost constant threats. Throughout our childhood, it seemed as though every day there was word of some white man who intended to kill him. We had seen Dad work hard to achieve the dream of owning his own sawmill only to have someone burn it to the ground. Many of the people in our community faced the same treatment and lived with the same angst. We were not impervious to the fear those threats engendered, either—during the early part of my life, my dreams at night were filled with images of white people killing my father. Yet we learned to overcome those fears, and one of the ways in which we did that was to act unafraid. Rather than give in to fear and hand our lives over to its control, we confessed the promises of God, trusted in His will, and acted as if we knew no fear.

While still adjusting to the role of pastor's wife and new mother, Coretta was catapulted into the midst of a heated protest. Many would have cowered in the face of such sudden and immediate pressure, but she did not. Just as Martin and the black community stood at a divine moment in history, Coretta had reached a decisive moment in her own personal history. No longer bound by the limitations others sought to impose upon her, she stepped into the fullness of the realization that, no matter what white people said, she had been created by God for a purpose and supplied by Him with all that was necessary to blossom in that moment.

Though not unemotional, Coretta was a cerebral person. She was not ruled by sentimentality but by reason and rational thought. I do not mean to imply that she had no sense of emotion, but it was not the primary lens through which she viewed the events of her life. That approach and her staunch unwillingness to act as if she was scared allowed God to lift her above the turmoil of events around her and established in her a core of inner strength few people have possessed.

19

Christmas 1955

On Christmas Eve 1955, Coretta brought five-week-old Yolanda to our parents' home near Marion. As they celebrated with their three children and their first grandchild, Mother and Dad felt a little richer but also more anxious that year. Coretta and the baby were driven to Marion from Montgomery by a friend. Martin joined us the following day. The bus boycott made it necessary for him to remain in Montgomery that Christmas, except for Christmas Day. He arrived in time to have dinner with the family.

Between "oohs" and "aahs" over the baby, the bus boycott in Montgomery was the main topic of conversation. Everyone wanted to hear the story straight from Coretta and Martin. Those who lived outside Montgomery had difficulty believing blacks there had united on their own behalf. Blacks in Montgomery had never shown any initiative before, and no one anywhere in the country had tried a protest of that scale.[1]

Both Coretta and Martin were calm and confident about what blacks in Montgomery were doing, but they refrained from making any predictions about the outcome. Although they appeared neither anxious nor fearful, we all felt the battle they faced would be long and difficult. However, no one dared speak of the worst, certainly not at Christmastime. Instead, we talked around the subject.

At one point, our aunt Cornelia Osburn asked Martin, "Aren't you afraid of losing your credit?"

We knew she was not concerned about his finances. Martin seemed taken aback by the question at first. "Lose my credit?" Then he realized she was really asking about his life. He smiled and said, "No, I'm not afraid of that. To lose my credit would be a small price to pay for freedom."

After dinner that evening, the rest of us went back to our normal lives. Martin, Coretta, and baby Yoki returned to Montgomery. There they found the struggle had just begun.

During the month of December, designated members of the MIA held several meetings with city officials and representatives of the bus company in an effort to reach an agreement that would bring an end to the boycott. Convinced their demands were modest and fully justified, blacks were not willing to end the protest until their stipulations had been met and their goals achieved. The city and the bus lines were equally intransigent. As a result, negotiations broke down.

When blacks refused to compromise, the opposition resorted to many different forms of harassment. As president and chief spokesman for the MIA, Martin became the main target of their efforts. Since the beginning of the protest, he and Coretta had received threatening telephone calls and letters.

In January, those calls increased in such proportions that the telephone in their home rang all day and most of the night. The telephone rang constantly, apparently the result of a coordinated effort. Often, the caller would hang up as soon as the receiver was lifted, then immediately dial again. At home most days, Coretta felt the brunt of that abuse. When someone was actually on the line, she heard insults peppered with offensive language, most of it aimed at Martin. Some of the callers made threats on Martin's life.

False rumors about the leaders of the protest, especially Martin, were rampant. Blacks were told by their white employers that their leaders were riding in big cars while they were forced to walk, that "outside agitators" were there stirring up trouble only to make money from the protest. A rumor was spread, which some people outside Montgomery believed for a time, that Martin had purchased a new Cadillac for himself and a Buick station wagon for Coretta.

On Sunday, January 22, an announcement appeared in the *Montgomery Advertiser* indicating the city commissioners had reached a settlement with a group of prominent black ministers. The announcement was intended to inject confusion among blacks and to coax them back aboard the city buses Sunday morning. The Sunday edition of the paper was printed Saturday night for distribution early Sunday morning. As the paper was being prepared for the printing press, a report about the announcement ran over the Associated Press newswire.

Far away in Minnesota, Carl Rowan, a reporter for the *Minneapolis Tribune,* saw the wire report. Rather than risk publishing an erroneous story, he called Martin to verify the information. The call reached Martin late Saturday night. He assured Rowan the report was in error, then began calling members of the MIA executive committee. The committee notified ministers in all the black churches about the erroneous announcement set to appear in Sunday's paper. The pastors, in turn, told their congregations the following morning. Outmaneuvered, the opposition became desperate.

When the boycott first began, protesters who regularly used the bus service sought their own means of alternative transportation. Some rode with friends who had cars, others walked, but most people took a taxi. Glad to have the extra business, taxi drivers were accommodating and helpful. That worked well for the first few days, but as the boycott continued, the ad hoc system became untenable. During the first week of the boycott, the city had threatened to arrest taxi drivers who did not charge the city-mandated minimum fare. Martin and other MIA leaders realized a more reliable and less onerous alternative was required if the boycott was to hold.

Drawing on the experience of previous attempted boycotts in Baton Rouge, Louisiana, the MIA executive committee prepared a plan to coordinate those people who owned cars and those who did not. Predetermined collection points were established throughout the city where people in need of a ride could gather in the morning and evening. Blacks who owned cars were assigned to locations in a manner that evenly distributed the available vehicles. Those needing a ride had only to get to the collection point. Those with a car needed only to stop at a single location to pick up and drop off. The system worked well—so well, in fact, that the city decided to do something about it.

As the new year dawned, the city embarked on a "get tough" approach to the boycott. All three city commissioners openly joined the White Citizens Council. Black people were arrested and sometimes jailed for minor and even fictitious traffic violations. Drivers in the car pool were stopped and questioned about their licenses, insurance, and places of employment. People waiting at the collection points were told by policemen that they were violating laws against hitchhiking. Others were told they would be arrested and charged with vagrancy if they were found "milling around in white neighborhoods." Martin was arrested and jailed for allegedly speeding, a seemingly minor infraction.

Martin's arrest brought him face-to-face with the unspeakable fear that haunted most black men of his day, the fear of death. Many African American men who were arrested and taken to jail were later found swinging from a stout limb of a tall oak. In the South, lynching had long been a grim reality few wanted to confront. For

Martin, being jailed forced him to confront the fact that the struggle in which he was engaged might cost him his life.

The arrest came at a vulnerable time for Martin. His prominent position as president of MIA put him at the forefront of every decision, every meeting, every rally. When a decision was required, everyone wanted to know what Martin thought. When things went well, others wanted to share the credit, but when things went poorly, they second-guessed his choices. Leading such a disparate group had required enormous amounts of time and energy.

That night, after Martin was released from jail, he reached an emotional and spiritual breaking point. Alone in the kitchen at the parsonage, he began to contemplate leaving his role as president of the MIA. As the night grew late, he searched his mind for a graceful way to extricate himself from the boycott and go back to being simply the pastor of a prestigious church. But try as he might, he could not find a way, and in desperation he began to confess to God the weakness he felt inside. Suddenly, the pall began to lift from his spirit, and he saw that the faith he had professed had been what he described as an "inherited" religion, one he had obtained from his father and grandfather, both of whom were ministers. To be effective, his faith in God must become personal. He must know God for himself. The moment of introduction came that night at the kitchen table when God became not merely a theological concept, but a real and personal Savior. In his spirit, Martin heard God whispering to him, "Martin Luther, stand up for righteousness. Stand up for truth. And lo, I will be with you. Even until the end of the world."[2] From that moment on, Martin Luther King Jr. was never the same.

Far from deterring the protesters, the increased belligerence only made them more determined. The car pool system drew riders and drivers together. People who did not normally associate regularly with each other found themselves waiting together for a ride or jammed onto the seat of a car. Thrown together by circumstances, they were soon bound together in spirit.

Later that January, with revenue in serious decline, the bus company cut service on bus lines operating in black neighborhoods. The move infuriated blacks throughout the city who saw it as more evidence of the city's real attitude toward them. With every attempt to beat the protesters down, the sense of brotherhood in black neighborhoods became even more real.

While the MIA's leadership planned and coordinated the physical operation of the boycott, the zeal and morale of the black community was maintained by weekly mass meetings that rotated from church to church. One had only to attend those meetings to see the superficial labels of rank, class, and creed melt into a spiritual bond of hope and faith. The intellectuals arrived at the meetings as early as the uneducated. The eloquent manifested as deep an involvement in the religious rituals of the services as the least articulate.[3]

Traditionally, the black church has been a church of emotion and fire. That spiritual quality was reflected in the mass meetings. In the refining fire of adversity, college professors, doctors, lawyers, cooks, porters, maids, and even derelicts rediscovered their common identity and common faith in Christ. Over and over again, visitors who came to Montgomery to attend the meetings would say, "What you are doing here in Montgomery is the greatest development that we have seen in America in the twentieth century." The influence of the drama could be felt across the South and throughout the nation.

Through the first four weeks of January 1956, tensions continued to rise as the city and the bus company attempted to pressure the MIA and the black community to capitulate. Encouraged by the bellicose and obstinate response of elected officials, militant white citizens took things a step further. Buses were struck by gunfire and rocks. White husbands forced their wives to stop assisting their black housekeepers with rides and other acts of kindness. The telephone calls to Coretta and Martin's home became more aggressive, and threats on their lives increased. As events would prove, those threats were not idle rhetoric.[4]

20

Bombing

On the evening of January 30, Martin left home to attend a mass meeting. Coretta stayed behind with Yolanda. Martin rode to the meeting with Roscoe Williams, one of a group of black men who were becoming active members at Dexter. Roscoe's wife, Mary Lucy, stayed at the house with Coretta and the baby.

With the men gone, Coretta and Mary Lucy moved to the living room where they visited and watched television. Little Yolanda was down the hall in her room fast asleep. A short time later, Coretta began to feel uneasy. Though she could not articulate what was wrong, she had a sense of foreboding. She did her best to keep her concern to herself, but as she sat with Mary Lucy, she actively listened, straining to hear the slightest sound of anything out of the ordinary.

A few minutes later, there was a noise from outside, like the sound of a brick hitting the front steps. In an instant, Coretta sprang to her feet and darted down the hall. Startled, Mary Lucy hurried after her. As they moved past the guest room, an explosion rocked the house.

Shards of glass and splinters of wood filled the air as the blast ripped through the front wall of the house, tearing off part of the porch and destroying the picture window in the living room. Thick black smoke filled the house. Cold, wintry air rushed through the gaping hole.

Awakened by the blast, Yolanda cried out from her room. Coretta picked her up and held her close. With Mary Lucy beside her, they slowly crept down the hall to review the damage.

The sofa and chair where they had been sitting were across the room, ripped and ruined. Tables and the collectibles Coretta had carefully arranged were in disarray. Pictures that remained on the wall hung at precarious angles.

As she stood there, surveying the damage, her first thought was to call someone, but everyone she would call was at the mass meeting. She could call the police, but she was not sure how they would respond. Then a voice called out, "Is anybody hurt?"

For an instant, Coretta felt a pang of fear strike her soul, but almost as quickly she recognized the voice as that of her neighbor. The two of them hugged each other and then turned again to view the damage. When Coretta mentioned her hesitancy about calling the police, the neighbor told her she had already notified them.

Just then, the telephone rang. When Coretta answered, a female voice cried out, "Yes, I did it. And I'm just sorry I didn't kill all you bastards." Shaken by the anger in the voice, Coretta had little time to dwell on it. By the time she hung up the phone, people were arriving from every direction.

When news of the bombing reached the mass meeting, the evening's program was speedily brought to a close. Martin urged everyone to go home and remember their commitment to the philosophy of nonviolence. That philosophy, so crucial to the effectiveness of their message, was facing a severe test. The last thing he wanted was to give the Montgomery police an excuse to unleash their brutal force on black neighborhoods.

Instead of going home, many of those who had attended the meeting went to the parsonage to view the damage for themselves. Emotionally charged and ready for action, they gathered on the lawn and in the street outside the house. When Martin arrived home, about fifteen minutes after the incident occurred, he had to push his way through a large crowd. As he wound his way toward the front steps, he could see those assembled were armed with guns, knives, and anything else that could be used as weapons.

The police attempted to clear the streets so traffic could move by, but their orders were ignored. When they tried to press the issue, some in the crowd responded with threats. After years of enduring personal insults and indignities, blacks that night were on the verge of responding in anger. Martin overheard one man say to a white policeman, "I ain't gonna move nowhere. That's the trouble now. You white folks is always pushin' us around. Now you got your .38 and I got mine. So, let's battle it out."[1] The crowd, which was growing larger and becoming more unwieldy by the minute, was ready to explode.

Inside the house, Martin spoke briefly with Coretta, who was calm and composed. Then he looked in on the baby. Finding them both unharmed, he turned to the issue of the crowd outside and their angry unrest.

Mayor Gayle met Martin in the dining room, along with Police Commissioner Sellers and several white reporters. There, he listened while the city officials expressed their regrets that "this unfortunate incident has taken place in our city."[2] By then, the crowd outside had become louder. Pessimists in the room felt that Montgomery was in for an unavoidable catastrophe.

From the dining room, Martin moved to the front porch. There, with the mayor on one side and the police commissioner on the other, he turned to face the crowd. He paused for a moment, his eyes focused on the faces before him, then raised his arms in a gesture for quiet. A hush fell over those gathered on the lawn and quickly moved to those standing in the street. All eyes focused on Martin.

In a tone free of strong emotion, Martin told the people that his wife and baby were safe and unharmed and so was he. Then, speaking clearly and forcefully, he said,

> Now let's not become panicky. If you have weapons, take them home; if you do not have them, please do not seek to get them. We cannot solve this problem with retaliatory violence. We must meet violence with nonviolence. Remember the words of Jesus: "He who lives by the sword will perish by the sword." We must love our white brothers, no matter what they do to us. We must make them know that we love them. Jesus still cries out in words that echo across the centuries: "Love your enemies; bless them that curse you; pray for them that despitefully use you." This is what we must live by. We must meet hate with love. Remember, if I am stopped, this movement will not stop, because God is with the movement. Go home with this glowing faith and this radiant assurance.[3]

Martin's remarks were met with affirmation from the crowd. There were shouts of "Amen" and "God bless you." Those who had only moments before called for a violent response now stood with tears streaming down their faces.

While Martin had been speaking, a photographer took a picture of him flanked by the mayor and police commissioner. That picture made the front page of the next day's newspapers in towns and cities across the nation. Once again, the bus boycott was the focus of national attention.

Like other efforts to stifle the boycott, the bombing of Martin and Coretta's home worked to solidify the black community's commitment to the protest and to the notion of resisting evil in a spirit of love. Prior to that moment, the notion of love and forgiveness had been only an ideal, a statement made in a speech, a philosophy discussed over lunch. The bombing gave protesters an opportunity to make that ideal the focus of an emotional commitment.

Self-defense came as naturally to black people as it did to whites. Exercising the nobler, higher instinct of responding in love required restraint and discipline. When the black community responded in that manner, an act meant for their destruction became yet another instrument in God's hands for transforming Martin, Coretta, and those involved in the protest from mere reactionaries to an indomitable force for good.

That night on the lawn outside the parsonage, the protesters reached a crucial moment in the struggle against bigotry and racism, a moment not unlike the one Martin had experienced a few nights before at the table in the parsonage kitchen. From that point on, there would be no turning back. The work ahead required participants who were not ruled by fear. Those who were willing to go forward, to press on toward the goal of freedom and liberation, would risk everything, even their lives. That night, with the acrid smell of smoke from the bomb burning in their nostrils and surrounded by policemen waiting to pounce at the least provocation, the protesters crossed the commitment line. In exercising self-control, they gained mastery of themselves and the moment. To outsiders, to the uninitiated, their response perhaps looked like weakness, but standing there, listening to Martin, they put on the armor of God, an armor not made by hands but by the Spirit for a battle that would be fought as much in the spiritual realm as in the physical. Equipped and ready, they were prepared to face the hardships that would lead them to the end they so desperately sought.

For Coretta, the moment was equally important. Though she did not speak about it at the time, she too had reached a moment of crisis, a moment when the theoretical became real. Later, after the protest had proved successful, she reflected on those hours and days following the bombing.

> I had to face what seemed to be the inevitable consequence if we continued the struggle. Yes, even death. For the first time in my life religion became really real. I had prayed before but never before had I realized the power that is in prayer. In my prayers I said, "Lord, I've done all that I can do, believing that we are right. Now I leave it up to you. I ask not for help to do my will but thine." Before long I had stopped worrying and I haven't worried since. God gave me the strength, the faith, and the courage to stand up and say, "If I die—and if my husband should die for His cause in trying to bring about His kingdom on earth, then what a noble way to die."[4]

For Coretta, as for Martin, the events of that January were critical. In those four short weeks, they both had been to the edge of despair and stared death in the eye.

There, they found strength and courage in their relationship with God. More than a resolve to press forward with the boycott, their decision that month was a commitment to fight for social and economic justice wherever that fight might take them. By the time January ended, they had surrendered themselves without reserve to the work of the Holy Spirit and abandoned themselves to the mission of transforming the South. They had no idea of the scope of the adventure that awaited them.

21

Staying

News of the bombing spread quickly. Across the state in Marion, our parents heard about it on the radio. They started out immediately for Montgomery. Dad felt Coretta and the baby should come to live with them until things cooled off. By the time he and Mother arrived at the parsonage, Coretta and Martin had gone to the home of a church member where they planned to stay until the parsonage had been repaired.

When Dad announced that he and Mother were there to take Coretta and Yolanda home with them, Coretta's reply was polite but swift. "I can't go. I really wouldn't be happy if I did. I want to stay here with Martin."

Dad did not give in quickly, but when he saw he was not going to change Coretta's mind, he reluctantly accepted her decision.

Later that night, Martin's father arrived from Atlanta. Like our parents, he had heard news of the bombing on the radio. And, like our parents, he did not bother to call ahead. He simply climbed into his car and started toward Montgomery.

When Daddy King arrived, he tried to persuade Martin not only to get his wife and child out of town, but to resign as pastor of Dexter. He wanted Martin to move to Atlanta and join him as co-pastor at Ebenezer Baptist Church. Martin resisted and explained again the nature of the work they were trying to do in Montgomery. His father thought remaining there was a bad idea. "Better to be a live dog," he said, "than a dead lion."

That was a tense and trying time for Coretta. Fear hung thick in the air. Everyone around her was frightened and worried, but she would not be deterred. Standing by her husband and being there when he needed her was important to her. The more the two fathers pushed them to leave Montgomery, the more Coretta and Martin resisted. Coretta never wavered in support of Martin, the protest, or the people to whom they were ministering.

The next morning at breakfast Martin smiled across the table at her, "Coretta, you have been a real soldier. You were the only one who stood with me."[1]

Coretta wanted to be no place else. Although living on the edge of a precipice, she found those days thrilling and exciting. No one knew for certain what would happen. Each day brought a new challenge, a new obstacle, and a new lesson. She was proud to be in the fight and proud to work alongside her husband, to sense the movement of God, to hear His voice and catch His vision, and to see that vision come to pass. For her it was a wonderful time to be alive and a blessing to live at the center of change. The dangers were real—as real as a bomb on her front porch—but she did not want to be anywhere else, and she was determined to stay.

Except for a few brief trips to Marion and Atlanta to visit family on holidays and special occasions, Coretta remained in Montgomery throughout the most perilous phase of the struggle. During those times when she was away, she could hardly wait to return. She wanted to know, firsthand, all the daily developments. For her there was no substitute for being on the scene, at the center of events, where the spirit of the people could be felt.

Restoring the parsonage took almost two months to complete. Along with the necessary repairs, workmen installed floodlights at each corner of the house. For several months afterward, unarmed watchmen guarded the house around the clock. At the same time, members of Dexter kept a nightly prayer vigil near the residence.

For Coretta, the bombing had quickened her understanding of the fragile nature of life. No security system could offer foolproof protection. Anyone bent on taking their lives could find a way to do it. Guards and lights could not prevent it. The only real security was the security that came from within, from knowing the worthiness of the cause in which they were engaged and trusting that God would see them through. Resorting to conventional forms of protection would be an act of capitulation, one that would contradict the philosophy of nonviolence they espoused. "After the bombing, when the tension was still high, the members of our church decided to take turns in spending the night in our home (before the watchman was hired), but my husband would not let them arm. He said that in a nonviolent movement people should not bear arms. Bob Williams, a friend who taught at the state college, would come and he would sleep with a shotgun beside his bed. Every time a car stopped, Bob would jump. Also, following the bombing someone bought a gun and gave it to Martin. We kept it for a few weeks and then Martin decided he didn't want a gun in the house and had it removed."[2]

The parsonage bombing forced MIA leadership to face the stark reality of their cause. What had been a political exercise was now far more serious. From that moment on, protesters would know each time they took to the streets they were putting their lives on the line. Realizing that, Martin and the executive committee took a closer look at their strategy. One area that received their immediate attention was their use of the legal system.

Immediately following Rosa Parks' conviction, her attorney, Fred Gray, filed a notice of appeal. Mrs. Parks had been charged with violating the city's segregation ordinances by refusing to give up her seat on the bus. Those ordinances were based on underlying state statutes. At the time, an appeal of her conviction seemed the best way to challenge the constitutionality of Alabama's laws requiring segregation. Now, in the wake of the bombing, Gray sought a way to move things forward more rapidly.

By the night of January 30, city officials had made clear their intent to frustrate the boycott at every turn. Their increasingly belligerent tactics empowered radical citizens to take matters even further. Gray and other attorneys involved in representing the protesters in court realized Rosa Parks's appeal would meet with continual delays. Years might pass before the case reached the Alabama Supreme Court, a necessary step in taking the case ultimately to the US Supreme Court. Even then, there was the possibility that an appellate court could reverse Mrs. Parks's conviction on other grounds and never reach the segregation issue.

With that in mind, Gray suggested they file a separate petition in federal court asking the court to determine whether Alabama's statutes met requirements imposed by the US Constitution. Unlike state judges, federal judges were appointed for life and were not directly subject to the political process. Freed from the need to campaign for reelection, they were somewhat removed from the influence of public sentiment. They also tended to have a worldview that was more cosmopolitan than their counterparts in state court. The move would remove the case from much of the stalling and delaying tactics it would face in the state court system. Even if they lost at trial, the case could be appealed through the federal system where the possibility of success was much greater than in state court. MIA leadership agreed.

On February 2, Gray filed a petition in federal district court on behalf of Aurelia Browder, Susie McDonald, Claudette Colvin, and Mary Louise Smith, all of whom had been either arrested or otherwise removed from a city bus for failure to comply with Montgomery's segregation ordinances. The case became known as *Browder v. Gayle*.[3] The petition sought a determination that Montgomery's segregation ordinances and the underlying Alabama segregation statutes violated the Fourteenth Amendment of the US Constitution. If effective, the petition would require the desegregation of Montgomery's bus service.

The reaction to that filing was swift and powerful. That night, a bomb tossed from a passing car landed in front of E. D. Nixon's home. The explosion could be heard for miles but did little damage to Nixon's house. Nixon was not at home, having left earlier for his job as a Pullman porter.

A week later, on February 10, a crowd of twelve thousand whites jammed the Montgomery Coliseum to hear a bevy of politicians decry the latest attempts to alter or destroy the South's segregated traditions. The keynote speaker that evening was Senator James O. Eastland from Mississippi. Those who attended went home more determined than ever to oppose any changes in southern culture.

The next week, Montgomery County circuit court judge Eugene Carter ordered a grand jury to consider whether leaders of the bus boycott ought to stand trial for violating an obscure Alabama statute prohibiting economic boycotts. On February 21, the grand jury returned indictments against ninety-eight of Montgomery's finest black leaders.

Martin and Coretta were out of town when the indictments were issued, but their absence did not stop MIA leadership from responding. As the first warrants were served, word of the pending arrests spread. Rather than wait for police to serve them with arrest warrants, prominent members of the protest went down to the police station together and surrendered en masse. Some went voluntarily to see if they had been indicted, too. The indictments became a badge of honor among the protesters. Many of those who had not been indicted were disappointed at being excluded but remained at the jail anyway to sign the bonds of those arrested.

When Martin returned to Montgomery the following day, he surrendered also. Coretta and a crowd of supporters greeted him when he emerged from the jail. What had been planned by city and county officials as a threat to the protesters turned out to be a great boost for their morale. Once again, the dignified and humble manner in which blacks conducted themselves stood in stark contrast to the conduct displayed by city officials and made plain the just nature of the protesters' cause.

Meanwhile, the petition filed by Fred Gray in federal court seeking to desegregate Montgomery's bus service continued to make its way toward trial. The case was scheduled to be heard by a three-judge panel that included Richard T. Rives, Frank M. Johnson Jr., and Seybourne Lynne. Rives served on the federal court of appeals in Atlanta. Lynne was a federal district court judge from Birmingham. Johnson served on the federal court in Montgomery but was a recent appointee to the bench. Something of an outsider, he had been born and reared in Winston County, the lone county in Alabama where Republicans held significant influence.

Although he had not served on the bench long, Johnson was known to be a man of integrity.[4] While the case awaited trial, attention turned to the criminal cases in state court.

Of the ninety-eight black leaders who had been indicted by the Montgomery County grand jury, only Martin was actually tried. His case was heard on March 19, and after a three-day trial, he was convicted. Judge Carter fined him $500. Martin filed a notice of appeal and was released on bond pending the final outcome.

Later that spring, testimony was heard in the federal court desegregation case. Each of the plaintiffs testified about how they were treated while onboard the city buses.[5] The case was heard without incident. Issues raised in the case were taken under submission, awaiting final decision at a later date. Everyone in the black community hoped for the best.

Through the summer of 1956, Montgomery sweltered under blistering heat. Mass meetings continued, serving as a way to keep morale high among the protesters and as a means of disseminating information. The bus boycott, already in its sixth month, had become a way of life. Transportation continued to be an issue, but as time passed, people adapted, learning to allow extra time in their schedule for more cumbersome travel.

Using funds raised from Martin's increasingly hectic speaking schedule and contributions received from around the world, the MIA purchased station wagons for the carpool system. A local agency initially insured them, but later their coverage was mysteriously dropped. Without insurance, legally the cars could not be driven. After several frantic phone calls, the Alexander Agency, a black-owned business in Atlanta, placed insurance coverage with Lloyds of London for the vehicles. With the added capacity of the larger automobiles, the car pool system became even more efficient than before.

By June, leadership roles within the protest had become well-established. Everyone knew what to expect from the city and how to respond. With events falling into a predictable rhythm, Coretta and Martin took a vacation. Driving with the Abernathys, they toured the Southwest, eventually arriving in San Francisco, California, where Martin was to speak at the annual NAACP convention. He and Coretta were in California when they received news that the federal court in Montgomery had reached a ruling in the bus desegregation case. Voting two to one, the judges found Montgomery's segregation ordinances and the underlying Alabama statutes unconstitutional. Everyone was elated, but their joy was quickly tempered by the continuing judicial process.

The city responded to the decision in *Browder* by filing an immediate appeal. The case would be heard again by a federal appeals court in New Orleans. Implementation of the lower court's decision was still months away if at all.

In August, after a tense but peaceful summer, violence erupted once again when a bomb exploded outside the home of Robert Graetz. A white minister who served on the MIA executive committee, Graetz was despised by many in the white community who felt he had betrayed them. The bomb blew out windows and did other damage to the house. Graetz and his family were away at the time and escaped injury. Rather than deter his involvement in the protest, the bombing became a source of encouragement.

That September, Coretta went with Martin to a meeting of the National Baptist Convention in Denver, Colorado. Martin appeared on the program and gave an address updating the crowd on the Montgomery bus boycott. The Reverend Joseph H. Jackson, president of the convention and a powerful African American minister from Chicago, introduced Martin to the crowd. They were friends at the time, and Jackson was eager to promote Martin. Later, Jackson would split with Martin and spend much of his energy and time opposing the use of civil disobedience in civil rights reform.

Coretta also appeared on the program. On September 7, she sang a solo at one of the convention worship services accompanied by Martin's mother, Alberta Williams King. Although Coretta had continued to sing with the Dexter choir, most of her time and attention had been devoted to caring for Yolanda. Now, almost two years after her last concert, she was ready to sing on her own once again.

The trip to Colorado brought Coretta welcome relief from the late-summer heat of Montgomery and the constant focus on details of the bus boycott. Invigorated by the experience and by the spiritual vitality of the conference, she began to think again of returning to her own work as a singer. Later that month after returning to Montgomery, she gave a concert at Dexter and began to seek additional opportunities to sing.

In October, the city filed a petition in Montgomery County circuit court seeking an injunction against the MIA to halt the car pool. In its petition the city argued that the car pool system infringed on the bus company's exclusive transportation franchise. That case posed a far more serious challenge to the boycott than any of the city's other legal efforts.

Prior to that point, the city's efforts to use the legal system—enforcement of motor vehicle laws, threats by police against protesters as they gathered at the car pool collection points, and close monitoring for traffic law violations—had amounted to little more than harassment. Though aggravating and inconvenient, those actions could not deter the protesters from continuing. Even the wholesale arrest of MIA leadership for violating anti-boycott statutes could not prevent the boycott from going forward. But without the car pool system, maintaining participation in the boycott would be extremely difficult.

That same month, Coretta traveled to Mobile where she gave a concert at the I. L. A. Auditorium.[6] The concert was sponsored by the Young Adult Fellowship at Warren Street Methodist Church. The pastor there, the Reverend Joseph Lowery, was an ardent supporter of the Montgomery boycott.[7] At that concert, Coretta sang classical pieces along with traditional spirituals. Emma Willis organized the event and obtained sponsorship from a number of Mobile businesses. Coretta was pleased with her performance and glad to be singing again.

Meanwhile, the legal cases surrounding the boycott continued to go forward. The following month, the city of Montgomery's petition for an injunction went to trial. The economic impact of the boycott had been widespread, affecting not only the city bus service but downtown businesses as well. That the city would be successful in obtaining an injunction against further car pool activity seemed all but certain. Then, while testimony in the case was still being heard, the US Supreme Court issued a decision affirming the ruling of the three-judge panel in the federal bus desegregation case. As news of the Supreme Court's decision spread through the courthouse, trial of the injunction case was recessed, never to be resumed.

Once again, protesters were elated at the outcome. The US Supreme Court had ruled in their favor. A government body outside the state of Alabama had heard their cause and agreed with them. Yet, just as with earlier rulings in the case, that joy was cut short by the city's response. Determined to go down fighting, the city filed a motion asking the Supreme Court to reconsider its opinion. Doing so delayed final resolution of the matter yet a little longer.

As December approached, the boycott reached its twelfth month. It had been a year of difficulty and danger, but the protesters were finally within sight of victory. To mark the first anniversary of the boycott, Harry Belafonte and a group calling themselves In Friendship arranged a gala fund-raiser at the Manhattan Center in New York.[8] One of the principal participants in that group was a successful attorney named Stanley Levison. Martin and Levison struck up a friendship almost immediately. Levison had followed details of the Montgomery boycott and rather quickly recognized the broader nature of its implications. Long an advocate for fundamental change in American society, he was eager to assist Martin in developing those implications and exploiting the opportunity revealed by the boycott's success. The two became close friends and remained so the rest of Martin's life.[9]

Staged as a fund-raiser, the Manhattan Center event was held on December 5. The event was organized by Mrs. Ralph Bunche, Mrs. James Pike, and Mrs. Roy Wilkins. It featured performances by Coretta along with Harry Belafonte and Duke Ellington. Coretta worked hard to prepare for the evening, drawing on music she had prepared for concerts earlier in the year. In her previous concerts she had used music to convey a message, but the message was much less overt and was carried primarily by the lyrics of the compositions she performed. For this event, she added additional pieces and wove together songs, dramatic readings, and poetry to tell the story of the Montgomery boycott and the fight for freedom.

One of the songs she sang that night, "My Feet Are Tired," was composed by Frances Thomas, Coretta's former teacher at Lincoln School. Mrs. Thomas had visited Coretta the previous summer and experienced the spirit of the mass meetings. At one of those meetings she heard the often repeated phrase, "My feet are tired but my soul is rested." Inspired by that phrase, she returned home and penned a song to express her sentiments about the protest. A second song, "Lord, I Can't Turn Back," was written by Robert Williams, a professor of voice at Alabama State College. He was inspired to write it upon hearing the news that Martin had been arrested on the anti-boycott indictment.

Coretta performed well and was enthusiastically received by the audience and by other performers on the program. As a result, she began to think of using that format in a series of concerts at other venues across the country. While she felt her roles as wife, mother, and homemaker were important, she nonetheless continued to have the sense of the calling to sing she had received as a student at Lincoln School. She wanted to make a difference, not merely entertain. With Yolanda a little older and the pace of the boycott beginning to ease, she began to look for ways to use her talent and training to promote the larger aims of their work.

In the days that followed, the Supreme Court denied the city of Montgomery's request to reconsider the ruling in the desegregation case. In a pattern of delay and obfuscation that would be repeated many times thereafter in other southern cities, the Montgomery city commission refused to implement the court's order until official documents arrived.

The Supreme Court's official mandate of judgment was received by the federal district court in Montgomery on December 20. With the entry of a final order in the case, the city and the bus service had little option but to obey the ruling.

The following day, December 21, 1956, three hundred eighty-two days after it began, the Montgomery bus boycott came to an end. That morning, Martin, Rosa Parks, Ralph Abernathy, and a white man named Glenn Smiley, who had helped Martin gain a deeper understanding of nonviolent protest, boarded a city bus near the parsonage. After paying the fare, they took a seat near the front of the bus and rode unmolested through the city.

Christmas that year was an especially joyous season of praise and thanksgiving. Blacks celebrated a year of struggle, survival, and ultimate victory. There had been many trying moments and many miraculous breakthroughs. Yet, in spite of the odds against them, they had prevailed. Segregation was still the law of the land and there would be many more protests and battles to fight, but for that Christmas season, Martin and Coretta joined the congregation at Dexter in celebrating the victory in Montgomery.

22

Southern Christian Leadership Conference

With the dawn of 1957, the South remained steeped in racial inequality. Trapped in remnants of plantation culture, the South found itself enslaved by the evil it had so readily embraced, which obliterated the rich history and traditions of the African American community. While that evil—the notion that one person could own another, that one race was superior to another, that one race held an inherent right to control another—oppressed blacks, it ensnared whites to the destruction of their own souls. Yet, in a strange twist, the same culture that trapped the South in bigotry and ignorance also made it a place ripe for revolutionary change.

For one thing, southerners generally were more religious and more religiously aware than northerners. Blacks and whites ate at separate restaurants, drank from separate water fountains, and attended separate churches, but the Gospel they heard on Sunday morning came from the same Bible, and they knew it. Whites often used Scripture to justify southern apartheid, and blacks used it as encouragement for a soon-to-be-arriving better day, but a high percentage of both groups regularly attended church services and had a good working knowledge of common Biblical stories and events.

Not only that, the South remained predominantly agrarian. In the 1950s, a large portion of Southern families, both black and white, still lived on farms. Even professionals who did not earn a living directly from the land lived in a manner and enjoyed activities that put them in close touch with nature. Many southern whites had grown up in homes that were just as poverty-stricken as those of the typical black family. Whites might not have cared for blacks, but they still knew the names of their black neighbors. Because of that commonality, nonviolent protest, with its emphasis on love, forgiveness, and community touched a common chord that reached across color lines. Even so, the battle for widespread, systemic change was not easy.

The bus boycott had been born out of the need to respond to an unjust and immoral policy. Swept up in that response, Coretta and Martin came to embrace nonviolent protest as a means of expression consistent with Biblical teachings. They had no illusions, however, concerning the depth of opposition to change in the South or the practical means by which it could be addressed.

The experiences of a year of protest had convinced them that full equality for blacks in America would require changes in the law. Bringing those changes to pass would be a daunting task. Segregationists held control of the state legislatures in each of the southern states, rendering moot any attempt to use the state legislative process to address the ills those same legislatures had created. By the end of the Montgomery boycott, Coretta and Martin were convinced change would come only through federal intervention.

In the spring of 1956, President Eisenhower submitted to Congress proposed legislation that would strengthen the federal government's ability to intervene in instances of voting rights abuses. That legislation, however, met with strong opposition from Southern Democrats. As a result, it languished in congressional committees.[1]

Supreme Court decisions in *Brown v. Board of Education* and *Browder v. Gayle* had gone a long way toward destroying segregation, but those decisions had arisen from a protest context. By exposing the true nature of segregation, protest in the streets put moral and political force behind African American demands for equality and justice. As Coretta and Martin considered their lives beyond the Montgomery protest, they looked toward using that combination—protest and federal action— as a way of prying the South free from the clutches of racism. In late December 1956, Coretta and Martin traveled to Baltimore to attend the annual Omega Psi Phi Conclave. Martin had been selected as the fraternity's Man of the Year and was to be honored at a banquet there. My husband was a member of that fraternity, so we joined them for the festivities. At the time, our former Lincoln School music teacher, Olive J. Williams, was living with her elderly parents in Baltimore. Coretta came up a day before the convention, and the two of us went to see Miss Williams. We had a great time visiting with her and remembering our days at Lincoln.

Later that weekend, we attended the banquet at which Martin was honored. Stanley Levison was there and sat with us at our table. After the banquet, we all went back to Coretta and Martin's hotel room. As the evening wore on, conversation turned to the Montgomery protest and whether that protest had broader applications than merely to desegregate Montgomery buses. Levison argued the protest had revealed a means of changing not only the South, but the entire nation. Martin was intrigued by the idea and suggested they call a meeting of black leaders to explore the subject further.

In January 1957, Martin issued an invitation to selected leaders asking them to come to Atlanta to discuss racial and economic issues facing blacks. Entitled the Southern Negro Leaders Conference on Transportation and Nonviolent Integration, the meeting was to address the broader implications of the Montgomery experience. Martin and Ralph Abernathy were the driving force behind the effort. Black leaders from across the South attended.

As the conference was about to begin, a series of bombings struck Montgomery. Robert Graetz's home was hit again, and this time it was destroyed. Moments later, a bomb exploded at Ralph Abernathy's home. Later that night, bombs exploded at several black churches in and around Montgomery, inflicting significant damage. Ralph and Martin were forced to return to Montgomery. In their absence, Coretta and Fred Shuttlesworth, a minister and activist from Birmingham, conducted the conference sessions.

Coretta had taken an active part in the Montgomery protest and was familiar with the issues Martin wanted to address. In addition, the concerts she had performed around the region had taken her to churches very different from Dexter and the other black Montgomery congregations. Pastors from some of those churches were in attendance at the Atlanta conference. Many of the ministers in whose churches she had not performed had visited in her home. They knew full well the strength of her character and personality.

In other ways, perhaps, Coretta was better suited for the task of chairing the conference than Martin. She understood the nature of the participants and was sensitive to the fragility of their egos. Male pride and jealousy had been a constant threat to the MIA and the bus boycott. Her leadership of the meetings tended to dampen that rivalry. She also was comfortable working with men. Coretta's ability to steer them without threatening their pride proved invaluable. The work she and Fred accomplished in those meetings laid the groundwork for all that was to follow.

Martin and Ralph returned for the conclusion of the conference, after which the group issued telegrams to President Eisenhower, Vice President Nixon, and Attorney General Herbert Brownell asking them to put the weight of the federal government behind a call for compliance with the Supreme Court's decision in *Brown* and its implications. They asked Brownell for direct federal intervention and protection for blacks.

By the following month, with no tangible federal help likely, a second conference was held in New Orleans. Ninety-seven black leaders from across the South attended. At that meeting, the attendees formed a permanent organization to address civil rights issues on an ongoing basis. The organization adopted the name Southern Leadership Conference. Later, it would be renamed the Southern Christian Leadership Conference (SCLC) to denote the spiritual nature of its origins and purpose. Martin was elected president. Ralph was chosen as treasurer.[2] With the motto, "To redeem the soul of America," they began the work of shining the bright light of truth on the nation's attitudes and policies toward blacks. Some of those who attended that organizational meeting paid with their lives to see that motto become reality.

At the conclusion of the New Orleans meeting, Martin announced that if President Eisenhower did not speak out in favor of desegregation in the South and call for immediate passage of pending federal civil rights legislation, SCLC would conduct a march on the nation's capital. Martin was ready to apply the lessons he had learned in Montgomery to a larger context.

In March, at the invitation of Kwame Nkrumah, Coretta and Martin joined Ralph Bunche, Adam Clayton Powell, and A. Philip Randolph on a trip to Ghana.[3] On March 5, 1957, they attended a celebration marking the passage of Ghana from a British colony to a free republic. Vice President Nixon also attended. Martin, unable to resist an opportunity for political access, approached Nixon and broached the subject of a vice presidential visit to the South to see the conditions there for himself. Nixon appeared cool toward the idea but suggested Martin contact him when they returned to the United States.

By May, Eisenhower had made no further public statement regarding desegregation, and the attorney general had provided no direct assistance to remedy voter registration discrimination. At an April planning session in New York, Martin insisted the march on Washington, now called the Prayer Pilgrimage for Freedom, should go forward. A. Philip Randolph, founder and president of the Brotherhood of Sleeping Car Porters, agreed. Roy Wilkins, president of the NAACP, was less enthusiastic. Wilkins saw SCLC as a challenge to the NAACP's dominance and was not supportive of the kind of protests Martin had waged.

For his part, Martin had chafed at Wilkins's insistence on using the judicial system as the sole means of effecting change. Martin had stated his frustration in no uncertain terms and, in spite of Wilkins' objections, had shown an inclination to take his grievances beyond the courthouse and into the street. Wilkins, who viewed himself as the nation's senior black leader, had taken offense at some of Martin's comments.

Nevertheless, the pilgrimage was announced for May 17, 1957, the third anniversary of the Supreme Court decision in *Brown v. Board of Education*. Bayard Rustin and Stanley Levison began working to organize the event.

When the march was announced, Martin had suggested a crowd of fifty thousand would turn out. He worked diligently to publicize the event and to ensure that blacks attended in numbers sufficient to send Congress and the Eisenhower administration a strong message. Crisscrossing the South, as he would many times in subsequent years, he divided his energies between pastoral duties at Dexter and preparing for the march. Coretta, pregnant with their second child, remained at home with Yolanda.

The actual response for the pilgrimage was half the number Martin and SCLC had hoped. Still, it was an impressive effort. The highlight of the day was a series of speeches delivered from the steps of the Lincoln Memorial. Others on the program were accomplished orators and far better known, but by the end of the day, Martin had become the crowd favorite. Using his penchant for turning a phrase, he made a compelling argument for federal action to ensure the right to vote as the only available means of confronting the root causes of the problems facing blacks in the South.

> Give us the ballot and we will no longer plead to the federal government for passage of an antilynching law; we will by the power of our vote write the law on the statute books of the southern states and bring an end to the dastardly acts of the hooded perpetrators of violence.
> Give us the ballot and we will transform the salient misdeeds of bloodthirsty mobs into the calculated good deeds of orderly citizens.[4]

Martin's phrase "Give us the ballot" became the tagline for news stories nationwide with his picture featured alongside front-page accounts of the speech. Before the following day ended, he was a national celebrity. He had come to Washington largely unknown and found himself on the steps of the Lincoln Memorial surrounded by established black figures of far greater notoriety, but he left that event the leader of the Civil Rights Movement and a person with whom all others would be forced to reckon.

The pilgrimage did not produce the dramatic breakthrough Martin and Coretta had hoped for, but it succeeded in obtaining a response from the Eisenhower administration. On June 13, Vice President Nixon and Labor Secretary James P. Mitchell met with Martin at the vice president's office in Washington. There, Martin described in detail the effects of segregation on the South in general and on African

Americans in particular. Neither Nixon nor Mitchell offered tangible solutions, but Martin was pleased that, at last, someone in Washington had listened thoughtfully to the black community's grievances.

Through the remainder of the summer, Eisenhower continued to avoid public comment on desegregation. His intransigence in bringing the force of his office to bear on the plight of blacks and in support of the Supreme Court's recent decisions left Martin and Coretta frustrated. That frustration would be short-lived; events in the South would soon compel the president to act.

For more than two years, federal courts had worked with state and local school boards to implement the Supreme Court's ruling in *Brown v. Board of Education*. That effort proved slow, cumbersome, and difficult. Successful integration of public schools was inconsistent in the North and nonexistent in the South. In an effort to quicken the pace of integration, the NAACP targeted key southern locations as tests for compliance with the court's decision. In September 1957, they focused their attention on Arkansas.

When the school year began, nine black students appeared for registration at Central High School in Little Rock. They were met by an angry mob of white parents accompanied by troops from the Arkansas National Guard, who had been sent by the governor to bar the black students from entering the school. When police secretly slipped the students into the school by another door, riots broke out. With the city in disarray and the state refusing to honor the Supreme Court's decision, President Eisenhower deployed elements of the 101st Airborne Division to restore order and escort the students into the school.

During that same month, Congress finally acted. Driven by the Montgomery boycott, the nation's response to the Pilgrimage for Freedom, and events in Little Rock, Congress overcame southern opposition and enacted civil rights legislation. Though not comprehensive and weakened by amendments, the Civil Rights Act of 1957, as the legislation became known, sought to combat state resistance to black voter registration. By that act, Congress established the Civil Rights Division of the Department of Justice, giving it the power to supervise elections. It also established the Civil Rights Commission.

In October, Coretta gave birth to the couple's second child, Martin Luther King III. His arrival gave Coretta extra duties at home and diverted her attention from her growing popularity as a concert artist. She remained at home caring for her children through the remainder of that year, but her heart was still committed to a calling she had known since childhood and which had become more defined through the years. She longed to make a difference and was certain her work lay in the cause she had come to fully embrace that night two years before when the bomb exploded on their front porch. Although primarily occupied with two small children, whom she adored, Coretta also longed to be on the stage—not merely entertaining but using the arts and her well-trained voice to make a difference in the liberation of African Americans and the improvement of the human condition.

23

Atlanta

As 1958 began, Martin continued to divide his time between his responsibilities at Dexter, his obligations to the MIA, and his attempts to infuse life into the fledgling SCLC. The church, well-organized and efficient, continued to do well. The other two organizations struggled.

Both SCLC and the MIA shared a common interest in promoting voter registration drives. Sometimes those efforts overlapped. When they did, it caused internal bickering and jostling for position. That dissension drew time and energy away from their objectives. At the same time, requests for speaking engagements arrived from all over the nation. Martin accepted as many of those opportunities as his schedule allowed and did his best to push SCLC forward with voter registration efforts.

Having recovered physically from the birth of her second child, Coretta was active, too. While caring for their children, she began working to return to the concert stage. On April 25, she made her first concert appearance of the year at Parker High School Auditorium in Birmingham, Alabama. Her performance was sponsored by the Omicron Lambda Chapter of Alpha Phi Alpha Fraternity. For that concert, she changed some of the songs in the first half of the show but continued with the basic format established at the New York gala two years earlier, telling the story of the Montgomery boycott. She was accompanied by Ralph Simpson, an instructor at Alabama State College. For Coretta, the concert was important both as a continuation of her professional career and as a way to participate in the Civil Rights Movement. She was as committed to the Movement as Martin and was equally effective in her own right. Her concerts offered the audience an emotional connection to the message of social, economic, and spiritual transformation, but they did so in an intensely personal way. Music proved a powerful medium not only for conveying a message, but for changing hearts. She recognized that power and intended to use it at every opportunity.

In the fall, Martin traveled to New York to participate in a youth march supporting school integration. While there, he held several events to publicize the release of his first book, *Stride Toward Freedom,* the story of the Montgomery bus boycott. At a book signing in Harlem, he was confronted by a woman named Izola Curry. With no warning or provocation, Curry took a letter opener from her purse and stabbed Martin in the chest just above his heart. With the letter opener protruding from the wound, Martin was rushed to Harlem Hospital. The tip of the opener had lodged perilously close to his aorta. Doctors later told him had he sneezed, he likely would have died. Several hours of surgery were required to repair the damage. Coretta flew from Montgomery that night and spent the next two months in New York helping nurse him back to health.

While Martin recovered from the stab wound, SCLC languished. Coretta helped with administrative details, handling correspondence and fielding questions from the press, but only Martin could provide the energy and focus needed to keep the organization moving forward. Well-wishers sent cards and letters of support, many of which contained contributions, but money remained a problem.

Recovery and recuperation from the stab wound required extended care over a protracted period that kept Coretta and Martin in New York through most of October. With Martin unable to travel, Coretta filled in for him at previously scheduled speaking engagements. One of those events came near the end of October when she appeared in Washington, D.C., at the Youth March for Integrated Schools. The march had been the brainchild of A. Philip Randolph as an opportunity to call attention to the need to integrate public schools and to give people living in the North the chance to show their support. With ten thousand protesters looking on, Coretta delivered a speech on Martin's behalf.

Not long after the Washington march, doctors released Martin to travel, and he returned with Coretta to Montgomery. There, on December 1, Coretta gave a concert at Holt Street Baptist Church. Her performance once again followed the earlier format, telling the Montgomery boycott story through songs and dramatic readings. The congregation at Holt Street received her with enthusiasm. The church had been the site of the initial mass meeting held at the beginning of the boycott. Martin had been introduced as MIA president there, and members of the church had been instrumental in making the protest a success.

Martin continued to recover, and over the next five months, he returned to a heavy schedule of speaking engagements. He and Coretta also began detailed planning for their much-anticipated trip to India.

Viewing the excursion as a leisurely time to study the teachings of Gandhi in his native setting, Coretta and Martin departed for India in February 1959, five months after the stabbing incident. Anticipating a time of rest, they arrived to find a heavy schedule of travel and public appearances. Martin was assigned to speak almost as much as he did at home, and Coretta was provided with a number of opportunities to sing. In between those events, they were able to meet with a number of people who had been taught and trained by Gandhi, and Coretta and Martin were astounded at the changes nonviolent protest had produced. However, they were deeply troubled by the rampant poverty they encountered.

Near the end of March, Coretta and Martin returned to the United States and a life even more hectic than before. Martin's speeches had been the primary source of income for SCLC. In his absence, that income had gone lacking. When he returned, he found the organization financially destitute. He embarked immediately on a national speaking tour in an effort to keep the work afloat.

For most of that year, Coretta was occupied at home, tending to her two young children and assisting with duties at the church. Her only concert of 1959 came on October 9 when she performed at Greenwood Missionary Baptist Church in Tuskegee, Alabama. Grennetta Ross accompanied her.

Located near Tuskegee Institute, a historically black university, Coretta's performance at Greenwood gave her the opportunity to appear before an audience of young college students.[1] Martin had spoken at the church several years earlier, telling the story of the Montgomery boycott. Now, Coretta had an opportunity to demonstrate that story through song and dramatic readings. She relished the chance to impart to an emerging generation the same kind of mission-oriented enthusiasm she had received while attending Lincoln School and Antioch College.

By the end of 1959, Martin had spent very little time tending to his obligations at Dexter. Life for him had changed. When he had accepted the position as pastor at Dexter, he had done so with the intention of establishing a career as a local pastor. Since that time, events had taken him far from the traditional role of minister. By the end of the boycott, his vision had moved from issues facing the pastor of a congregation to the issues facing America. Those issues could no longer be adequately addressed from the pulpit of a church in Montgomery, Alabama.

Consequently, in January 1960, after agonizing deliberation, Martin resigned as pastor of Dexter. That month, he and Coretta moved their family from Montgomery to Atlanta where Martin became co-pastor of Ebenezer Baptist Church. There he worked alongside his father. The move lightened Martin's pastoral burden and gave him a broader base from which to operate.

What had begun as isolated, localized protests in Montgomery and other southern cities had reached the cusp of regional momentum and offered the potential for effecting permanent change. That momentum had faded in the ensuing years since the Montgomery boycott, mainly attributable to the division of Martin's attention. To succeed, the Movement needed the full-time attention of a leader capable of galvanizing local protests into a national revolution. Living in Atlanta and working from Ebenezer Baptist Church gave Martin the platform from which to coordinate those protests and lead them to a new level. Atlanta also offered cultural and educational opportunities for personal growth in a cosmopolitan environment. Coretta especially needed that.

24

Albany

In February 1960, only six days after Coretta, Martin, and their family arrived in Atlanta, students in North Carolina staged the first of what would be many sit-ins in an attempt to desegregate dining facilities. The protest was held in Greensboro, North Carolina, and touched off a wave of similar protests across the South. Later that month, Martin traveled to Durham where he met with the leaders of the sit-ins. At his suggestion, they formed a coordinating committee to assist them in their work. Later that year, the group became a permanent organization called the Student Nonviolent Coordinating Committee (SNCC).

Sit-ins proved an effective, nonviolent means of drawing attention to the discriminatory practices of prominent regional and national stores. Gradually, sit-ins moved from North Carolina to other states in the South. In October a sit-in was held in Rich's Department Store in downtown Atlanta. Back then, many department stores had a small luncheon café where shoppers could pause for refreshments or a light meal. Rich's let anyone shop in the store but only served white patrons at the lunch counter. Martin joined the students that day as they occupied seats at the counter and asked to be served. When the manager told them to leave, they politely remained in their seats. Shortly after that, they were arrested and taken from the store to Fulton County Jail. Other protesters from that event were released within a few days, but Martin remained in jail. Coretta called to find out why. What she heard was alarming.

Earlier that year, sometime around May, Coretta and Martin had had dinner with Lillian Smith, a prominent southern novelist.[1] Afterward they drove Smith back to Emory Hospital where she was undergoing treatment for cancer. On the way, a policeman spotted Smith in the car with Martin. Lillian Smith was a white woman. The policeman wanted to know what a white woman was doing in a car with two African Americans. The license plates on the car had expired, and Martin, newly moved from Alabama, had not obtained a Georgia driver's license within the required time frame. The incident occurred in a part of Atlanta located in DeKalb County, and Martin was issued a citation to appear in DeKalb County Court.

When Martin appeared in court on charges related to the expired tag and out-of-state driver's license, he was found guilty. He was fined and sentenced to four months in jail. The sentence was suspended, and Martin was placed on probation. As a condition of probation, Martin was ordered not to violate the law for a period of one year. Martin thought the case had been disposed of and did not realize he was on probation. His arrest at the sit-in in Rich's was a minor offense, but it violated the terms of his probation on the prior charge. Authorities in DeKalb County wanted him transported there for a hearing.

A few days later, a hearing was held in DeKalb County before Judge Oscar Mitchell to determine whether Martin should go to prison on the earlier traffic charge. The judge wasted no time in sentencing Martin to serve the previously suspended sentence. Martin's attorneys filed a notice of appeal and asked that he be released on bond. Mitchell scheduled a hearing to consider the appeal bond issue. Coretta and Martin assumed he would remain in the county jail until that hearing.

Late that night, Martin was roused from his cell, handcuffed, and led outside to a car. He had no idea where he was going. Two deputies drove through the night with Martin sitting in back. One can imagine the thoughts that went through his mind. Once again, he faced the real prospect of death. All our lives we had heard stories about black prisoners who were taken from their cells at night and were never seen or heard from again.

That night, the car ride ended at the Georgia State Prison near Reidsville. Martin was issued a prison uniform and escorted to a cell. No one knew Martin had left the county jail until his attorney came to court for the appeal bond hearing. When Coretta found out, she feared Martin would be killed.

At the time, John F. Kennedy was campaigning for president. Kennedy was a Democrat. His opponent, Richard Nixon, a Republican, had been generally favored in the black community. Most blacks regarded Democrats with suspicion, especially in the South. Democrats from Southern states who controlled the party were staunch segregationists. While Martin remained in prison, Coretta called Harris Wofford, who was a member of Kennedy's campaign staff. Wofford got word to Kennedy, who telephoned Coretta to offer his assistance. Later, Kennedy's brother Robert phoned Judge Mitchell to insist that Martin be released.

While their efforts carried little official weight, the Kennedys' involvement buoyed Coretta's spirits. Martin's father, who had previously endorsed Richard Nixon, was so moved that he decided to vote for Kennedy in the upcoming presidential election. He urged members of his congregation to do so as well. Nixon, who had refused to comment on the situation, was written off as weak.

Finally, Judge Mitchell held a hearing on the appeal bond issue. Martin's attorneys presented their argument, and Mitchell agreed. Eight days after being arrested, Martin was released. Coretta and Martin had been tested by the incident. Coretta, who was pregnant at the time with their third child, found it particularly distressing. Yet they persevered and emerged more convinced than ever that they had no choice but to fight racism in every place it was found.

Traumatic as those days had been, events moved forward at a rapid pace, leaving them little time to reflect. SNCC continued to negotiate with Atlanta merchants about integrating their businesses. Martin joined in that effort and continued speaking around the country. Each month saw him increasingly away from home.

In January 1961, Coretta gave birth to their third child, Dexter. By then, Yolanda, the oldest of their children, was an active six-year-old. With a newborn and a four-year-old requiring attention, too, caring for her growing family kept Coretta occupied at home most of that year. Martin's already hectic schedule took him away from Atlanta for extended periods. Coretta had always enjoyed keeping an orderly home and concentrated on maintaining a stable environment for their children. She remained as cognizant of her calling as before, but during that period of her life, she worked toward fulfilling that calling through the rearing of her children. With an overtly conscious effort, she sought to instill in them the same drive and desire for change she had received from our parents and the faculty at Lincoln and Antioch. God was at work in the world, and she wanted her children involved with Him in that effort.

That spring, the focus of demonstrations shifted to interstate transportation in a series of Freedom Rides designed to test enforcement of Supreme Court decisions that had ruled against segregation in interstate transportation.[2] Organized by the Congress of Racial Equality (CORE), riders headed south from Washington, D.C., much like the Fellowship of Reconciliation some twenty years earlier. Traveling aboard two Greyhound buses, the group encountered little difficulty as they made their way through Virginia, North Carolina, and down to Atlanta. Martin met them at the bus station before they continued on to Alabama.

On May 14, outside Anniston, Alabama, the first bus of Freedom Riders was attacked by an angry white mob. The bus was set on fire. When the second bus arrived at the Anniston terminal, whites attacked it, too. Later that day, the lone remaining bus arrived in Birmingham. There, the riders were again met by an angry mob. Several riders were seriously injured.[3]

In December 1961, Martin went to Albany, Georgia, to speak at a mass rally. Black leaders in Albany, with the help of SNCC organizers, were protesting against enforcement of Albany's segregation ordinances on city bus lines and in the interstate bus and rail terminals. Though he had gone there only to give an address, Martin spent the night and led a march the following day. That led to a protracted involvement in the ongoing Albany boycott that occupied Martin's time through most of 1962.

Albany was a vicious city. I worked there as a professor at Albany State College during the 1956–57 school year. Many times I saw white men walking the streets with shotguns on their shoulders. It was a mean, scary place.

The boycott forced the city of Albany to shut down its bus service and had a serious financial effect on downtown businesses, but the Movement was undermined by internal strife and bickering. During the course of his involvement there, Martin was arrested several times and spent a number of weeks in jail. Through the summer, he shared many long, hot days in a cell with fellow protestor Ralph Abernathy. Concerned for their safety, Coretta and Juanita Abernathy visited them there and found conditions deplorable. Without air-conditioning or proper sanitation facilities, the cells were reminiscent of something one would expect in a Third World country. The women were appalled to find their husbands confined in such a place, but understood their mission and obligation to the Movement. Still, Coretta and Juanita could not help but cringe as their children asked once again why their fathers, ministers and advocates for others, were in jail.

Opposed by an intransigent city commission, the Albany movement led to little in the way of tangible results. Still, Martin and the SCLC leadership learned valuable lessons about organizing protests. Truly effective change in Albany was made more difficult by the lack of registered black voters. Viewing the protest from a cell at the county jail, Martin realized the indispensable power of voter registration as a way of gaining leverage on elected officials. Those lessons from Albany would be put to good use as SCLC turned its efforts toward Birmingham.

25

Birmingham

Early in 1962, Fred Shuttlesworth suggested SCLC focus its attention on conditions in Birmingham. He felt that Birmingham's reputation made it the key to unlocking the South. With years of experience quietly leading opposition to Birmingham's segregation policies, Shuttlesworth made a compelling argument.

Later in the decade, news reporters gave Birmingham great notoriety as "Bombingham." We knew the city by that name long before the reporters arrived. Even in the early 1950s, we heard stories of whites bombing the homes of black leaders who dared to speak out on racial issues. Notable among those whose homes were damaged was Arthur Shores, an attorney who often represented the NAACP.[1]

Birmingham was an industrial city undergirded by northern business interests and controlled by a powerful all-white political structure. Led by Public Safety Commissioner Eugene "Bull" Connor, Birmingham police had a reputation for brutally opposing public protests and demonstrations. When union representatives had attempted to organize workers in the area's steel mills, Connor had not hesitated to use force against outside "organizers." If he was heavy-handed with white protesters, we knew he would be rough on blacks. Birmingham was a place where racism was as important as religion. Both blacks and white moderates lived under a cloud of fear. In the 1950s and 1960s, it was a violent place for thinking people to live.

While Martin focused on Birmingham and southern segregation, Coretta turned her attention to the broader issue of international peace. The previous year, a group calling itself Women Strike for Peace held a protest march in Washington, D.C. Founded by Bella Abzug and Dagmar Wilson, the group hoped to gain support for an international agreement banning nuclear weapons. Their immediate concern that year was the pending negotiations for a treaty banning atmospheric nuclear testing. Though led by experienced organizers, the group was composed of typical middle-class white women, most of them mothers and homemakers.[2]

One of the primary forums for international disarmament negotiations was with the United Nations Committee on Disarmament, a permanent arm of the UN which met in Geneva, Switzerland. In the spring of 1962, members of Women Strike for Peace approached Coretta about joining a delegation to the committee. Intrigued by the grassroots nature of the effort and motivated by her commitment to the broader implications of nonviolence, Coretta agreed.

The delegation departed Atlanta aboard a Swissair flight on April 6. When they arrived in Geneva, the group received a cool reception from the United States' representative, Arthur Dean. Apparently taking issue with the notion that the United States was stalling the talks, Dean suggested the group should talk to the Soviet Union's delegation, implying they were the stumbling blocks to a meaningful treaty. Refusing to cower to Dean's curt dismissal, the women did just as he had suggested. Valerian Zorin and Semyon Tsarapkin, senior members of the Soviet negotiating team, gave the women a warm and cordial welcome.

Talks in Geneva eventually resulted in the Limited Test Ban Treaty. When President Kennedy signed the agreement, Coretta had the satisfaction of knowing she had participated in making history. The success of that effort marked the beginning of her long involvement with the Peace Movement.

Coretta did not realize it at the time, but her involvement with Women Strike for Peace and her meeting with the Soviet delegation caught the attention of the FBI. The agency had opened a file on her earlier when Kwame Nkrumah had invited her and Martin to Ghana. As her involvement in the Peace Movement increased, the agency took an even greater interest in her affairs. She was not subjected to the kinds of abuse Martin received, but throughout the 1960s, and even later, she was the subject of increasing interest.[3]

In September of that year, SCLC held its annual convention in Birmingham, and Martin had an opportunity to experience for himself the kind of sentiment that gave the city its notorious reputation. While Martin addressed the convention, a white man came from the crowd and made his way toward the front. Brash and unafraid, he charged the podium where Martin stood and struck him in the face with his fist. Shocked and astounded, Martin nevertheless refused to retaliate or strike back. Several men from the dais wrestled the assailant to the ground, but Martin refused to press charges. Bull Connor intervened and arrested the man anyway. The attack was the kind of behavior Martin expected. Connor's response was not and left Martin wondering if the protest in Birmingham might be less confrontational than he had first thought. He would soon find out Birmingham's reputation under Connor was well deserved.

In January 1963, Martin, Ralph Abernathy, and Fred Shuttlesworth met with President Kennedy and Attorney General Robert Kennedy in an attempt to convince them to introduce much-needed civil rights legislation. Although President Kennedy was sympathetic, he indicated he had no plans for proposing civil rights legislation that year. Instead, he wanted to push legislation on other domestic issues. The president thought any movement by him in the area of civil rights would divide Congress and weaken the chances for any of his domestic legislation to pass.

Following their meeting, Martin and other SCLC leaders felt they had no choice but to go forward with plans to force a confrontation in Birmingham. They hoped they could win real concessions on segregation issues from local white leaders and force the federal government to act. Martin communicated their intentions to the president and indicated he would expect federal assistance if violence erupted.

Unlike Albany, strategy and financial support for the Birmingham crusade was prepared well in advance. Martin envisioned a protest involving large numbers of participants, many of whom would be arrested. In order to assure maximum involvement, SCLC needed the ability to offer participants bail immediately upon arrest. Doing that would require a substantial sum of money. A committee was formed for the purpose of raising the necessary funds.

In conjunction with the fund-raising effort, Martin and Fred Shuttlesworth attended a meeting with Harry Belafonte in his New York apartment. Harry gathered seventy-five prominent people from the New York area, all of whom had pledged their support. At that meeting Martin and Shuttlesworth spoke of the dangers and difficulties protesters would likely encounter. Thousands of dollars would be needed to post bail bonds. Those present that night agreed to help. The Western Leadership Conference and the Virginia SCLC affiliate did as well. The NAACP Legal Defense Fund agreed to provide legal assistance for any cases that reached court.

Toward the end of January 1963, James Bevel, Dorothy Cotton, and James Orange were sent to Birmingham to begin the fieldwork necessary for an effective protest. Their primary duty was to recruit and train marchers for the public demonstrations. Bevel, Cotton, and Orange held mass meetings and workshops in which they presented details about nonviolent demonstration methods. They also collected commitment cards from those willing to go to jail.

In March 1963, Coretta gave birth to her and Martin's fourth child, Bernice. I had been attending graduate school in Boston the prior year but became ill. A few months earlier, Coretta had come to Boston to see about me. When she discovered how sick I was, she insisted on taking me home with her. I didn't want to give up on school that year, but I was glad to be with her and to be in their home when Bernice was born on March 28.

About two weeks after Bernice was born, Martin, Ralph, Wyatt Walker, and Andrew Young left Atlanta and joined SCLC staff in Birmingham. They set up headquarters in the Gaston Motel. Coretta was concerned about their safety but not overly distraught. I'm sure Martin would have rather stayed at home, but he felt compelled to go. He loved his family, but he was driven by a sense of purpose and calling that was much larger than his own desires.

Plans called for the protest in Birmingham to begin during the Easter season with a boycott of downtown stores. Martin was certain this would lower retail sales at a time when shopping was usually brisk. By doing so, he hoped Birmingham businessmen would respond in favor of the protest's demands as a way of protecting their own self-interests. Martin understood capitalism and wanted to use it as a way of driving the business community toward economic justice. Loveman's, Pizitz, and Woolworth department stores were selected as targets.

In the next stage, after the boycott was in place, a small march was planned through downtown streets to the courthouse to emphasize the beginning of SCLC's voter registration drive and to reinforce the boycott. At the same time, sit-ins would begin at lunch counters in downtown stores.

As April approached and the date for the first protest actions drew near, NAACP leadership and others involved in planning the protest suggested they should delay action. Birmingham had held its mayoral election just weeks before. Results from that contest put white moderate Albert Boutwell in a runoff with Connor, an avowed racist. If the protests began before the runoff election, they might tip the vote toward Connor. The runoff election was scheduled for April 2. Protest leaders agreed to delay their efforts until the following day.

When Boutwell won the runoff, many argued that the protest should be delayed even further. The election results, they said, suggested racial attitudes in Birmingham were changing. A protest now might derail that natural move toward a more progressive stance. Martin disagreed.

Aside from the fact that elaborate plans for the protest were in place and people were ready to go, Connor remained public safety commissioner. The election of Boutwell had been occasioned by a change in Birmingham's form of government. Birmingham had previously been governed by commissioners in a strong commission/weak mayor format. The change switched the government to a mayor-council form with the mayor in a much stronger position. Commissioners elected under the prior form had been elected to terms that had not yet expired. Connor and others refused to hand over control of their offices until their original terms ended. Immediately following the runoff, Boutwell filed suit asking the court to remove the commissioners from office. A decision in that case would not take long. Martin wanted to march while Connor was still in office.

As public safety commissioner, Connor controlled the city police. Working from that position, he had become a major source of power for radical segregationists, a stronghold from which they attacked blacks with impunity and intimidated any who favored a progressive stance. Connor maintained a façade of public decency, but beneath the surface Martin was certain Connor was a vile and hateful man. Martin believed a march while Connor was still in office would bring his racist nature to light and let the public see how evil and dangerous racism really was.

On April 3, the protest went forward as planned. Students from nearby Miles College conducted sit-ins at lunch counters in downtown department stores. Blacks began to boycott those same stores. When those conducting the sit-ins refused to leave the stores, they were arrested. At first, policemen were courteous, but as other students stepped in to take the vacant seats, police frustration grew and their conduct became more belligerent.

Later that same week, marchers took to the streets. Beginning from Sixteenth Street Baptist Church, they slowly walked toward the downtown district. Not as many marchers participated as Martin had hoped, but they proceeded just the same, conducting a march every day. Police responded by arresting them, too. Soon several hundred protesters were incarcerated in the Birmingham jail.

As days passed and the sit-ins and marches continued, Birmingham business leaders became increasingly concerned. The boycott had decreased sales from blacks, but more than that, the marches and subsequent arrests had scared away potential white customers. Apprehensive about the economic effects of a protracted disruption, business owners contacted Fred Shuttlesworth, Arthur Shores, and others about negotiating an end to the protest.

Birmingham's black community had made their demands clear from the beginning— desegregate store facilities, hire blacks on a nondiscriminatory basis, drop charges against jailed protesters, and create a biracial committee to work out a timetable for further desegregation. Meeting in secret with white business leaders, Shuttlesworth and several other local leaders held to those basic demands. While the two sides talked, marches and sit-ins continued.

The marches continued, more protesters went to jail, and merchants steadily lost money from declining sales. One week into the protest, the businessmen were ready to accede to the protesters' demands. City commissioners, however, were unwilling to cooperate. At the same time, Connor became increasingly adamant in opposition to any agreement. To make his point, he filed a petition in Jefferson County Circuit Court seeking an injunction barring the demonstrators from further marches. His request was quickly granted.

When the ruling was made public, Martin promptly announced that the injunction would be disobeyed. A march was scheduled for April 12, Good Friday. He intended to go forward with the march. The symbolism, he felt, was appropriate for what the protesters faced.

Once again, not everyone agreed with Martin's position. Some felt that, as nonviolent protesters, disobeying the court's order would contradict the principles for which they stood. In addition, the SCLC bail bond fund was depleted. With no money for bail, protesters could not be guaranteed quick release from jail. If Martin and the leadership disobeyed the court's order, they could be incarcerated for a considerable length of time. Confronted just hours prior to the march, Martin asked for time to meditate on the decision and retreated to his room at the motel. Half an hour later, he emerged dressed in work clothes. His decision was obvious.

"I've decided to take a leap of faith. I've decided to go to jail. I don't know what's going to happen; I don't know whether this Movement will continue to build up or whether it will collapse. If enough people are willing to go to jail, I believe it will force the city officials to act or force the federal government to act. So I am going today."[4]

From the motel, Martin and the others rode to Zion Hill Church where the march was set to begin. There, he spoke to a mass meeting, making plain to those who gathered that he was prepared to go to jail for whatever length of time was required. At the conclusion of his remarks, he stepped from behind the pulpit and started up the aisle toward the door.

Outside, he was joined by fifty or sixty protesters. Together, they set off down the street. Blacks who had come to observe them and urge them on lined the way. The streets were filled with policemen, too. At first, as the march proceeded from the church, the policemen merely watched, but as the protest drew closer to the downtown area, Connor ordered his men to arrest the demonstrators. Martin and Ralph were arrested along with all the others.

Inside the Birmingham jail, Martin and Ralph were held in separate cells. Cut off from the world outside, Martin had little news of the fate of the other protesters or whether the demonstrations were continuing. Alone in a hot, stuffy cell, he sat on the bare steel frame of a cot and thought about all that had transpired.

Meanwhile, the protest continued in the streets of Birmingham. Staff organizers from SCLC and SNCC worked tirelessly to recruit participants for the daily marches. On Easter Sunday, Martin's brother, A. D. King, led a march from his church on the north side of the city. After several blocks, he and those with him were arrested and taken to jail. Others joined in the effort the following day, and the marches continued unabated.

While Martin sat in jail, Coretta was at home in Atlanta with her children. Martin, confined to a cell, had been unable to telephone her. She had heard nothing from him since the night before the march. She knew that Martin and those on the march with him had been arrested, but she had received no further information about him. Conditions in the Birmingham jail were not much better than what she had observed in Albany. She had heard reports that prisoners there were forced to live in dire circumstances. I was with her during that time and could see how concerned she was for Martin's safety. However, discipline and action were the hallmarks of Coretta's life, and rather than wallowing in worry, she moved into action.

When Sunday came and Martin still had not called, Coretta attempted to telephone President Kennedy to ask for his help. He was out of town as was the vice president, but a White House operator suggested the press secretary, Pierre Salinger, might be able to help. After talking to Salinger she waited to see what would happen. A few minutes later Robert Kennedy, the attorney general, called her. He assured her they would do everything possible to contact Martin and find out his condition.

Monday came, and still Coretta had not heard from Martin. Then, that afternoon President Kennedy called. He informed her that the FBI had been ordered to investigate the situation in Birmingham and assured her that Martin would call her shortly. A few minutes later, Martin called, and the two were able to talk.

Coretta was relieved to know that Martin was well, but she was not satisfied with the way things were developing. He had been in jail too long and held there without the ability to contact anyone. One thing Coretta had learned from experience was the value of public exposure. Even officials with the hardest hearts often changed their conduct when they knew someone was watching. That was why she had wanted the president involved. She wanted officials in Birmingham to know that someone else knew what they were doing. But Coretta was never one to leave things to others. If public awareness was necessary, she would make certain they knew she was watching, too. The following Thursday, April 18, Coretta and Juanita Abernathy flew to Birmingham to see for themselves how their husbands were being treated.[5]

After Coretta and Juanita visited the jail, conditions improved for Martin and Ralph. They were allowed to leave their cells to exercise and were given the opportunity to shower and shave. During one of those moments of civility, Martin was provided a copy of the *Birmingham News*. A group of white clergymen had published a statement in the newspaper voicing their criticism of the demonstrations. Their statement deeply disturbed Martin, and he began drafting a response letter on the margins of the newspaper and scraps of toilet paper. That writing is now known as the "Letter from a Birmingham Jail." In it, he set out the reasons for the demonstrations in Birmingham. He went on to describe the philosophy of nonviolent protest and the reasons why current conditions compelled him and others to acts of civil disobedience. The document became a primer for nonviolent protesters.

Eight days after Martin's arrest, Clarence Jones, an attorney from New York, arrived in Birmingham. Martin was glad to see him, but Martin was even more excited by the news Jones brought. Thanks to the efforts of Harry Belafonte, fifty thousand dollars had been raised for the bail fund.

26

Fire Hoses ... and Dogs

After Martin was released from jail, he and the Birmingham protest faced a new and more serious challenge. Whether from sympathy or fear of trouble, Birmingham's white citizens had stayed away from downtown stores. Their absence compounded the economic effect of the boycott. That they had not openly opposed the marches seemed like a good sign. Adult blacks, however, had been unwilling to participate in numbers sufficient to make the kind of bold statement SCLC wanted to make. Without their participation, the marches would appear to be only the thinly supported work of outsiders. As long as whites felt black residents were apathetic to their own condition, city leadership would never take steps to implement even the most moderate changes.

With the national media beginning to lose interest, James Bevel, an SCLC staff member, suggested they use high school students in the next march. Martin was hesitant at first. The use of children in a march was a risky move. The sight of young people leading a protest seemed to carry a message of desperation. Others agreed. Protest marches were dangerous, and placing children in that situation seemed unwise. Bevel argued just the opposite. Children, he suggested, offered a message of innocence and hope. No one could resist the plea of a child.

Reluctantly, Martin approved only an invitation asking students who were interested in participating to come to the Sixteenth Street Baptist Church on May 2, 1963. He planned to provide them with a full and frank presentation of what they might expect and rudimentary instruction in nonviolent protest. He was willing to pursue the notion but was less than enthusiastic about the result it might bring.

While others sounded a note of alarm, Bevel saw inclusion of the students as the moment of opportunity for which they had been waiting. When the students arrived at the church, he quickly organized them into groups. Without waiting for final approval, he sent them out from the church in successive waves. A few blocks from the church, the police were waiting. By the time the third wave of marchers reached the police lines, hundreds of students had been arrested. Images of Birmingham policemen herding school-age children into custody filled the evening news.

Though Martin had not ordered the marches, he was pleased with the result. The students were orderly, and their enthusiasm was contagious. News outlets picked up the story and gave the protests renewed exposure. Birmingham police had treated the students in a firm and authoritative manner but had not used excessive force.

The next day, Bevel organized another wave of student marchers. Before anyone could stop him, the students left the church and headed downtown. Encouraged by reports from the day before, crowds lined the streets to watch and cheer the marchers. Unlike the day before, however, things soon turned ugly.

When the marchers reached Kelley Ingram Park, they were met by police, some of whom were accompanied by dogs. Firemen stood nearby with high-pressure water hoses manned and ready. As the young marchers approached, torrents of water were unleashed against them. The force of the blast from the hoses sent students tumbling down the street and across the sidewalks. The water pressure was so intense it ripped the clothes off some marchers. As they clung to trees in the park for protection, the jets of water tore the bark from beneath their outstretched fingers.

With marchers soaked, confused, and in disarray, Connor ordered the police to move forward with the dogs. The sight of snarling, trained attack dogs sent the protesters scurrying. Many who had been knocked to the ground by the blasts from the hoses lay in the street unable to move. Others were injured by club-swinging policemen.

The crowd that had gathered on the sidewalks to watch was incensed at the treatment accorded the protesters. Bottles and rocks sailed through the air toward the policemen and firemen. News cameras caught it all on tape.

Like most of the nation, Coretta watched the events of that day via televised news reports. She was appalled at the treatment the protesters received and was concerned for Martin's safety. Still, she had long since come to terms with the danger involved in the work to which they were committed.

A march on Sunday met with similar treatment. Onlookers joined in the melee, throwing rocks and bottles. With the jails filled to capacity, Connor used the fire hoses again in an attempt to disperse the crowd. Reporters from around the world had poured into Birmingham to cover the events. Newspapers and television broadcasts across the nation carried graphic and disturbing images of the day's events.

In response, Robert Kennedy dispatched Burke Marshall, his chief civil rights assistant, and Joseph F. Dolan, assistant deputy attorney general, to see if a truce could be reached. Worried that Kennedy was more interested in containing the political repercussions of the violence than in winning justice for blacks, Martin was skeptical of Marshall's presence. Martin had seen the shifting sands of political interests in the Albany protest. Suspicious of attempts to negotiate, he was convinced that only new federal laws could bring about the changes he and the SCLC leadership sought.

Almost from the moment of his arrival, Marshall dispelled Martin's doubts. Instead of strong-arming the parties, he focused on the group most obviously affected by the protests—the downtown businessmen and merchants. Acting as mediator, Marshall assisted in keeping lines of communication open and in arranging the continuing secret meetings between protest leadership and downtown merchants.

Marshall met separately with representatives of the downtown businessmen on several occasions but without much progress. Then, on May 7, in an effort to bring new life to the talks, he met with a much larger group. Throughout the morning, the merchants remained deeply entrenched in opposition to even the most minor demands of the protesters.

At noon, the group left the building to eat lunch. While they had been meeting, thousands of blacks had quietly assembled on the downtown streets and sidewalks. When the businessmen came from the building, they stepped into a sea of blacks. Orderly and solemn, the crowd joined in singing freedom songs. The discreet witness of so many blacks had a powerful effect that touched the heart of one of the businessmen in a way that forced him to confront the evil and unjust nature of his racial attitudes. When the group returned from lunch, he spoke in favor of working something out; eventually the others joined him.

When Marshall informed Martin that representatives from the business and industrial community wanted to meet with him to work out a settlement, Martin responded by ordering a twenty-four hour halt to demonstrations. He then traveled across town to join in the meeting.

After hours of discussion, the twenty-four-hour moratorium on marches came and went without an agreement on the protesters' demands. Once again, leaders in the black community were divided on whether to return to the streets with yet more marches. Martin, however, was convinced the marches and the disruption they caused had been the only real source of power and leverage against the downtown merchants. Unable to reach a negotiated agreement, he ordered a resumption of the marches. Once again, Connor and the police responded by arresting protesters as they neared the downtown district.

Finally, on May 10, faced with continuing disruption of business, the merchants agreed to terms addressing the protesters' demands, including desegregation of lunch counters in downtown businesses, hiring of blacks—not only in industry but in clerk and sales positions—cooperation in releasing protesters from jail, and creation of an interracial committee to address future issues. Final implementation was contingent on a court order upholding Boutwell's victory in the mayoral election, but the agreement contained everything for which the protest leadership had hoped.

27

Bombs

The agreement in Birmingham brought an end to the marches and demonstrations. Protesters were released from jail, and order was restored to the streets. A tenuous, uneasy peace settled over the city, but it did not last long.

News that businessmen had agreed to the protesters' demands infuriated segregationists. Ku Klux Klansmen, who had been conspicuously absent from the marches, responded with violence in a wave of terror that seemed designed to incite the black community to react in ways that would destroy the progress they had worked so hard to attain.

On Saturday night, May 11, 1963, the home of the Reverend A. D. King, Martin's brother, was bombed. He and his family escaped unharmed, but most of the house was destroyed. That same night a bomb erupted near the window of Martin's room at the Gaston Motel. Martin had left town for a speaking engagement and was not in the motel at the time. Several people were injured. Had Martin been there, he would have been, too.

As it happened, the bombs went off about the time bars and clubs in the black neighborhoods were closing. Many of the people coming from the bars did not have the discipline of the Movement and had no understanding of what was really occurring. As word of the bombings spread, thousands of blacks poured into the streets, looking for a place to vent their anger. Police and firemen who responded to emergency calls from the blasts were met with a hail of stones and bottles. Violence spread as people took to the streets to express years of frustration. Cars were overturned and set on fire. The damage was significant. It seemed that whoever had planted the bombs was intent on starting a riot that would upset the recent agreement.

Governor George Wallace's state police responded by sealing off the African American areas of the city. Then they moved in with clubs and pistols, beating many innocent blacks. Anne Walker, wife of SCLC staff member Wyatt Tee Walker, was one of the victims. She was confronted by police and beaten as she attempted to enter her husband's bombed-out room at the Gaston Motel. Wyatt took her to the hospital for treatment. As he drove back to the motel, he was also attacked by state troopers.

The next evening, President Kennedy spoke to the nation in a televised broadcast. In his address he reiterated his commitment to establishing order and peace in Birmingham within the framework provided by the agreement reached earlier that week between protesters, downtown merchants, and city officials. To make certain that happened, he ordered three thousand federal troops into position near Birmingham and stood ready to federalize the Alabama National Guard. His resolve to bring federal pressure to bear on the situation brought a momentary lull to the violence.

Then, a few days later, the Birmingham Board of Education issued letters notifying parents that it had suspended or expelled more than a thousand high school students who had been absent from school while participating in the marches. Martin and other leaders of the protest decided to submit the school board's action to judicial review. With the help of the NAACP Legal Defense Fund, they filed a petition in federal court seeking an order reversing the school board's decision.

On May 22, a federal district judge in Birmingham upheld the school board's action. Just a few hours later, Judge Elbert Tuttle of the US Court of Appeals for the Fifth Circuit reversed that decision and strongly condemned the board's action.[1] That evening protesters in Birmingham gathered at a mass meeting to celebrate.

While the protest had been going on, the lawsuit regarding the final outcome of Birmingham's mayoral election had been making its way through state court. On May 23, the Alabama Supreme Court issued its ruling, deciding in favor of Boutwell and the newly elected city council. The court's decision officially removed Eugene "Bull" Connor from office.[2]

On June 11, not quite three weeks later, Alabama Governor George Wallace stood in the doorway at the entrance to Foster Auditorium on the campus of The University of Alabama in Tuscaloosa. He was blocking the entrance of two black students, Vivian Malone and James Hood, who were attempting to register for the coming term. Later that day, President Kennedy federalized the Alabama National Guard, and the two students returned. Flanked by the guard, now under the president's control and escorted by Deputy Attorney General Nicholas Katzenbach and a contingent of federal marshals, Malone and Hood once again attempted to enter the building. This time, after being confronted by the commander of the Alabama National Guard, Governor Wallace stepped aside and allowed the students to enter. They succeeded in registering for class, but the university campus remained hostile.

That evening, President Kennedy again spoke to the nation in a televised address. After detailing events in Birmingham and Tuscaloosa, he announced that he would ask Congress for comprehensive civil rights legislation. Finally, the federal government was stepping into the fight. The effort to dismantle institutional racism had turned a crucial corner.

As if to punctuate the need for that legislation, only hours after President Kennedy concluded his address to the nation, NAACP official Medgar Evers was shot and killed outside his home in Jackson, Mississippi. Racial tensions, already running high, reached critical levels.

28

Washington, D.C.

As he had promised in his address to the nation, President Kennedy sent a civil rights bill to Congress on June 19, 1963. Emulating the Civil Rights Act of 1875, the bill offered by Kennedy included provisions to ban discrimination in public accommodations and authorized the attorney general to enforce court decisions against states that continued to operate segregated public school systems. Coretta was elated that President Kennedy had taken that action but was frustrated that it came only after Martin and others had risked their lives to bring the need for it to light.

Slowly, with painful steps that often seemed frustratingly small, the revolution that had begun with Rosa Parks's decision on the bus that day took hold of the nation's conscience. By the summer of 1963, institutional racism in the South was in retreat, and the change which blacks long had sought was poised to sweep across the nation. The quest for political and economic equality—the fight to free blacks from oppression at the hands of whites and to free whites from the evil that blinded their eyes to justice—was gaining momentum and becoming a movement. Passage of the newly introduced civil rights bill was critical to that movement's success. Coretta and Martin were determined to see that happen.

From the beginning of the Montgomery protest through the darkest days of the demonstrations in Birmingham, Coretta and Martin had sensed they were in an uphill fight. After Birmingham, though much remained to be accomplished, they began to sense momentum gathering behind the cause of integration, inclusion, and equality.

With the US Supreme Court in the lead, federal courts had issued decisions that, with few exceptions, consistently applied the court's reasoning in *Brown v. Board of Education.* Although the effort in Albany had been less than successful, Montgomery and Birmingham had been examples of how nonviolent protest could lead to effective political change. Leaders of the major civil rights organizations—the NAACP, SNCC, SCLC, CORE, and the National Urban League—had made great strides toward their goal of extending the full privileges of citizenship to all people regardless of race or color. Now, they were on the verge of monumental federal legislation. With it, the federal government would have the authority to intervene when local officials were reluctant to act. Presidential leadership would still be critical, but federal officials would wield far more power than before, which they could exercise without direct presidential intervention. One more dramatic push would assure that the civil rights bill received swift passage.

A protest march capable of sending a galvanizing, triumphant message—one that would convince Congress to act and one that would invigorate blacks everywhere—could only be held in the nation's capital. But that march could not be like any other held thus far. For the march to be effective, participants would have to conduct themselves in a dignified, orderly manner. They would have to come from all across the nation, and they would have to include more than just blacks. White participation was crucial. Congress needed to see that the question of civil rights was not merely a black issue, but one that affected people of every race and color.

Like the earlier Pilgrimage for Freedom in 1957, the idea of a march in support of the civil rights bill came from A. Philip Randolph. As first proposed, the theme of the march was to focus on the need of African Americans for jobs and freedom. Martin wholeheartedly supported the idea as did the SCLC leadership. That theme rang true in Coretta's heart as well. CORE's James Farmer also supported the idea, but not everyone involved in the Movement agreed.

Whitney Young of the National Urban League declined to participate. Roy Wilkins of the NAACP was less than receptive. Undaunted, Randolph and the others went forward with plans and set a tentative date for sometime in August. When their plans were made public, President Kennedy invited leaders from the major black organizations to a meeting at the White House.

Kennedy was concerned that a protest march would send the wrong message to Congress. In order to gain passage of the bill, he needed the support of moderate Republicans from the West and Midwest. Having few if any black people in their districts, they often viewed racial issues less emotionally than did those from other regions of the country. They tended to favor passage of the act, but a march with the clear aim of applying force to Congress might drive them in the opposite direction. Kennedy felt many in Congress who would otherwise vote for the bill would be reluctant to support it if they thought they were being forced to do so.

Martin, Randolph, and Farmer argued in favor of the march and did their best to convince President Kennedy. Wilkins and Young were noncommittal. The meeting ended without a decision, but Kennedy had made it clear to the group that he did not favor the march.

At the conclusion of the meeting, Kennedy took Martin aside and guided him to the White House Rose Garden. There, he warned Martin that the FBI was concerned about Martin's ties to Stanley Levison, whom they had long suspected of being a member of the Communist Party. The FBI also was concerned about the political ties of an SCLC staff member. Martin listened politely but was not moved by what he heard. Levison had been Martin's friend long before he had met the Kennedys and had stood with him through some very trying times—a stance that rested solely on friendship and from which Levison had nothing to gain. Such was not the case with the FBI. The FBI director, J. Edgar Hoover, had made public his opposition to Martin and the Civil Rights Movement in clear and unambiguous terms. Martin was appreciative of the president's concern but declined to sever ties with Levison and told the president as much.

The public announcement of the march and the meeting at the White House pushed Wilkins and Young reluctantly toward support for the march. What had begun as a jostling of male egos soon became a witness of unanimity in the black community. Randolph was named chairman of the event. Bayard Rustin and Walter Fauntroy handled most of the planning and details for the actual event.

With careful, meticulous work, the march began to expand in scope, moving beyond jobs and freedom to include the cause of civil rights. The focus of the event subtly shifted away from protest and more toward the strategic nature of the pending legislation. As much as was possible, marchers were trained and briefed on the kind of conduct expected. Groups beyond the black community were recruited. For example, Walter Reuther, leader of the United Auto Workers, endorsed the march, and he and many union members turned out to support it.

The National Council of Churches took up the cause with enthusiasm and organized groups at churches across the country. With their help, meals were provided to participants. Travelers coming from across the nation were able to stop at previously designated churches along the way for free meals or just for a rest. Their effort gave participants a sense that God was behind both the march and the Civil Rights Movement. What had begun as a political concept became a spiritual pilgrimage.

When discussions first began about a march in the nation's capital, Martin was skeptical that it would be a success. He wondered how many would attend and whether they would do so in numbers sufficient to make the necessary statement. Once again, he faced the dilemma he had encountered in Albany and Birmingham. While the march was necessary, it was a risky venture. Strong participation would send a clear message of public support for the bill to Congress. Weak participation would send the opposite, and the bill would be doomed to failure. Martin need not have worried.

The march was scheduled to begin at the Washington Memorial and proceed across the National Mall to the Lincoln Memorial. By Wednesday, the day of the event, over two hundred thousand people had gathered. It was far more than organizers had expected. Even more to their liking, many of the participants were white. Better still, everyone conducted themselves in an orderly and solemn manner. The march became less a protest and more a statement of national will and intent. The people of America had seen the ugly face of racism, and they wanted it no more.

At the Lincoln Memorial, each of the major leaders addressed the crowd. They were met with enthusiasm and applause, but everyone was waiting for Martin. In spite of the internecine bickering, everyone associated with the Civil Rights Movement realized Martin was its public face. He was the one quoted in the newspapers, interviewed on television, and remembered by the people in the street. As the event at the Lincoln Memorial drew to a close, the crowd waited anxiously for him to take the podium.

Coretta had stayed up with Martin most of the night before, tirelessly working with him to perfect the remarks he would give that day. Line by line, phrase by phrase, they had labored over his speech with diligence. As the night turned to early morning, they had come to weigh almost every word for just the right emphasis, nuance, and feel. Coretta had gone to bed sometime around three that morning, but Martin stayed up even longer, going over and over the speech, trying to insure it had the correct cadence and rhythm. Finally, when dawn broke, he had given the speech to a typist. Now, hours later, looking out on the throngs gathered around the reflecting pool, their anticipation must have struck both Coretta and Martin as an affirmation of all they had endured during the previous seven years.

Martin and Coretta had been on a journey, one that began before the protest in Montgomery. Though they both had long held a sense of a greater purpose at work in their lives, they had come to the cause of civil rights by a curious combination of events. Nevertheless, they had confronted evil and had been led to discover a deep and abiding faith in God. They found there the courage and determination to see the protest through to its end even if it meant death. In Albany and Birmingham that determination had been tested, and they had found their will, in the end, adequate for the mission to which they now knew beyond all doubt they had been called. Now, standing on the steps of the Lincoln Memorial, they faced yet another test of that same determination.

When others on the program had concluded their remarks, Randolph came to the podium one last time. With a simple introduction, he announced Martin as the final speaker. Proclaiming him the "moral leader of our nation," Randolph stepped aside as Martin started forward.

Prepared text in hand, Martin squeezed between those gathered on the steps and came to stand before the bank of microphones that ringed the lectern. He began to read his prepared remarks. The crowd responded with intermittent, polite applause. They warmed some as he moved on to the body of the speech. Several people seated in the foreground encouraged him with comments.

"That's right," someone was heard to say.

"Yes, Lord," another remarked.

Though confident and forceful, Martin's cadence sounded a little stilted, as if he were holding in check the preacher that resided within him. Then, halfway through the address, he likened the Declaration of Independence and the Constitution to promissory notes signed by our Founding Fathers. Those notes had been issued not merely to whites but to blacks as well. But the notes issued to blacks had been returned marked "Insufficient Funds." The crowd responded with enthusiasm. Martin's voice relaxed, and his cadence changed to the easy rhythm he used in the pulpit.

With the crowd now picking up the tempo, Martin's mind cleared of all else but the moment. Freed of distraction, the Holy Spirit began to work. Martin was no longer a public figure giving an address before a large audience at a prominent national landmark, but rather a preacher exhorting his congregation. His voice took on new, fervent emotion, and he remembered a sermon he had given many times before, one that played on the notion of a dream. Not a dream born of slumber, but a national dream—the American Dream of opportunity and equality. As he addressed the audience that day, he sensed the appropriateness of that sermon for them. Gently, seamlessly, he slipped from the prepared text to the message that lay deep in his spirit. With his voice clear and strong, he moved into an extemporaneous exposition of the dream to which he had given his life. "Even though we face the difficulties of today and tomorrow, I still have a dream. It is a dream deeply rooted in the American Dream. I have a dream, that one day this nation will rise up and live out the true meaning of its creed, 'We hold these truths to be self evident, that all men are created equal.' I have a dream that one day on the red hills of Georgia, the sons of former slaves and the sons of former slave owners will be able to sit down together at the table of brotherhood. I have a dream . . ."[1]

The dream portion of the address lasted five minutes, but it was the oratorical moment of a lifetime and a defining moment for Martin Luther King Jr. Today, almost no one remembers the first twelve minutes of that speech. Even fewer remember the allusion to our founding documents as promissory notes, but many can recite from memory portions of the final lines.

Following the speech, Martin and others who had organized the event were invited to the White House. There, they met with a jubilant President Kennedy. The march and accompanying speeches had been a resounding success. Televised to the nation and abroad, the speeches from the Lincoln Memorial had struck precisely the correct tone. What many had feared would become an unsettling and unruly gathering had become instead a national chorus, a clarion call for racial justice and equality perfectly framed within the context of the American experience.

At its heart, the nonviolent movement was a movement rooted and grounded in love. Not an easy, sentimental love, but the purposeful, self-sacrificing devotion demonstrated by Jesus. The kind of devotion that moved a man to give himself to a cause larger than his own self-interest, without regard for life or safety or the assurance of success as a precondition. In the summer of 1963, blacks across the South had shown that kind of love. In Montgomery, Albany, and Birmingham, in the face of bombings and beatings, dogs and fire hoses, they had stood against the voices of racism and tyranny without returning violence for violence, and in so doing they had shown by their own conduct the moral righteousness of their demands.

On the steps of the Lincoln Memorial, the voices of change reached a crescendo that would ensure passage of the new civil rights bill and would propel the country forward in a decade of transformation and self-examination unlike any it had ever experienced before.

29

Sixteenth Street Baptist Church

The March on Washington was a success in every respect. Event leaders had hoped for one hundred thousand participants. The crowd, in fact, was twice that number. Although originally conceived as a protest, the marchers were orderly, considerate, and respectful. Speeches from the Lincoln Memorial were carefully crafted to send the correct message; they were edgy and honest but not vicious or unduly provocative. The nation watching on television heard articulate, erudite speeches and witnessed a surprisingly pro-American event. Yet for all the progress that had been made, the nation and particularly the South remained deeply divided. Little more than two weeks after the march, violence erupted again. And, once again, Birmingham was the focus.

Earlier that year, in April and May, the Sixteenth Street Baptist Church, located a few blocks west of downtown Birmingham, had been the rallying point for those who participated in the Birmingham protest. Marchers who set off toward downtown had gathered in front of the building near the steps that faced south toward Sixth Avenue. Many evenings the church's sanctuary was the sight of mass meetings that invigorated tired protesters. Weary from a constant barrage of racial epithets and the daily risk of bodily harm, they obtained there a renewed spirit and the energy to persevere. During the height of the protest, the church had received numerous bomb threats, some of which disrupted services and programs, but no explosions had occurred and no bombs had been found. That all changed on the morning of September 15, 1963.

In the early morning darkness that Sunday, an automobile came to a stop on the east side of the church. A white man emerged from the car carrying a box. He hurried toward the building and placed the box in the well of a basement window a few feet from the northeast corner of the building. Moments later, he returned to the car and drove away.

Inside the box was a bomb made with ten sticks of dynamite wired to a time-delayed fuse and a battery. Tucked out of sight, it sat unnoticed as those silent, still hours gave way to the gray light of dawn.

As the sun rose over the city, the small rectangular box sat quietly in the window well. Lights came on in the apartment building across the street. Tired feet moved past on the sidewalk. A truck rumbled by, followed by the soft sound of a passing car. The scent of brewing coffee wafted from an open window. All the while, time ticked slowly past.

Later that morning, worshippers gathered for Sunday services. Adult Sunday school classes met upstairs. Children's programs convened in the basement. Car doors slammed shut as the congregation arrived. Friendly voices echoed along the street as friends greeted each other. Moments later, footsteps clicked against the sidewalk as worshipers moved inside. In a few minutes the sound of music drifted from the building.

Then, as the timing device in the box reached the hour of 10:22, a switch snapped closed. Electrical current shot through a twisted tangle of wires. In an instant, all ten sticks of dynamite detonated in a horrific explosion that ripped a gaping hole in the wall of the church building.

Bricks sailed through the air. Cars parked along the street were tossed aside by the force of the blast. Windows on the east side of the church shattered. Smoke and dust filled the building. And beneath the rubble lay the mangled bodies of four young girls who had been in the downstairs bathroom on the opposite side of the wall from the bomb.

Men rushed around the corner of the building and combed through the debris. Moments later, anguished cries filled the air as the bodies were carefully lifted from the basement. As might be expected, emotions ran high.

News of the attack spread quickly throughout the black community. Ministers at the church and others in surrounding areas called for blacks to exercise restraint, but many refused to heed the ministers' voices. Throughout the day, violence erupted in several locations across the city. One young boy, who had been throwing bricks at the police, was killed by officers as they chased after him. Another child, riding his bicycle along the roadway, was gunned down by whites in an indiscriminate and senseless act of hatred.

News of the bombing struck Coretta and Martin hard. After all the work in Birmingham, they realized racial hatred was still deeply entrenched there. Coretta, as a mother, was particularly affected by the loss of the children and the harsh reality that the struggle for freedom would take such innocent lives.

The following day, President Kennedy issued a statement condemning the bombing and blaming Alabama Governor George Wallace for creating an environment that permitted such conduct. The governor's defiance of federal court desegregation orders, the president argued, had empowered segregationists to commit acts of violence against blacks. Martin returned to Birmingham and spoke at a joint funeral for three of the slain children.

In the days and weeks that followed, Martin and the SCLC leadership discussed their response to the situation in Birmingham. Several wanted to return to the streets with protest marches and reinstitute the boycott that had been effective in the spring. Others wanted even stronger action. Serious consideration was given to a march on Montgomery, the capital of Alabama. While discussion continued, Martin maintained a heavy schedule of speaking engagements, sometimes delivering two or three speeches in a single day. In between speeches, the discussion continued as Martin and the SCLC leadership searched for an appropriate response to the attack on the church.

Early in November, Coretta attended a Women Strike for Peace rally in New York. She addressed the group at a meeting held at the National Baptist Church. Later, they marched from Central Park to the United Nations Headquarters. Timed to coincide with the second anniversary of the group's formation, the march celebrated the successful completion of the Limited Nuclear Test Ban Treaty. The group was received at the United Nations by Secretary General U Thant.

Three weeks later, Coretta and Martin were at home in Atlanta when they learned President Kennedy had been shot. First reports indicated only that he had been seriously wounded. Martin was enjoying a rare day in his study upstairs when the news broke. Coretta joined him near the television as images from Dallas played across the screen. Together, they watched in silence as Walter Cronkite told the world the awful truth. The president was dead.

Visibly shaken, Martin sat on the sofa and continued to watch the news reports. Coretta sat with him. After a while Martin sighed and said in a grim voice, "That could happen to me." He remained in a somber mood the rest of the day.

Over the previous two years, Coretta and Martin had come to know President Kennedy and considered him a friend. Twice Coretta had called him when Martin was incarcerated, and both times he had stepped forward to offer assistance. He could have ignored her phone calls as other politicians had, but he had not. Instead, he had marshaled the power of his position and turned it in her favor.

In the years since President Kennedy's death, many have criticized his actions regarding the Civil Rights Movement, suggesting he was reluctant to get involved for fear it would become a political liability, then was willing to act only for his own political gain. Politics did influence his decisions, but Coretta and Martin understood and respected that. Kennedy, after all, made no effort to hide the fact that he approached the issue from a political perspective. In the end, however, he made the right decision. Faced with the overwhelming brutality of racism, he set aside political expediency and ordered the Justice Department to intervene. When attempts at intervention revealed the paucity of federal options, he pressed Congress for new legislation, what would become the Civil Rights Act of 1964. No member of his cabinet, save the attorney general, had supported introducing the civil rights bill, believing it could not overcome opposition from southern congressmen; a view also held by Vice President Lyndon Johnson. Despite the opposition in his own administration, Kennedy had introduced the bill. Had he lived, his decisions regarding Birmingham and the March on Washington in 1963, his confrontation with Governor Wallace over integration of The University of Alabama, and his clear support for blacks in their fight for racial and economic equality might well have cost him reelection. He came to the fight reluctantly—almost everyone did—but once in that fight, he gave his best effort to see it through to the end.

Later that weekend, Martin traveled to Washington, D.C., to attend the president's funeral. Coretta stayed in Atlanta with the children and watched the events on television. She and I talked by telephone several times during that period. In those conversations she relayed to me how deeply the president's death had shaken Martin, what he had said about the shooting, and his speculation about his own fate. This was not the first time we had talked about it. Martin seemed to have an inner sense of what lay ahead for him. Those of us who had seen the anger on the faces of white racists knew his comment was not baseless speculation. The threat of death at the hands of violent men had been with us all our lives. We didn't treat it with a cavalier attitude, but neither did we cower or shrink from our calling. Coretta knew that evil men plotted against her husband every day. She knew they were not above attacking her, either. Yet she pressed on with her work in the Movement and insisted that Martin do so as well.

30

St. Augustine

In the aftermath of the Kennedy assassination, Martin might have liked a few days to spend alone reflecting on the events that had transpired that year. He could have used the rest and would have welcomed the opportunity to collect his thoughts, but it was not possible. Invitations to speak continued to arrive, pouring in from across the country. He accepted as many as his schedule would allow. In between speaking engagements, discussion of a widespread protest in Alabama continued, but the effort to organize events languished. Several proposed marches were adopted, then delayed, and staff assignments were slow to materialize. Much of the delay was due to continuing disagreement among staff members about what to do next. In addition, Martin's extended speaking tours made quick resolution difficult. As the president and visionary force behind SCLC, he was needed to make decisions about where and how to conduct the protests. He wanted to be there, but with income from his public appearances once again providing the major source of funding for the organization, he had little choice but to accept as many speaking engagements as possible.

In March 1964, SCLC held its convention in Orlando, Florida. Representatives from the black community in St. Augustine approached SCLC staff about helping with their efforts to desegregate the city. Robert Hayling led a group there that was trying to make progress against a strong Ku Klux Klan organization with ties to the chief of police and the sheriff. Numerous violent incidents had occurred, including the death of a Klansman.

SCLC established the group from St. Augustine as an official affiliate and a few days later sent staff members to see what could be done. By the end of March, students arriving in Florida for spring break were recruited for a major demonstration.

The event resulted in the arrest of several hundred protesters, including the mother of the governor of Massachusetts. Her arrest attracted the attention of national reporters. With the focus on St. Augustine, plans for a protest in Alabama slipped further behind.

From May to July, Martin made repeated trips to St. Augustine. He spoke at mass meetings, encouraging the protesters to remain faithful to the cause of their own liberation. As with most actions he supported, Martin also took to the streets, joining protesters in a march through the downtown business district. One of those marches led to his arrest, and he spent a week in the St. Augustine jail.

In between trips to St. Augustine, Martin crisscrossed the nation delivering speeches and conducting church services. He traveled almost constantly. When he was not on the road, he was working on his next book. Coretta saw less and less of him.

As with the Birmingham protest, Martin and St. Augustine leaders attempted to use economic pressure on white business owners to reach a negotiated settlement. St. Augustine's economy was heavily dependent on tourism. As a result, many of the protest marches were held at night when the restaurants and bars were most active. After the first few marches, St. Augustine businessmen were eager to resolve the situation.

At the same time, under President Johnson's watchful eye, the civil rights bill was making its way through Congress. The new law would require that many of the demands put forth by St. Augustine protesters—integrated lodging and dining facilities and nondiscriminatory hiring practices—be implemented regardless of the protest's outcome. As that became more obvious, the only issue remaining open for argument was whether to appoint a biracial committee to address future difficulties. That issue was finally resolved on July 1, and both sides claimed victory. Though the result was not as overwhelming as in Birmingham, Martin was able to leave St. Augustine on a positive note.

Since the beginning of the Montgomery bus boycott, Martin had felt that real progress in the South would be made only with the help of federal intervention. He used every opportunity to assert his views on the matter at a national level. President Eisenhower, though interested in maintaining order, had shown little interest in the fundamental issues black people faced. President Kennedy had been reluctant at first, but when events brought to light the true nature of racism, he came to see that federal help was indispensable. To facilitate that, he had proposed the civil rights bill as a means of empowering the federal government to force desegregation of businesses, schools, and government. The March on Washington seemed to point toward the inevitability of the bill's passage. Then, with Kennedy's assassination, the measure hung in limbo. President Johnson, a southerner from Texas, was known as a ruthless politician, but one who also was very practical and pragmatic. Still, many blacks, including Coretta and Martin, were suspicious of his commitment to the civil rights struggle. They were pleasantly surprised when he put the full weight of his office behind passage of the bill. It received final approval in late June and became known as the Civil Rights Act of 1964.

On July 2, 1964, only a day after concluding the agreement in St. Augustine, Martin arrived in the nation's capital for the president's signing ceremony. President Johnson gave Martin one of the many pens he used to sign the official document. With his signature, Johnson placed the mandate of federal law behind many of the demands protesting blacks had supported with their feet and with their lives. Coretta watched the ceremony on television from Atlanta.

Passage of the Civil Rights Act changed the landscape of Martin's efforts. After July 1964, the issue was no longer about getting whites to accede to protesters' demands, but rather was about enforcing the law. On that subject, Martin and Johnson had differing views.

The year 1964 was a presidential election year. Johnson faced a formidable opponent in Barry Goldwater, the Republican nominee. Goldwater's unabashed conservatism appealed to southern whites, many of whom had been Democrats. Kennedy's public support of the Civil Rights Movement and Johnson's all-out effort to win passage of the Civil Rights Act alienated many in that group. Goldwater's popularity threatened to take the South for the Republicans. Conventional wisdom suggested the Democrats could not win the election without southern support. Johnson wanted to delay desegregation activity until after the election to avoid further alienation of southern whites. Martin felt black people had waited long enough.

On July 21, Martin flew to Mississippi for a week-long tour of the state. SCLC was engaged there with other civil rights organizations in what was dubbed Freedom Summer—a summer-long effort to register black voters and test application of the new Civil Rights Act. Using college students, many of whom had been recruited from northern universities, SNCC and CORE had taken the lead in that effort.

Coretta was apprehensive about the trip. Of all the southern states, Mississippi was the most viciously racist. Many people outside the South thought of Alabama as the seat of racism, but Alabama was tame compared to Mississippi. It was truly the heart of darkness in the Deep South. Several SCLC staff members were concerned about the Mississippi trip and voiced their worries, but most of them realized Martin had to go. Since June, three young student volunteers—Andrew Goodman, James Chaney, and Michael Schwerner—had been missing. Almost everyone assumed they were dead. SCLC had a smaller presence than the other organizations working in the state, but Martin had the public name. His presence not only would encourage those already working there, but also would draw the attention of the national media to the plight of the missing students and help expose the depth of racial attitudes there. An FBI detail drawn from surrounding states accompanied Martin on the trip. Martin concluded the Mississippi journey without incident and returned to Atlanta. Coretta was relieved to have him safely home.

With trouble in St. Augustine no longer occupying his schedule and passage of the Civil Rights Act secured, Martin turned his attention to long-delayed plans for a protest in Alabama. In the weeks following the bombing of the Sixteenth Street Baptist Church, Martin and the SCLC leadership had evaluated Alabama for ways to draw attention to the evils of segregation. They were hoping to use those efforts to put pressure on local policy and practice and also to force the federal government to intervene. Now, with the Civil Rights Act made law, their thinking shifted to the enforcement of the new provisions. However, a review of the practices in Alabama showed that many businesses were complying with the new act. Consequently, Martin saw no need for the widespread protest he had earlier envisioned.

In August, Coretta and Martin took their children to New York to attend the World's Fair. The trip was supposed to be a family vacation. At the same time, the Democratic National Convention was meeting in Atlantic City, New Jersey, a short distance down the coast. Martin spent much of his time in New York trying to ensure that a convention delegation from Mississippi that included representatives of the Mississippi Freedom Democratic Party (MFDP)—instead of the all-white official Mississippi delegate group chosen through a process that excluded black voters—was seated. The delegate controversy arose because of Mississippi's voting practices, which denied African Americans an opportunity to participate in the electoral process. Shut out of that process, advocates formed the MFDP as a means of challenging the national Democratic Party's tolerance of Mississippi's actions. After tense negotiations, the MFDP was offered two at-large seats at the 1964 National Convention while the official, all-white Mississippi delegation was seated. Neither side was happy with the compromise.

The following month, Coretta, Martin, and Ralph Abernathy flew to Europe. As with the trip to India, what had been conceived of as a leisurely trip proved to be quite the opposite as Martin was booked with speaking engagements almost every day. The highlight of the trip was an audience with Pope Paul VI. Following that meeting, the pope formally endorsed the Civil Rights Movement. Martin was pleased to receive official international recognition for the Movement, and his spirits seemed lifted by the occasion, but he was a tired man.

After returning to the United States, Martin again launched into a frenzied schedule of speaking engagements. Having fought so hard to gain the public's attention on issues of racial equality and economic justice, he found it difficult to avoid any opportunity to address a public gathering. That heavy schedule, however, meant Coretta saw even less of him than before.

In October, Martin returned to Atlanta exhausted. Coretta felt he was more drained and empty than at any point previously. With her encouragement and that of his doctor, he checked himself into St. Joseph's Infirmary for rest and recuperation. He was asleep in his hospital bed when, on October 14, 1964, Coretta called to inform him that the Norwegian Nobel Committee in Oslo had awarded him the Nobel Peace Prize. Later that morning, she called to share the news with me at my home in North Carolina. I was excited that Martin would receive such a prestigious award, but Coretta and Martin were absolutely elated. They saw it as the imprimatur of international recognition and approval for their work, and it was.

After President Johnson won reelection in November, Martin assembled the SCLC leadership for a retreat in Birmingham. There, they refocused their effort on Alabama—this time with an eye toward voter registration. Selma became the center of attention. Tentative plans were made for a rally there in January. A local judge had issued an injunction barring mass meetings, but SCLC was prepared to test that order and risk going to jail if necessary.

While Martin traveled the country, Coretta, who had been left home with the children in Atlanta, grew somewhat restless with her lack of direct contribution to the Movement. She began to think of ways she could contribute beyond caring for the children and maintaining a stable home. Deep inside herself, she wanted to be more active in her support of the cause. As she searched for that greater outlet, she turned again to her original dream of a concert career.

Using the program from the 1956 gala event where she sang with Harry Belafonte— a program she had altered and improved in subsequent performances—Coretta developed an event that combined her musical talent with readings and narrative to tell the story not just of the Montgomery boycott, but of the entire Civil Rights Movement. She updated the program, taking the story through present events with songs carefully selected to convey the struggle and pain of African Americans. She planned to conduct the concerts as a fund-raiser for SCLC and worked to organize concerts in numerous locations across the country. Martin was rather skeptical about the concerts actually raising much money, but he encouraged her effort.[1]

While she worked to establish concert dates, Coretta devoted time each day to practicing the songs and getting her voice in shape. At the same time, her voice had developed a different tone—taking on a richer, fuller resonance—since the days when she had studied at the New England Conservatory. Subsequent events in her life had also imbued her presentation with a deeper sense of passion.

On November 15, accompanied by Jonathan Brice, she gave her first of many Freedom Concerts at the Town Hall in New York City. The event was co-chaired by Frances Lucas, Coretta's best friend from her Antioch days, and Marian Logan, who was an activist in the New York area. Proceeds from the concert benefited SCLC and the Goodman-Chaney-Schwerner Memorial Community Center. The performance was well attended, and Coretta sang well. Afterward, she attended a party in the apartment of Helen Phillips.[2]

In December a large group of family and friends joined Coretta and Martin for the trip to Norway where Martin received the Nobel Peace Prize. The award was officially conferred at a ceremony in Oslo on December 10, 1964.[3] Because the invitation came late, I was not able to make the trip, but for those who did it was the trip of a lifetime.

Several years later, in February 1971, Coretta and I traveled to Europe on a seven-country tour to promote her book, *My Life with Martin Luther King, Jr.*[4] During that trip Coretta visited Stockholm for an audience with the King of Sweden. One evening while we were there, we had dinner with a small group of dignitaries that included members of the Nobel Committee. Gunnar Myrdal was among those who attended. Myrdal had conducted a definitive study of race relations in the United States in the early 1940s.[5] Consequently, he and I struck up an immediate friendship. He took great pride in speaking with authority on race relations in America, although some of his insights were not accurate.

At dinner that evening in 1971, I had the distinct privilege of sitting beside the gentleman who had suggested that the committee name Martin for the 1964 Nobel Prize for Peace. He felt the prize would strengthen the Movement by giving it the kind of prestige that such recognition carried. Coming as it did on the heels of a wearisome year, it gave Martin renewed energy for the struggle ahead.

During the Christmas holidays of 1964, Martin and I discussed the coming year. With the Civil Rights Act now law and Johnson elected to a full term, SCLC turned its attention to testing compliance with the new law and to pushing for a specific voting rights bill. As we talked, Martin seemed in a particularly serious mood. During that conversation, he said, "Edythe, I've been to the mountain top, but we're going to the valley. And somebody is going to die."[6]

As the year drew to a close, Martin and the SCLC leadership made plans to support congressional action on the voting rights bill. Only federal registrars, he insisted, could remedy voting discrimination, and for that Congress would have to pass a law specifically authorizing the use of such registrars. Johnson, though sympathetic to the cause, repeatedly stated his desire to delay new civil rights legislation in favor of his broader domestic agenda.

At an SCLC retreat held in late December at the Gaston Motel in Birmingham, Martin and the leadership committee searched for a location from which they could launch a voter registration campaign designed to expose discriminatory registration practices. As the protest in Birmingham had prodded a reluctant Kennedy to act, they hoped a new protest specifically aimed at exposing voter rights abuses might prompt Johnson to do the same. They quickly settled on Selma, Alabama, as the perfect location.

31

Selma

Although the Civil Rights Act of 1964 was a landmark piece of legislation, its one glaring weakness was the lack of specific guarantees regarding the right to vote. Widespread use of poll taxes and literacy tests together with restricted access to county registrars severely limited the number of blacks in the South who were registered to vote.[1] Those blacks who managed to gain access to a registrar, pass the literacy test, and pay the poll tax often found their application for registration rejected because of some inadvertent, insubstantial clerical error on the registration form. Abuse and neglect of the law was widespread. Nowhere was that abuse more apparent than in Alabama's Black Belt.

Selma, the seat of government for Dallas County, was located in the heart of the Black Belt, less than sixty miles from our childhood home. The site of numerous antebellum plantations, the Black Belt remained a region trapped in the plantation culture. Hidden beneath a thin public veneer of civility, racial bigotry was as alive there in the 1960s as it had been a hundred years earlier. Dallas County sheriff Jim Clark, an avowed racist and a figure not unlike Birmingham's Bull Connor, was known to have little tolerance for blacks who moved beyond their accepted place in Selma society. Together, the combination of segregation and personality made it the setting SCLC needed.

On January 2, 1965, with the help of the Dallas County Voters League and SNCC, a rally was held in Selma at Brown's Chapel AME Church. A crowd of approximately seven hundred people attended. Martin spoke that evening about the need to register as many black voters as possible. Experience had shown him the ballot box was the most certain way to effect change in local governmental policy. Over the next two weeks, the SCLC staff trained protesters in nonviolent tactics.

While SCLC focused on plans for Selma, a small package arrived at the office in Atlanta. When it was opened, a staff member discovered it contained a tape recording. The office was constantly inundated with mail, much of it in response to Martin's many speeches. Many of those responses included personal notes, memorabilia, and tape recordings of his addresses. Coretta had undertaken the task of responding to Martin's personal correspondence. Part of that work included organizing and cataloging tapes of events where he spoke. Even then, she had a sense of the historic nature of what they were doing and of the value of his speeches and papers. Later she would make a concerted effort to gather those papers into a central archive, but it was an effort built on her long-held interest in preserving a record of events, an interest she had pursued from the beginning of the first protest in Montgomery. SCLC staff members were glad to have her help and set aside personal mail for her attention. The envelope with the tape recording was placed in a box with other similar items and delivered to the house.

As Coretta worked through the mail, she came to the envelope and took out its contents. Inside was the tape accompanied by a letter. Coretta glanced at the letter and knew right away it was trouble. She also knew from where it had come. The letter made vile accusations against Martin, accusing him of infidelity and other acts. From that, she surmised what was on the tape and knew it was nothing more than another attempt to drive a wedge between the two of them. Neither she nor Martin took the substantive matters on the tape recording seriously. However, they were both displeased that the FBI would make such a threat against them.[2]

Since the Montgomery bus boycott, Coretta and Martin had been aware the FBI was watching them. They had not known their conversations with Stanley Levison were being recorded, but they knew they were being watched. Over the ensuing years, that surveillance intensified. Rumors about Martin, Coretta, and others involved in the Movement regularly circulated among newspaper reporters. All of the stories were instigated by the FBI. Informants had been recruited or planted in all the major civil rights organizations. With information gleaned from those sources, the FBI sought every opportunity to disrupt the Movement's work. The tape in that envelope was one more of those efforts. Coretta saw it for what it was and discounted it immediately.

With preparations in Selma complete, on January 18, Martin and John Lewis, president of SNCC, led a group of four hundred voter registration applicants on a march from Brown's Chapel to the Dallas County courthouse. There they were met by Sheriff Clark.

Clark and several deputies barred the group from entering the courthouse and ordered them to move to an alley at the side of the building. From there, he assured them, the registrar would call them one at a time to come inside, take the Alabama literacy test, and complete the registration application forms. The group dutifully moved to the alley and waited all day, but no one was called inside to begin the registration process.

The following day, another group marched to the courthouse. They were confronted by Clark just as the day before, but this time the group refused to move into the alley. When they refused to obey his repeated demands, Clark arrested them. The next day protesters again marched to the courthouse but this time in successive waves. They, too, were arrested and led away to jail. By the third day, more than two hundred protesters were in custody. The arrests received national media attention.

Later that week, in response to a petition filed by the NAACP Legal Defense Fund, federal district judge Daniel Thomas issued an injunction against Dallas County officials prohibiting discriminatory voter registration practices. The following Monday, protesters appeared at the courthouse once again and attempted to register. As before, they were met by Sheriff Clark; only this time he was much rougher, striking a female protester with his nightstick as she lay helpless on the ground. Reporters covering the incident snapped photos of the attack, and by the next morning, images of the confrontation were on the front pages of newspapers everywhere.

On February 1, Martin and Ralph Abernathy led yet another march to the courthouse. The entire group was arrested and sent to jail. Martin and Ralph spent the week sharing a cell. While they were confined to jail, Coretta and Juanita Abernathy came to Selma to check on them. That same day, Malcolm X arrived in town.

Denied access to Martin, Coretta retreated to the home of a friend to decide what to do next. Later that day, she was informed that Malcolm X intended to speak at Brown's Chapel. For all of her involvement in and support of the Movement, Coretta had not participated heavily in the mass meetings. However, with Martin and Ralph in jail, she decided to attend the noon meeting. Malcolm X advocated the use of militant civil disobedience, including violence, a position in direct opposition to Martin's commitment to nonviolence. Malcolm X was a persuasive speaker with a winsome personality and a reputation for turning crowds on their heads. Coretta was interested in hearing what he had to say and wanted to be there to counteract anything he might say that would conflict with the nonviolent approach in which she and Martin believed.

That afternoon, Coretta sat quietly in Brown's Chapel and listened to Malcolm X's address to the mass meeting. She found nothing particularly upsetting in his presentation, but she as well as everyone else in the building knew the kind of protest he sought. When he had concluded his remarks, Coretta took the pulpit and gave an eloquent and succinct discourse on nonviolent resistance and the reasons why blacks could not win a physical confrontation against a white majority. When she finished, she and Malcolm X exchanged a brief greeting.[3]

While Martin and Ralph waited behind bars, Judge Thomas issued another order requiring the Dallas County Board of Registrars to end its tactics in delaying registration of black voters. That order suspended the use of literacy tests to qualify potential voters. On Friday, a congressional delegation arrived to review conditions in Selma. That same day, President Johnson issued a statement reiterating the right of all citizens to vote. Martin, still in jail, felt momentum shifting in the Movement's favor.

Two weeks after Malcolm X's visit to Selma, Martin bailed himself out of jail and traveled to Washington, D.C., to attend a meeting with President Johnson. As they discussed the situation in Selma, Johnson expressed his intention to introduce a voting rights bill as soon as Justice Department attorneys could prepare an acceptable draft. A few days later, Martin returned to Selma, buoyed by the president's decision.

On the evening of February 26, as SCLC expanded its effort to surrounding counties, protesters held a march in Marion, our hometown and the county seat of Perry County. The courthouse was a short distance from Lincoln School. Beginning at a downtown church, protestors intended to march through the business district to the county courthouse. One block from the church the marchers were confronted by Alabama state troopers. As the two groups faced each other, the street lights went out. In the resulting darkness, the troopers charged the protesters. Jimmie Lee Jackson, the nephew of a woman that Coretta had known since high school, was shot by one of the troopers. He died later that week. Coretta was devastated.

A memorial service in Jimmie Lee's honor was held on the Perry County courthouse steps. A crowd of over two thousand turned out in the rain to hear Martin give the eulogy. Afterward, Martin called for a march from Selma to Montgomery to protest conditions in the region that had led to Jimmie Lee's death. That demonstration was scheduled for March 7.

On the afternoon of Sunday, March 7, protesters assembled at Brown's Chapel and marched in a column through the streets of Selma to the Edmund Pettus Bridge. As they crested the top of the bridge, they saw a line of state troopers and sheriff's deputies blocking the road ahead. Several of the deputies were mounted on horseback. The protesters marched to within a few feet of the troopers where they were ordered to turn around. When they failed to immediately obey, the troopers charged forward, wielding nightsticks. Tear gas canisters exploded, sending a gray cloud of gas over the protesters as they scrambled to get out of the way. Cheered on by white bystanders, mounted deputies spurred their horses and plunged into the crowd. The bodies of injured marchers littered the highway in an incident that became known as Bloody Sunday.

Film crews caught the event on tape. Television networks interrupted their early evening programs to broadcast news reports of the day's events. Accounts of the brutal attack were replayed again on Monday and splashed across the front pages of newspapers everywhere. The nation shared the marchers' outrage.

After meeting with the SCLC leadership and assessing the aftermath of the march, Martin announced the marchers would resume their trek the following Tuesday. He extended an invitation to ministers around the world to join him in this task. President Johnson, concerned about a repeat of Sunday's incident, sent intermediaries to broker a deal that would avert a confrontation. At the same time, NAACP attorneys filed a petition asking federal district judge Frank M. Johnson to issue an injunction against the Dallas County sheriff and Alabama state troopers prohibiting them from impeding the march. After reviewing the petition, Judge Johnson issued a temporary injunction barring the proposed march pending a hearing in his court the following week.

In Selma, Martin was determined to continue with the march as planned. Intermediaries redoubled their efforts to reach a deal that would avert another bloody encounter in the streets.

At the last minute, Sheriff Clark agreed to hold his men at bay if the marchers would turn around when they reached the police line at the bottom of the bridge. Reluctantly, Martin agreed. He had not wanted to defy the court's injunction but felt compelled to act in the face of the brutalities foisted upon the protesters by Sheriff Clark the previous Sunday.

As agreed, on Tuesday Martin led the marchers over the Edmund Pettus Bridge to within a few feet of the waiting line of troopers and deputies. After kneeling in prayer there, they turned around and walked back to Brown's Chapel. Many were angry with Martin and felt he had betrayed them; however, Martin was certain Judge Johnson would decide in their favor when the hearing was finally held, and he did not want to taint that process. He also knew that if they proceeded in their attempt to continue down the highway, the marchers would receive even harsher treatment than they had the Sunday before.

That following week, Governor George Wallace contacted the White House and asked for a meeting with the president. President Johnson agreed, and the two met that Thursday. Wallace, who had his eye on national politics, hoped to score political points with his constituency by confronting the president. He and Johnson had a brisk exchange in the Oval Office, then Johnson led Wallace to the Rose Garden for a press conference. With the unsuspecting Wallace looking on, Johnson recounted the atrocities committed by Alabama state troopers in Selma and berated the state for its treatment of marchers who, after all, were only pursuing their right to vote. Then Johnson announced that he was introducing to Congress that day a comprehensive voting rights bill.

On Monday, Johnson addressed a joint session of Congress where he announced again the introduction of a voting rights bill and detailed the reasons why it was necessary. In clear and unequivocal terms he stated, "It is not just Negroes, but really it is all of us, who must overcome the crippling legacy of bigotry and injustice. And we shall overcome."[4] Those words—we shall overcome—taken from the title of a protest song that had become the Movement's anthem, resonated in the hearts of black people everywhere. The following day, as if to illustrate once more the need for the legislation, SNCC protesters who had gathered outside the state capitol building in Montgomery were attacked and beaten by Alabama state troopers.

Later that week, Judge Johnson concluded hearings on the NAACP injunction petition and issued an order prohibiting further impediment to the proposed Selma-to-Montgomery march. When Governor Wallace announced the state could not afford to protect the marchers, President Johnson federalized the Alabama National Guard and ordered them to provide security.

On March 21, three thousand protesters set out on the fifty-four-mile march to Montgomery. Martin led the column. Walking next to him was Cager Lee, the eighty-two-year-old grandfather of Jimmie Lee Jackson, who had been killed during the protest in Marion and whose death had provided the impetus for the Selma-to-Montgomery march.[5]

Camp sites were preselected and arrangements had been made to provide meals, toilets, and other accommodations. A few days later, outside Montgomery, Harry Belafonte, Sammy Davis Jr., and other nationally known entertainers provided a show for the marchers. Coretta, in between spring concert dates, joined them to perform on stage. The next day, March 24, 1965, the march proceeded to the state capital.

From the steps where Jefferson Davis had been sworn into office as president of the Confederacy, Martin and other Movement dignitaries addressed a crowd of twenty-five thousand. Coretta, our parents, Martin's parents, and many others flanked them.

Selma, for all its trouble, produced precisely the result SCLC had desired. Provoked by persistent marches, Sheriff Clark revealed to the world the face of racial bigotry. His reaction showed the nation that racial prejudice and discrimination was not limited to Birmingham, but was a condition that pervaded the South. Congress debated the voting rights bill through the summer of 1965, finally passing it in August. On August 6, President Johnson signed it into law as the Voting Rights Act of 1965. That great achievement, however, came at a heavy price.

In addition to Jimmie Lee Jackson, the Reverend James Reeb, a white minister from Boston, was beaten to death by white men in Selma. Reeb was among the many clergymen from around the country who joined Selma marchers after the "Bloody Sunday" attack by state troopers at the Edmund Pettus Bridge. Viola Gregg Liuzzo, a white housewife from Detroit, was shot and killed by Klansmen while ferrying marchers back to Selma after the march ended in Montgomery. Four men were arrested the next day and charged with her death.

When Martin told me the previous Christmas that they were going into the valley and some were going to die, he was speaking of himself as one of the victims. In the years following Birmingham, Martin became preoccupied with the possibility of his own demise—a concern not unjustified by the circumstances. He had seen the face of evil in Montgomery, Albany, Birmingham, and St. Augustine, and he had seen it again in Selma. Men fully capable of the most horrendous and personal acts of violence walked the streets of southern towns and sat in the pews of southern churches. The longer the fight lasted, the more certain Martin became that his own death would come at their hands. Coretta understood this was the risk they took in struggling for the cause to which she and Martin were called. Though she did not welcome the prospect of death, she was reconciled to the possibility and prepared to pay the ultimate price.

32

Freedom Concerts

The year 1965 saw two major events in the life of the Civil Rights Movement. One was the Selma March. The other was a lesser known, but equally important, series of concerts performed by Coretta. Those concerts were known as Freedom Concerts.

Working from the format of the Town Hall concert held in December 1964, Coretta sought to use her soprano voice and her love of music to tell the story of the Civil Rights Movement to people who might not otherwise attend a civil rights rally. By using a concert format, she could combine her creativity and love of the performing arts with the compelling message of the African American struggle for social and economic justice. She also was convinced the concerts would be great fundraisers. With the help of Xernona Clayton, she scheduled a five-city, nine-day West Coast concert tour. The tour was planned for the first week of March. Coincidentally, the tour began just as events were heating up in Selma. As events unfolded, the first six months of the year became one of the busiest periods of Coretta's life.

Beginning in San Diego, where she performed to a packed house of three thousand at the newly opened San Diego Civic Theatre, Coretta moved up the West Coast, stopping at major cities along the way.

In Los Angeles, she performed at the Second Baptist Church. Thomas Kilgore Jr., the pastor, had been active in civil rights protests since before Martin entered the ministry. He had been instrumental in planning the Pilgrimage for Freedom in 1957 and the March on Washington in 1963.[1] His congregation helped organize the event and was excited to play host to Coretta. A capacity crowd of over two thousand attended the concert.

While she was in Los Angeles, Women Strike for Peace honored Coretta with a luncheon at the Beverly Hills Hotel. She was delighted to see some of the people with whom she had worked in the peace movement. Several at the luncheon had traveled with her in the group that lobbied the nuclear disarmament conference in Geneva three years earlier.

At San Francisco's Third Baptist Church she drew the largest response of the tour. A crowd in excess of three thousand people turned out to claim one thousand available seats. By then, the country had learned of the bloody assault on protesters at the Edmund Pettus Bridge in Selma. For many, attending the tour became a means of registering their support for the protesters. It also was an occasion for others to register their disapproval. During the remainder of the tour, Coretta was inundated with death threats and bomb scares. Still, she was not deterred, and the tour continued to the next stop in Portland, Oregon.

At her final concert, held in the Garfield High School auditorium in Seattle, Washington, Coretta discussed with the audience events that had occurred in Selma. Alluding to the threats against her and Martin, she said, "You realize that what you are doing is pretty dangerous, but we go on with the faith that what we are doing is right. If something happens to my husband, the cause will continue. It may even be helped."[2]

By the third week of March, Coretta was home in Atlanta. Her West Coast concert tour had raised a total of twenty thousand dollars for SCLC. It also gave people in the western United States an opportunity to hear a firsthand account of events in Selma and of other work in the Civil Rights Movement. Attending her concerts became an act of support for the cause of racial equality and justice. When she had first suggested doing the concerts, most of the male SCLC staff members had been skeptical. As checks from concert proceeds arrived, they were forced to admit the venture had been an overwhelming success.

Coretta returned from the tour just as the march from Selma to Montgomery was getting underway. She wanted to join the marchers immediately but had a prior speaking engagement at Bennett College in Greensboro, North Carolina. Martin encouraged her to keep that commitment and suggested she could join them later. Selma and Montgomery were fifty miles apart. Covering that distance would take several days. With his encouragement, Coretta left for North Carolina.

Bennett College, an all-female, historically black school, was instrumental in the earlier sit-in protests. Many of the students who participated in and around Greensboro were Bennett students, eager to brave white hostility in an attempt to integrate segregated department store lunch counters.[3] Coretta was glad to have the opportunity to speak to the college's student body, but she was also eager to join the protesters on the road to Montgomery.

When she finished in North Carolina, Coretta went immediately to join the trek from Selma to Montgomery. The night she arrived, marchers were camped on the outskirts of Montgomery. She joined Harry Belafonte's entertainment show on a makeshift stage and performed to the delight of the crowd. Among those performing that evening were Tony Bennett; Nina Simone; Peter, Paul and Mary; and Frankie Lane. The following day, Coretta continued on with the marchers into Montgomery.

Three days after the march ended, Coretta returned to the road with a series of spring concerts on the East Coast. Unlike the first portion of the tour, which took her to less hostile regions of the country, this series of concerts took her through the heart of some of the most racially segregated areas in the South. The list of locations where she performed reads like a historic tour of key 1960s civil rights venues.

On March 28, 1965, Coretta appeared at a concert in Albany, Georgia, one of the most insidiously segregated cities in the nation. Only a few years earlier, Martin and many others had been jailed while protesting Albany's segregated transportation facilities. That spring, as Coretta arrived, segregation was still very much a problem in southern Georgia.

At the beginning of April, she took a short break from the concert tour to attend a dinner in Detroit honoring Rosa Parks. After the Montgomery boycott had concluded, Parks had moved north to live with family members. Rather than marking the end of her involvement in the Civil Rights Movement, her relocation had served only to expand interest in her and the story of how the boycott began. Coretta was delighted to address the audience that evening and recount for them the significance of Parks's courage.

Two weeks later, on April 16, Coretta held a concert in Tuscaloosa, Alabama, the scene of unrest two years earlier when Governor George Wallace stood in the entrance to Foster Auditorium in an attempt to prevent black students from registering for class. Only a presidential order federalizing the Alabama National Guard had forced Wallace to step aside.

The First African Baptist Church in Tuscaloosa was pastored by Martin's friend the Reverend T. Y. Rogers Jr. The concert there came on the heels of the violence in Selma and the March to Montgomery. Racial tensions were running high throughout the city and across the state. Appearing there was an open invitation for trouble, but Coretta refused to cower.

In May, Coretta went to Chicago for the Fifteenth Anniversary Celebration of the Women's International League for Peace and Freedom. The meeting was held at the Conrad Hilton Hotel. She addressed the gathering on the subject of "Peace, Jobs, and Freedom."

Coretta returned to Atlanta and performed in concert there on May 9. Though Atlanta was one of the more progressive cities in the South, it was by no means a racially peaceful location. In spite of advances made through the sit-ins and lunch counter protests several years before, many private businesses remained segregated, in flagrant violation of the recent Civil Rights Act. The previous summer, a pistol-waving Lester Maddox, owner of Atlanta's Pickrick Restaurant, had refused to serve blacks. His action was a clear violation of federal law, yet his conduct won the admiration of many whites in Georgia. A staunch segregationist, he sold wooden axe handles at his restaurant, which he suggested should be used to defend private property against forced integration. One week after Coretta's concert, an all-white jury acquitted Maddox of assault charges arising from that earlier incident. The following year, 1966, he won election as Georgia's governor. Georgia had come a long way in addressing its racial problems, but it still had a long way to go.

The spring concert tour ended in May with a performance in Philadelphia. Coretta appeared there on May 23, 1965, at the First African Baptist Church. After completing a series of concerts and speaking engagements that had taken her across the nation, Coretta had cause to be proud of her accomplishments. Capacity crowds had greeted her at every stop and provided donations that helped make the protest in Selma possible. Reporters provided coverage of her appearances, and concert reviews were favorable. She had successfully combined her love of the arts with her commitment to the cause of economic and social justice. It was a success she would repeat in coming years as she refined her message and expanded her audience.

33

Watts

As the protest in Selma drew to a close, Martin turned his attention to the plight of blacks in the North and the task of transforming the Civil Rights Movement, which had been largely a southern effort, into a national endeavor. Doing that forced him to confront the much deeper problems that lay at the root of the nation's troubles— economic disparity, systemically unequal opportunity, and a white power structure unwilling to do anything about either.

Martin also faced difficulties within SCLC. Longstanding staff conflicts created a climate of turmoil and strained relationships. Money, always an issue, was especially tight. At the height of the Selma protest, when news media portrayed daily the excessive responses of Dallas County sheriff's deputies and Alabama state troopers, an abundance of contributions had flowed in. Then, as the demonstrations began to ebb and the march from Selma to Montgomery went forward without incident, the stream of money coming to SCLC dried up. As in the past, the organization was forced to rely on income from Martin's speeches to help fill the gap.

At the same time, Coretta and Martin turned again to the broader issue of international peace. Earlier that year, on March 2, 1965, while addressing a group at Howard University in Washington, D.C., Martin voiced opposition to the war in Vietnam. It was the first time he spoke publicly on the issue. It would not be his last.

Three months later, on June 8, 1965, Coretta spoke at the Emergency Rally on Vietnam held at Madison Square Garden in New York. The rally was sponsored by SANE—the National Committee for a Sane Nuclear Policy—and chaired by veteran actor Ossie Davis. Already known for her stance against international violence in general and the Vietnam War in particular, Coretta was ahead of Martin on the issue and kept up a consistent presence in the Peace Movement. She had been at-tracted to the issue of international peace by the grassroots appeal of Women Strike for Peace—mothers interested in preserving a future for their children free of nuclear weapons—but it had been more than that to her. In the early years of their marriage, Coretta had searched for an area of involvement that was her own—a place where she could make a unique contribution separate from being the wife of Martin Lu-ther King Jr. The Peace Movement became that place.

Throughout the remainder of 1965, Martin maintained an almost unbearable speaking schedule, sometimes delivering a dozen addresses in a single day. He told reporters he was getting four hours of sleep each night, but often he functioned on less than that. Since moving from Montgomery to Atlanta and taking the co-pastorate with his father at Ebenezer, he had been away from home far more than he had been present. Many months he was there only a few days, often only for a single day. Con-stant travel took a physical toll on his body.

Martin knew his physical condition was not good, but more work than ever re-mained to be done. In many ways all that had happened up to that point—Mont-gomery, Birmingham, the March on Washington, and Selma—had served to bring the country only to the starting line. For all the gains we had made, the deeper under-lying issues—those that lay at the core of the nation's problems—were yet to be ad-dressed and were just then coming to light. Those issues, the ones that dealt with socioeconomic disparity, were not the kinds of problems that could be easily tackled in the South. For those issues, he had to move north where the economic differences were as great as the racial differences had been in the South. There, economic in-justice was not cloaked in genteel graciousness but in a disarmingly subtle coat of indifference, which many mistook for tolerance, making the task all the more dif-ficult. Martin was looking for a place in the North to begin again the work of cam-paigning for civil justice, and when he cast his eyes in that direction, his attention focused on Chicago.

Civil rights work in Chicago centered primarily on the issue of school segrega-tion. Despite court orders regarding implementation of the decision in *Brown v. Board of Education,* schools in Chicago were still segregated if not by policy, at least by practice. SCLC staff members had visited Chicago earlier at the request of the Coordinating Council of Community Organizations (CCCO), which worked in Chicago to address school desegregation. On July 6, 1965, Martin spoke at a church convention there. The trip afforded him an opportunity to view conditions in the city and to meet CCCO leadership. He was well received and, as a result, returned to Chicago later that month to speak at neighborhood rallies. Afterward, he led a march to city hall where he called for desegregation of the city's schools.

Those two visits convinced Martin of the need for further involvement in Chicago, but he was still interested in surveying the possibility of action in other northern cities. Nevertheless, what he saw in Chicago's slums and ghettos left him appalled.

On August 6, Martin traveled to Washington, D.C., where he attended the signing ceremony for the Voting Rights Act, a major piece of civil rights legislation made possible by the nation's reaction to events in Selma. Later that month, he presided over an SCLC convention in Birmingham. At the convention, Martin spoke out against the war in Vietnam, a theme he had broached in earlier speeches but dropped when staff members and others voiced opposition to including the issue in SCLC's agenda. Though he had worked to avoid the issue in subsequent speeches, the war troubled him greatly. In his speech to the Birmingham convention, he returned to it once again and proposed that SCLC send letters to leaders of the countries involved in the war, encouraging them to negotiate an end to hostilities.

For Martin, as well as for Coretta, opposition to the Vietnam War was a logical and inescapable extension of his commitment to nonviolence. He found opposition to violence in America—a proposition for which he repeatedly had laid his life on the line and to which SCLC owed its existence—incompatible with the promotion of violence in foreign countries.

In August, riots broke out in the Watts section of Los Angeles. Martin went there in an attempt to help restore order. The violence and destruction he witnessed left him dismayed. But looking beyond the immediate conditions, he was struck even harder by the economic plight that lay at the core of the riots. Seeing beyond the broken windows and burned buildings, he was confronted once again by the economic disparity he found inherent in American capitalism. That disparity dominated his thinking for the remainder of his life, and he came to see that single issue as the heart of the social problems facing the nation. Racial prejudice and bigotry were the surface issues, but the real problem was one of economic opportunity. People lived in slums and decrepit apartment buildings because someone else profited from them being there. As the issue dominated his mind, Martin came to see his calling to the ministry as a prophetic mission to address those fundamental ills.

While Martin moved toward the issues of class and economic disparity, President Johnson—who had espoused those same views earlier—moved away from them. Johnson, now in his first full term, was increasingly consumed by the escalating war in Vietnam. Enticed into the war by the notion that he could achieve a military victory abroad while achieving a social revolution at home, he found the war consumed both his time and the federal budget. Social programs, once the centerpiece of his presidency, were steadily eroded to pay for an ever-expanding war. At the same time, opposition to the war was growing stronger by the day. Martin's antiwar statements aggravated Johnson personally and drove him in the opposite direction of the social changes he previously hoped would define his administration and achieve for him a legacy comparable to that of Franklin D. Roosevelt.

Martin, for his part, had seen enough to know that America—even President Johnson—lacked the moral will to mount serious opposition to an engrained class disparity from which the white establishment profited so handsomely. Attacking the Bull Connors and Jim Clarks of America cost little. Solving the disparity in economic opportunity and distribution of wealth would cost much, and it was a political journey Johnson never would take. Martin was certain that if he addressed those issues, he would do so alone. By the fall of 1965, Martin already had committed himself to addressing socioeconomic issues, and he would not be dissuaded.

In October, an all-white Alabama jury acquitted one of the Klansmen accused of murdering Viola Liuzzo, the civil rights worker who had been shot while ferrying protesters from Montgomery back to Selma. Martin was incensed at the verdict and issued a call for protests in major Alabama cities. Staff members discussed cities in which marches could be held, but they were already stretched thin with efforts in Chicago and were hampered by a continued lack of funding. As a result, those protests never materialized.

Coretta continued her involvement in the Peace Movement. In October, she attended a banquet in Philadelphia sponsored by the Women's International League for Peace and Freedom. The following month she joined twenty-five thousand protesters in Washington for an antiwar march. She finished the year with a concert at New Bethel Baptist Church in Detroit.

The fact that Coretta came first to see the connection between nonviolent civil rights protest and opposition to the war raises the obvious question of whether and to what extent she influenced Martin's progression in that same direction. Having known her all my life and having seen them both on numerous occasions, I don't think she exercised that kind of influence over his thought. They shared vigorous and robust conversation about the issues they faced. She was a chief sounding board for his ideas and a promoter of his involvement in the Civil Rights Movement, but to say she steered him toward support of international peace would overlook the independence of his own thoughts and beliefs. She was at home with time to think and reflect while he was on the road before the public, doing the day-to-day work of bringing change to the nation. She had time to make the connection. It took Martin a little longer to reach the same conclusion as Coretta, but it was a delay caused by the demands on his time and attention. For her, the connection was much more cerebral and arrived at by contemplative analysis of ideas and concepts. Martin came to the issues of class disparity and international peace because of the emotional impact of the circumstances he encountered as he traveled the country and the world.

34

1966

In January 1966, Martin and Coretta rented an apartment in a rundown section of Chicago. After renovations were completed, Martin moved in and lived there three days a week. Coretta and the children came up during the summer. By their presence, they hoped to draw attention to the plight of Chicagoans living in slum conditions.

The more Martin saw of conditions in Chicago, the more despondent he became. Blacks in the South were subjected to racial bigotry, discrimination, and harassment, but they could own property and gain some degree of economic security. In the North, they were warehoused in poorly maintained apartment buildings where they were often forced to live without electricity or adequate plumbing. Stiflingly hot in the summer, the apartments were miserably cold in winter. As despondent as he was at the conditions, Martin was frustrated and angry with a city government that seemed not to notice the problem.

In February, desperate to gain the city's attention and equally desperate to address the real problems of ghetto life, Martin and SCLC staff members seized a dilapidated Chicago apartment building. They informed tenants that the SCLC was now the landlord and that rent payments would be used to repair the building. News reports criticized SCLC for its actions and questioned how they could legally do such a thing, but there was no official opposition. Martin and Ralph arranged for repairs to be made to the building and began removing trash from the halls.

That spring, Martin met with President Johnson to discuss a new civil rights bill that was pending before Congress. That bill would address the problem of all-white juries and the need for open housing, and make violence against civil rights workers a federal crime. Johnson introduced the legislation, but the prospects of passage were not very good. In spite of their differences over the war, Johnson needed Martin's support if he were to seek reelection. Martin saw continued federal intervention as the only hope for solving the nation's social problems and hoped the bill would receive the president's full support.

While Martin continued to move forward through the spring with work in Chicago, Coretta continued to develop her own identity as an advocate for civil rights and the broader issues of international peace and freedom. As her identity with these issues grew, she faced increased opposition.

On March 10, 1966, she traveled to Florida for a Freedom Concert at the Pasadena Community Church in St. Petersburg. Unlike her other concerts, which had been promoted as fundraisers for SCLC, this one was given to raise money for the Children's Interracial Organization, which operated a kindergarten and daycare. Pasadena Church was an influential church with an all-white congregation, but it was committed to healing race relations. The kindergarten and daycare were mixed-race facilities. Her activities for that event were closely monitored by the FBI and local police, who followed her every move.

During June, Coretta traveled to Flushing, New York, where she gave a concert sponsored by Antioch Baptist Church. The event was held in the auditorium at Flushing High School. Russell Goode accompanied her. A. C. L. Arbouin, pastor of Antioch, had served as pastor at Dexter several years before Martin. Living and working in New York now, he was well aware of the difficulties faced in transporting the Civil Rights Movement beyond the South and was glad to have Coretta before his congregation. Her presence helped draw attention to those obstacles and focused the church's efforts on the need for progress in the North.

On July 31, Coretta traveled to Houston, Texas, where she performed in a Freedom Concert at the Sam Houston Music Hall. Linda Joseph was emcee. By 1966, Texas was changing. That fall, just a few months after Coretta was there, Barbara Jordan was elected to the state legislature; she was the first black woman to ever serve in that body and the first African American to serve there since Reconstruction. Impressed by her ability, Houstonians later elected her to the United States House of Representatives. NASA's Manned Spaceflight Center, located in Houston in 1961, put the city in the international spotlight as a twentieth century city of progress. To many, it seemed the old ways were gone for good, but while Coretta sang inside the Music Hall, members of the Ku Klux Klan picketed on the streets outside.

Early that summer, James Meredith set out alone on a march from Memphis to Jackson, a march he called the Walk Against Fear. Courageous to a fault, Meredith in 1962 had been the first black student admitted to the University of Mississippi. He spent much of his life defiantly opposing attempts by whites to intimidate African Americans. His one-man march, which began in June, was one of those efforts.

A few miles south of Memphis, Meredith was shot. His injuries were not life threatening, but he did require treatment at a hospital in Memphis. News of the shooting traveled quickly through the black community. That afternoon, leaders from the major civil rights organizations descended on Memphis to visit Meredith in his hospital room. They arrived prepared to pick up the march where he had left off.

As black leaders gathered around Meredith's hospital bed, the vision of how the march should be carried out divided the civil rights organizations into two camps. The NAACP thought it should be a peaceful march, mostly a symbolic gesture aimed at gaining passage in Congress of the new civil rights bill. Stokely Carmichael, who was now president of SNCC, took a more militant stance, insisting the march should focus on eliminating black fear. At the same time, he argued that groups favoring the use of force should be included. Martin and members of SCLC, committed to nonviolence, found themselves in the middle. When discussions grew acrimonious, the NAACP withdrew its support, leaving Martin and Carmichael to resume Meredith's march. They did so in an uneasy alliance.

At first, only Martin, Carmichael, and a few others resumed the march. Soon, however, they were joined by many more. With no real logistical plans in place, SNCC and SCLC scrambled to solve food and lodging needs for a growing group of protesters. As the march continued, additional volunteers were recruited and assigned to conduct voter registration in the communities through which the march traveled. Several serious confrontations erupted with state and local police in a number of towns along the way.

As the march progressed, Martin became less and less satisfied with the manner in which SNCC promoted the use of force to press its demands. When Carmichael's phrase "Black Power" emerged as a slogan, the differences between Martin and Carmichael became difficult to conceal. Martin was convinced the use of violence would lead to overwhelming opposition from whites, eliminating any possibility of meaningful change. He repeatedly pointed out to Carmichael that blacks, at the time, comprised only 10 percent of the total population. To achieve their aims, they needed the help of moderate whites—help they would never get if they resorted to violence.

While the march continued across Mississippi, work continued in Chicago. Martin spoke at a rally at Soldier Field, then led five thousand protesters on a march to city hall. When they arrived, they taped a list of demands to the entrance of the city hall.

Late in July 1966, SCLC staff member Jesse Jackson began leading Chicago marchers through all-white neighborhoods to real estate offices in order to protest the lack of open housing. Protesters were verbally harassed and physically attacked by bottle-throwing whites. Newscasts reported the incidents. As in Birmingham and Selma, pictures appeared in newspapers across the nation. Martin was buoyed by the response and was determined to pressure Realtors to abide by Chicago's open housing ordinance.

When the marches threatened to disrupt city life, Mayor Richard Daley called for a summit of area black leaders. After weeks of negotiation, a deal was reached that called for implementation of most of the group's demands. Having lived through similar "deals" in Albany and St. Augustine, Martin was skeptical that it would lead to any fundamental change. Nevertheless, city officials and business leaders had made significant commitments that represented tangible gains for blacks. A number of groups were upset with the deal and accused him of selling out, but Martin was able to convince most of them to live by the agreement, at least for the time being.

In August, SCLC held its annual convention in Jackson, Mississippi. Coretta joined Martin for the event. She accompanied him to the airport on August 8, where they met Senator Edward M. Kennedy, the convention's featured speaker.

By September, the new civil rights bill was hopelessly blocked in the Senate. Undaunted, Martin continued to focus on economic issues and called for a guaranteed annual income for every adult citizen. At the same time, he grew more and more despondent over the results they had been able to achieve since the Selma protest. Viewing events of the 1950s and 1960s from the perspective of his experience in the North, he was convinced people who had voiced alarm over events in Birmingham and Selma were not so much in favor of blacks as against the images they saw of overt racism. They were against Bull Connor and against Jim Clark, but they were not committed to the work of achieving true economic justice.

Meanwhile, Coretta continued to travel the country conducting Freedom Concerts. Near the end of the month, she went to New Orleans for a concert hosted by St. Peter Claver Church, a primarily black Catholic congregation. The event was held at the Municipal Auditorium. In the ten years prior to her appearance, Louisiana, a staunchly segregationist state, had seen dramatic changes. Most of those changes were brought about by the Civil Rights Movement through the work of SCLC. New Orleans, a city of mixed races almost from the day of its founding, had led the state forward. Many of the changes in Louisiana had been dramatic and received considerable attention from news reports. Among them was an announcement made official two months after Coretta's visit that the National Football League would award the city a team. For Coretta, perhaps the greatest differences were not those visible to the national eye, but the smaller things, the changes in the details of life that touched people on a daily basis. She was in New Orleans only one night, but she spent that night as a guest at the Roosevelt Hotel just off Canal Street, something neither she nor any other African American could have done three years earlier. She was able to do that not by prior special arrangement but because it was now the law. She sang to a rousing crowd that night, then left the next morning to meet Martin in Dallas.

In October, Coretta sang in concert at Chicago's Dunbar High School. United Workers for Chicago sponsored her appearance. She finished the year with a Freedom Concert at New Hope Baptist Church in Granada, Mississippi, not far from Neshoba County where the bodies of Goodman, Chaney, and Schwerner had been discovered. As with her previous concerts, Coretta refused to be intimidated and was determined to bring the message of the Civil Rights Movement to the darkest corners of the nation.

෨

In 1967, Coretta and Martin took a four-week trip to Jamaica to allow Martin time to rest and work on a new book. When he returned to the United States, he picked up the issue of American involvement in Vietnam with a vengeance. That February he addressed a crowd in Los Angeles and called for an end to the war. In March he led an antiwar protest in Chicago with Dr. Benjamin Spock in which five thousand protesters participated. In April he preached to a crowd of three thousand at Riverside Church in New York, calling for an end to the war in his famous "Time to Break Silence" sermon. Later that month he participated in an antiwar protest in New York organized by the Spring Mobilization Committee. As part of that event, Martin, along with Spock and Harry Belafonte, led a group of 125,000 protesters on a march from Central Park to the United Nations Headquarters. Most civil rights leaders denounced his antiwar position, afraid of the consequences of parting with Johnson, who by then was committed to the war.

While Martin was in New York, Coretta was in San Francisco where she participated in a West Coast Spring Mobilization rally at Kezar Stadium. A crowd of thirty thousand began the day on Market Street, then marched through downtown San Francisco to the stadium where the band Country Joe and the Fish warmed the audience with antiwar protest songs. Later, a stellar group of public figures addressed the crowd. Coretta joined Julian Bond, actor Robert Vaughn, and Eldridge Clever in calling for an end to the war. In her remarks, Coretta reiterated the message she had stressed during the past two years—the same message Martin was giving that day in New York—that achieving justice in the United States required achieving justice in Vietnam. At its peak that day, protesters filled the sixty-thousand-seat stadium to capacity.

The following month, Coretta attended a second Spring Mobilization event at Lincoln Temple in Washington, D.C. Following the rally, she led a group of protesters to the White House where they attempted to deliver a petition to the president.

In spite of opposition from traditional civil rights supporters, Coretta and Martin continued to expand their relationship with antiwar groups. In fact, as spring gave way to summer, Martin announced the summer of 1967 would be a Vietnam Summer. The 1950s and early 1960s had been an era of civil rights. Now, the country needed to move to an era of human rights. He and Coretta were uniting the Civil Rights Movement, at least rhetorically if not in fact, with antiwar protest.

That August, the annual SCLC convention was held in Atlanta at Ebenezer. As Martin faced the crowded sanctuary, there was a marked difference in his countenance. I was not the only one to notice it. He was weary and exhausted, but the change was deeper than that. More pained than weary, his eyes seemed to be fixed on a destination only he could see. By the end of his keynote address, there was hardly a dry eye in the house. I was convinced that afternoon that he had a sense that the end of his life was not far away. He had deprived himself of much in life, traveling the country instead of spending time with his children. He had been beaten, stoned, and jailed; he had been reviled by his supposed friends and hounded by agencies of the federal government. And he had preached his heart dry trying to force the nation to face up to what he was sure were the critical issues of this age—economic injustice and moral apathy. Yet when he looked back over his life, he saw a paltry, insignificant result for a lifetime of work, and he recognized the enormity of what remained to be done. He was convinced that only mass disruption of daily life in major cities could call attention to the nation's problems in a way that would compel people and governments to act. From that, he envisioned a protest led by thousands of poor people descending on cities not for a day or two, but until the nation fully addressed its fundamental social problems. It was a magnificent vision, but one many of us felt he would not live to see come to fruition.

At a December SCLC retreat, Martin continued to ruminate over what he saw as little change despite a decade of effort. SCLC needed to start again. Mass nonviolent action was needed, perhaps even mass civil disobedience. For him, there was no point in integrating blacks into a nation whose values were so askew. As that discussion continued, he focused on Washington, D.C., developing the idea of a poor people's march on the nation's capital. Reluctantly, staff began to formulate a plan for the Poor People's Campaign—a massive multiracial transition of poor people from all over the country to an encampment in Washington where they would remain until Congress addressed their issues. Martin assigned someone to draft an issues statement and begin work on logistical needs. The campaign would start in April 1968. Their demands would be specific, concrete, and simple—full employment, guaranteed annual income, and a commitment to construct five hundred thousand low-income housing units per year.

For the remainder of 1967 and early 1968, SCLC staff worked to prepare for the Poor People's Campaign while still attending to issues in Chicago. Martin kept up a relentless schedule of speaking engagements, crisscrossing the country to raise money and garner support for the campaign. Already weary and depressed, he pushed himself to the brink of exhaustion.

35

Memphis

In January 1968, Coretta participated in a Women Strike for Peace protest at the capitol in Washington, D.C. Calling themselves the Jeanette Rankin Brigade, in honor of the first woman elected to the House of Representatives, five thousand women gathered for the rally. Afterward, they marched to a Congress of Women conference which Coretta co-chaired with Pearl Willen and Mary Clarke.

As Coretta continued to carve a place for herself in antiwar and women's rights groups, Martin moved toward greater involvement with organized labor. That spring, sanitation workers in Memphis went out on strike when the city of Memphis refused to recognize their union. The local union, some 1,300 members strong, was almost all black. The city's refusal to recognize the union quickly became a racial issue. Daily marches ensued, followed by a boycott of downtown businesses. A friend asked Martin to help.

One of Martin's greatest weaknesses was an inability to say no, especially to the request of a friend and particularly when the issue touched his sense of justice. Though already burdened with the work in Chicago and plans for a massive protest in Washington, he rearranged his travel plans to permit a brief stop in Memphis. There, he spoke to a large crowd at the Masonic Temple. The crowd was energized by his remarks, and Martin, now battling depression constantly, was refreshed by their response. When the rally ended, strike leaders invited him to return and lead a protest march. Martin agreed to return at the end of the week.

Later that week, as he had promised, Martin returned to Memphis and led a protest march from the Masonic Temple toward downtown. However, unlike previous protest marches, SCLC staff members had not been involved in the planning.

Along the way, marchers at the rear of the column broke out in violent attacks on area businesses. News reports attributed the violence to Martin and SCLC. Angry at the reports, Martin made plans to return to the city and lead a peaceful demonstration. Arrangements were made, and after a postponement for a late snow storm, the second march was scheduled for April 8.

Work on the Poor People's Campaign continued at a furious pace. Martin traveled the South promoting it and recruiting volunteers. Meanwhile, SCLC staff arrived in Memphis to organize protesters for the strike march in an effort to insure there would not be a repeat of the earlier violence.

Martin and Ralph Abernathy arrived in Memphis on the morning of Wednesday, April 3. While they were en route from Atlanta, the city of Memphis obtained a temporary restraining order from federal district judge Bailey Brown, which prohibited any demonstrations for a period of ten days. When Martin arrived in Memphis, he was taken to the Lorraine Motel. Federal marshals were waiting to serve him with a copy of the restraining order when he arrived. Within hours, SCLC staff recruited lawyers to fight the order. They arrived at the motel that afternoon. Martin spent the remainder of the day with them discussing their legal options.

That night, Ralph left the motel to attend a rally at the Masonic Temple. Martin, chronically exhausted and still battling depression, intended to remain at the motel and rest. When Ralph arrived at the rally, he phoned Martin and suggested he change his plans and come speak to the crowd. Weary but unable to say no, Martin dressed and rode over to the hall.

With a crowd of two thousand before him, Martin began slowly. His voice sounded tired and heavy. Words seemed to come to him slowly. As he moved into the address, he imagined a scene in which God posed a question to him, "If you could live in any age, what age would you choose?" Slowly, methodically, he took the crowd on a metaphoric journey through history, from Egypt to the present, suggesting he would like to live "just a few years in the second half of the twentieth century." The audience warmed to him, and he warmed to their response. Words came more freely. His voice grew stronger as he took on some of the form so evident years before.

In the middle of the sermon, he turned to the story of his life, leading the audience through what he had seen and done just as he had earlier led them through history. He recounted the protests in Montgomery, Birmingham, and Selma; the March on Washington; and the protest they faced right there in Memphis. Weaving together themes of journey, struggle, victory, and destiny, he portrayed for them the journey of a people from oppression to deliverance. Finally, as he turned toward the conclusion, he delivered the now famous words, "I have been to the mountaintop. . . . And

I've looked over. And I have seen the Promised Land. I may not get there with you. But I want you to know tonight, that we, as a people, will get to the promised land!" He held that thought for a moment, turning it first one way, then another, before finishing with a phrase he had used many times before, reminding them once again that God was with them and that, "Mine eyes have seen the glory of the coming of the Lord."[1]

The following day, April 4, Martin slept late. Judge Brown had granted a hearing to address the issue of whether the restraining order might be amended to allow a limited protest. While Martin waited for the judge's decision, he rested in the motel room. What he had thought would take a few hours soon stretched into a day-long ordeal.

At last, late that afternoon, Andrew Young returned with a report. The judge had agreed to their request. After a brief discussion and lighthearted banter, Martin sent the others from his room while he dressed for dinner. The hour was late, almost six. They were scheduled to eat at the home of a friend who was waiting to take them. A few minutes later, Martin finished dressing and stepped out to the balcony.

Lincoln School Reunion in the summer of 1968. Coretta and daughter Bernice (far left) and I with my son, Arturo, in my arms (second from right). Courtesy of the Coretta Scott King Estate.

Coretta on vacation in Jamaica with Naomi B. King and me, summer 1969. Courtesy of the Coretta Scott King Estate.

Coretta enjoying a moment at home playing Scrabble with her children. From left to right: Dexter, Bernice, Yolanda, and Martin III, c. fall 1968. Courtesy of the Coretta Scott King Estate.

Coretta in her King Center home office with son Dexter and an unidentified woman, c. 1969. Coretta established the office in her home in order to spend more time with the children. Courtesy of the Coretta Scott King Estate.

Coretta and me in her King Center home office, c. 1969. Courtesy of the Coretta Scott King Estate.

Coretta in India receiving the Nehru Award with Indira Ghandi looking on, c.1969. Courtesy of the Coretta Scott King Estate.

Coretta greeting the pope at the Vatican in 1969. I accompanied Coretta on this trip. Courtesy of the Coretta Scott King Estate.

Coretta and me watching my son, Arturo, in the basement of her Atlanta home. Courtesy of the Edythe Scott Bagley Estate.

Coretta delivering a message from the pulpit of St. Paul's Cathedral in London, England, March 16, 1969. She was the first woman to deliver a message from the pulpit. I was proud to accompany her on that mission. Courtesy of the Coretta Scott King Estate.

Coretta at home in Atlanta with Naomi King, Jessie Treichler, and Norman Treichler, 1972. Courtesy of the Coretta Scott King Estate.

Coretta with Ralph Abernathy at a 1199 Union luncheon, c.1972. Courtesy of the Coretta Scott King Estate.

Coretta (left) and me (far right) with two unidentified
women at our parent's fiftieth wedding anniversary in 1972.
Courtesy of the Edythe Scott Bagley Estate.

Me, Obie Leonard, and Coretta, Christmas 1972. Courtesy of the Coretta Scott King Estate.

Coretta and my parents, Bernice and Obie Scott, in Marion, Alabama, c. 1972. Courtesy of the Coretta Scott King Estate.

Coretta in her King Center office showing plans for the future King Center complex, c. 1976. Courtesy of the Coretta Scott King Estate.

President Carter signing legislation designating the King Historic Site in Atlanta, c. 1977. The site includes the King Center, the MLK Jr. Birth Home, and Ebenezer Baptist Church. Courtesy of the Coretta Scott King Estate.

Coretta marching in Atlanta for the King Holiday, c.1990. From left to right: family friend Jerry Dunfrey, Christine King Farris, Coretta, Jessie Hill, and me. Courtesy of the Coretta Scott King Estate.

Coretta and Vice President Al Gore enjoying a moment at the King Holiday Commemorative Service at Ebenezer Baptist Church in Atlanta, January 1997. Courtesy of the Coretta Scott King Estate.

Coretta with Nelson Mandela in South Africa celebrating his victory as the first president of the new "free" South Africa, 1994. Courtesy of the Coretta Scott King Estate.

Coretta and me visiting Mrs. Lawson during her later years in Yellow Springs, Ohio.
Courtesy of the Edythe Scott Bagley Estate.

Betty Shabazz, wife of Malcolm X; Coretta; Myrlie Evers-Williams, wife of Medgar Evers,
at the National Political Congress of Black Women's Breakfast during the Congressional
Black Caucus Weekend, September 1995. Courtesy of the Coretta Scott King Estate.

Coretta with Winnie Mandela and Christine King Farris at the King Holiday parade in
Atlanta on January 21, 1992. Courtesy of the Coretta Scott King Estate

V FRUIT

And these are the ones sown on good soil: they hear the word and accept it
and bear fruit, thirty and sixty and a hundred fold.
—Mark 4:2

36

April 4, 1968

Martin admonished us from the beginning that the Movement was larger than any of us. Many times he reminded us that if something should happen to him, the Movement would go on. He said those words in the early days of the Montgomery bus boycott, and he repeated them as the SCLC leadership entered Birmingham and Selma. The last sermon I heard Martin preach was on Labor Day Weekend 1967. He repeated that admonition to us then, too, in a strange sermon entitled "Seas of Separation." Like many others he delivered in the last two years of his life, it ended with a discourse on the final separation of death.

In January 1968, Coretta had major surgery. I went to Atlanta before she entered the hospital and stayed with her through the second week of February to help her recover. Martin was at home much of that time, but he was not the same person I had known earlier. His conversations and demeanor reflected deep and unresolved pain.

On February 19, the day I was to return home, Martin returned from Mississippi where he had been promoting the Poor People's Campaign. A portion of that proposed campaign was to include a march that would begin in Jackson and conclude in Washington, D.C. Someone had suggested a mule train should travel the entire route. Martin greeted the idea with enthusiasm. His eyes sparkled as he told us about it that morning.

As we talked, the three of us—Coretta, Martin, and I—ended up in the kitchen. Just as Martin was about to leave for his office, he kissed Coretta good-bye, then started toward the doorway to the stairs that led down to the garage. I listened to the sound of his footsteps as he reached the bottom, opened the door, and stepped outside. That was the last time I saw him alive.

Later that day, before leaving for the airport, I had a conversation with Coretta in her bedroom. Several weeks had passed since the surgery, but it had left her feeling tired and drained. She lay on the bed, relaxing as we talked. I mentioned an interview with Jacqueline Kennedy that had appeared in a recent issue of the *Ladies Home Journal*. We both admired Jackie's courage, poise, and dignity. In the interview she said that during the preparations for President Kennedy's funeral, she had been sustained by feelings of anger. Thinking about the terrible act of murder committed against her husband motivated her to keep moving. I don't remember the exact words I used as Coretta and I discussed the interview, but I remember the sense of foreboding that came over me while we talked. I foresaw something coming for Coretta, something dark and tragic, and I told her that she would need to be exceedingly strong in the coming days. She listened attentively but said nothing in reply.

Shortly after returning home from Atlanta, I accepted a teaching position at Cheyney State College.[1] I assumed the teaching duties of a professor in the English Department who had become ill. A few weeks later, I received a telephone call from the chairman of the Theatre Department at West Chester State College,[2] which was located nearby, inviting me to apply for an opening in his department. After seeing my credentials and interviewing me, he was anxious for me to join the faculty. The next step was an interview with two members of the department, one male and one female. On April 4, 1968, I met the two of them and the chairman for lunch. He and I continued to have a good rapport, but while we ate and talked, I came to feel uncomfortable with the others.

After lunch, the two faculty members showed me around their facility, and we discussed what my role in the department might be. In the course of that tour it became obvious they did not want me to join the department. The gentleman stated emphatically that despite my holding an MFA degree in directing and acting, I would not be directing any productions.

"Then what would I do?"

"You would work at the box office selling tickets," he replied.

The woman with us repeatedly asked, "How can you take this position when you have a two-and-a-half-year-old child?"

When my husband, Arthur, came home that evening and asked about the interview, I told him it had not gone well and I was sure I would have a difficult time there even if they offered me the position. At any rate, I had decided not to accept the job.

As we talked, the evening news on television showed a film clip of Martin speaking to a large crowd in Memphis. We heard him say, "Yes, we are going to march again," a reference to a march they had planned for the coming Monday. Arturo, our two-and-half-year-old son recognized his uncle. He toddled over to the screen and pointed to Martin's image. When the news ended, we switched off the television.

Sometime later in the evening, the phone rang. Our friend, Fran Lucas was calling from New York. "Martin has been shot in Memphis," she said, "He's on the critical list. Scottie, let's go to Atlanta."

"No! No! No!" I cried as I dropped the telephone, unable to say more. In my heart I knew this was the end. I didn't want Martin to die. I didn't want him to be gone, but I was certain he would not survive. What he had anticipated, what I had sensed during my last visit with Coretta, had now come to pass.

Throughout the evening, our telephone continued to ring as calls came from across the nation. I tried over and over again to reach Coretta, but her telephone stayed busy as did that of our parents. After numerous attempts, I was finally able to reach Dad.

"How is Martin?"

"He's dead," Dad replied. "He's dead."

And just like that, it was over. Martin's twelve years of ministry and advocacy for change had ended. When he confined his efforts to alleviating the suffering of his own race, many supported his work. Yet when he spoke out against the war in Vietnam, many turned on him. The American press, former friends and colleagues, and fellow civil rights leaders thought he should stick solely to the issue of race. They did not mind telling him so, either. Even the Reverend Billy Graham criticized Martin's stance on the war.

After talking to Dad for a moment, I hung up the telephone and paced the upstairs hallway, weeping bitterly. Arturo watched in silence. Eventually, I settled down and began pulling together things to take to Atlanta. Among the things I gathered were pieces of writing that I had composed about Martin and the Movement for previous occasions. They would be useful sources of inspiration in putting together Martin's funeral program. I was certain that would be one of my assignments. Martin's death was still unreal, but I did my best to prepare my mind for what lay ahead.

On Saturday, Edith Savage, a friend from Trenton, New Jersey, accompanied me on a noonday flight to Atlanta.

37

Friday

On Friday, April 5, 1968, Coretta traveled to Memphis to retrieve Martin's body. Senator Robert Kennedy provided an airplane and a young assistant for the trip. Martin's sister, Christine, and her husband, Isaac, accompanied Coretta, as did Jean Young, Juanita Abernathy, Dora McDonald, and several others. They waited on the tarmac in Memphis while the casket was placed in the aircraft. Coretta never left the plane. Some of the SCLC staff who had been in Memphis with Martin joined them for the return trip to Atlanta.

When Edith Savage and I landed in Atlanta Saturday afternoon, an SCLC staff member picked us up at the airport and took us to the house. Coretta was away making funeral arrangements when I arrived. Many of the details of Martin's death were still unknown. In response to the obvious threat, security officers were everywhere: in the street, on the lawn, and even inside the house.

Coretta's kitchen had become the nerve center of the family. Dora McDonald, who had been Martin's secretary, and Bernita Bennette, a friend and the wife of an SCLC staff member, had set up an area around the kitchen table as a temporary office. Xernona Clayton was there, too. Patricia Cook—she later married and became Patricia Latimore—who had assisted Coretta with the children, was in and out. Across the room, Coretta's housekeeper, Dorothy Lockhart, worked to maintain order around the stove. In keeping with a wonderful southern tradition, many people who came to the house brought food. Mrs. Lockhart, with the help of volunteers from Ebenezer and the community, coordinated meals and prepared special dishes as well. As I came through the doorway, I was immersed in a sea of rich aroma and a cacophony of noise.

The group in the kitchen greeted me with a hug, and we exchanged brief words of sympathy. I sobbed as we embraced each other, but after a moment I realized no one else in the room was crying. I straightened myself, squared my shoulders, and slipped down the hall to put my luggage in the guest room. If they were not going to cry, neither was I. A few minutes later, I returned to the kitchen. They put me to work immediately.

"We need to prepare a printed program for the service," Dora McDonald said. "Coretta wants you and Bernita to work on it."

I said, "Okay," and turned to the details that remained to be addressed.

People moved in and out of the room, relaying messages, getting something to eat, delivering one more pie or cake or casserole. All the while, the telephone rang constantly. We fielded hundreds of calls as we diligently worked to get everything in place.[1]

With the number of people already gathered in and around the house and the many expressions of sympathy pouring in, we realized Martin's death would evoke a tremendous outpouring of public grief. A large number of dignitaries had already indicated their interest in attending his funeral, and many had arrived in Atlanta. In addition, Martin's life and work had touched millions of ordinary Americans, many of whom felt compelled to express their appreciation and devotion by making a pilgrimage to Atlanta to participate in his funeral. In an effort to accommodate that fact and Martin's stature as a national leader, Coretta, his immediate family, and the SCLC leadership decided his body should be made available for viewing by the public. Having reached that conclusion, they needed to locate an appropriate site.

Ebenezer had been the spiritual center of Martin's life and the Civil Rights Movement, but the church's sanctuary could seat only slightly more than seven hundred people. The regular church congregation alone would fill it to capacity. Several people suggested alternative locations for the service, but those responsible for planning the event were adamant the worship service could be held nowhere but Ebenezer.[2] Still, they had to accommodate what was rapidly becoming an international occasion.

Morehouse College, Martin's alma mater, would have easily accommodated a much larger crowd, but Coretta and the King family were already considering a second, larger memorial service there as a way of allowing more people to attend a formal ceremony. As they deliberated over the issue, someone suggested holding the public viewing at Spelman College, another of Atlanta's historically black schools. Doing that would allow them to include more of Atlanta's black community in the event and also would give a nod to the spirit of unity we all felt.

When Coretta returned to the house late that evening, we were all still in the kitchen right where we had been since I had arrived. I don't remember the moment I saw her. That day was a blur of questions, answers, phone calls, and preparations for the funeral. I am certain Coretta and I hugged each other as we always did, but I do not recall what was said. There is a bond between sisters few men ever understand that often makes words unnecessary. We each knew what the other had borne—the pain, the joy, the trials silently endured—and we were able to convey that understanding with a nod, a tilt of the head, a knowing look in our eyes. Whatever we said that day, Coretta was glad to see me, and I was glad to be there for her. She gave us the latest information on the funeral arrangements, services, and locations. Dora, Bernita, and I reviewed our plans for the printed program with her, and with Coretta's approval, we put things in motion to have it printed.

Late that evening, people began to drift away from the house, and the phone rang only intermittently. After the children were put to bed, Coretta and I had a chance to visit for a few minutes and then headed off to bed. Both of us were exhausted. Coretta and I slept in the same bed that night as we had done when we were children back in Alabama. Lying there in the dark next to her, I found it difficult to comprehend all that had happened in our lives: the places we had been, the things we had seen and done, the changes in which we had been privileged to participate. It all seemed impossible and unbelievable; it was overwhelming one moment and like a dream the next. Sometime later, I drifted off to sleep.

When we awoke the following morning, Coretta's first words were, "I was crying when I woke up."

I replied, "So was I."

Sunday morning, the funeral home transferred Martin's body to Sisters Chapel at Spelman College. While attendants prepared the body for the public, Coretta, the children, and other family members attended the regular Sunday morning service at Ebenezer. Martin's brother, A.D., had joined Martin in Memphis the week before. While they visited at the motel, Martin discussed the sermon he planned to give. Using Martin's notes, A.D. preached the sermon that morning.

In the afternoon, Coretta, the children, and I went to Spelman College to see Martin's body and officially open the chapel to the public. When we arrived, mourners had already formed lines that stretched across the campus. I followed Coretta to the casket and glanced down at Martin's face, then quickly looked away. Bernice, who had turned five years old the week before, peeked into the casket and had the same reaction. Neither of us cared to linger long at his side. Some said the expression on his face appeared peaceful. Others said he seemed only to be asleep. I did not care for the way he looked.

Thousands waited in line for hours to see Martin one last time. Many filed past his casket with bleak, stony faces. Others wept openly. All of them had a story to tell of how Martin had touched their lives. I was glad we gave them an opportunity to remember him and to recount for each other what he meant to them.

38

Memphis March

During the course of that sad weekend, the question arose as to whether Coretta should go to Memphis for the march Martin had planned to lead that Monday. Some suggested her participation in the march might place her in physical danger. The night of Martin's death there had been riots and outbursts of sporadic violence in major cities around the nation. In Memphis, the governor called out the National Guard to ensure order. There was also a logistical question. Memphis was a long way from Atlanta, and Martin's funeral was scheduled for the following day.

Those of us closest to Coretta felt she needed to attend. Had he been able to speak, Martin would have insisted the march go forward. For that to happen, participation of the SCLC leadership was critical. Martin had given his life trying to help the workers in Memphis. He would have insisted that his death not hinder their progress.

The following morning, accompanied by her three oldest children, Coretta traveled to Memphis to lead the sanitation workers' protest march. Harry Belafonte and Ralph Abernathy went with her. Bernice stayed at the house with us.

When Coretta and the rest of the party arrived in Memphis, the marchers were ready and waiting. Coretta took her place at the front of the column, and they set off for city hall. Thousands joined in the march, and thousands more gathered along the route. Some came to support the sanitation workers. Others came to pay their respects to Coretta and the children. Unlike the earlier march that had been marred by violence, this one was orderly and calm—more of a memorial march for Martin than a protest march for the workers.

At city hall, the crowd assembled near the steps. Harry Belafonte gave a brief introduction, then Coretta stepped to the microphone. With all that was going on at the house in preparation for the funeral, there had been no time to draft a written speech for her, and besides it was not an occasion for a formal address. Instead, Coretta spoke from her heart.

> [Martin] often said, unearned suffering is redemptive, and if you give your life to a cause in which you believe, and which is right and just . . . and if your life comes to an end as a result of this, then your life could not have been lived in a more redemptive way. And I think that this is what my husband has done.
>
> But then I ask the question: How many men must die before we can really have a free and true and peaceful society? How long will it take? If we can catch the spirit and the true meaning of this experience, I believe that this nation can be transformed into a society of love, of justice, peace, and brotherhood where all men can really be brothers.[1]

Many were amazed that Coretta could speak in such moving and eloquent terms, not just about her husband—they might have expected that—but about the ideals for which he had worked so hard and died trying to promote. Those who only knew the public Coretta knew her as a mother and housewife, but she was much more than that. Since our days at Lincoln School, we had been socially aware and concerned about the issues around us. At Antioch College that awareness had deepened and matured. By 1968, Coretta was as married to the cause of racial and economic justice as she was to Martin. Commenting on her commitment to the Movement and how their lives had developed, Martin had said, "I wish I could say, and satisfy my masculine ego, that I led her down this path. But we walked down this path together."[2]

When Coretta spoke that day from the steps of city hall in Memphis, she drew upon her direct participation in the Movement. She not only had been a homemaker and mother, she had attended meetings, participated in discussions, marched, written, spoken, and sung for freedom, both alongside her husband and on her own. She was as well versed as anyone in the ideals that inspired Martin to a life of selfless service.

39

The Funeral

In the five days that followed Martin's death, thousands came to pay homage to a man, an age, and an idea that many felt could never die. Many more placed telephone calls and sent letters, telegrams, and flowers, and many sent money to further his cause, expressing the hope that Martin's work would continue. The millions whose lives he had touched found it inconceivable that the cause he so magnificently articulated would end. They were determined that it would not.

We had begun calling Martin's celebration a Festival of Love, a fitting tribute to a man who preached and lived his commitment to nonviolence. Atlanta's black community had exercised restraint consistent with his message of nonviolence. While people in other cities reacted to his death by rioting and indulging in acts of violence, those in Atlanta demonstrated to the world that they grasped the true meaning of his teaching. They sought to make Atlanta, at least during that period, the Beloved Community about which he often talked and dreamed.

In a spirit of love and cooperation, many people in Atlanta, white and black, made their homes available to out-of-town visitors. Others stepped forward to provide transportation for the many guests who descended on the city. Over three hundred cars, loaned and driven by their owners, attended to the transportation needs of mourners on the day of the funeral.

The service at Ebenezer was beautiful. The music and spoken word were soft, soothing, and transporting. It was a service Martin would have liked. At the conclusion, Martin's body was placed on a mule-drawn farm wagon—a gesture of support for his Poor People's Campaign. Then, with the famous and the unknown following behind, they took his body on one last march through the streets of Atlanta along a winding route to the campus of Morehouse College. My husband, Arthur, and I followed the casket with Coretta, her children, and Martin's family, part way through town. Then, a few miles from the church a car picked us up and carried us on to the Morehouse campus. Coretta and the family had to be in place when the crowd arrived, and the distance was too far for the children to walk.

Following the funeral and the burial, we all trooped back to the house. Somber and downcast, we were filled with an emptiness made all the more poignant by the realization that the service was over and Martin was gone. Perhaps we all would have benefited from a moment to let down and wail, but none of us did, at least none of us in the immediate family. All through the day, when I felt like crying, Martin's voice inside me kept saying, "Don't cry, Edythe. Do something!" Those words kept me dry-eyed and busy that weekend, and in my heart I resolved to "do something" for the Movement with the remainder of my life.

On Wednesday, the skies opened in a torrential rainstorm. Coretta's home was filled with people, but unlike the previous hectic days, we mostly chatted softly and sat around listening to the rain. I am sure some of those who were there found it hard to believe that Martin was actually gone and even harder to pick up their daily routine. Or perhaps they just wanted to be where their hearts had been for a long time. Coretta spent the day resting in bed.

Several of the people at the house that day were journalists conducting interviews. Simeon Booker, a reporter from *Jet* magazine, interviewed me. I knew him from my Antioch College days. We had lived in the same co-op house in Cleveland, Ohio, on the campus of Western Reserve University when I worked as a co-op student for the Cleveland Urban League.

Throughout most of the day, I kept an eye on Coretta. She had been constantly on the move since she had received the phone call from Memphis Thursday evening. She had spent much of the ensuing six days on her feet, greeting visitors and offering them words of comfort, even as they did their best to comfort her.

About two o'clock in the afternoon, I walked into Coretta's room. She sat up in bed and said in a voice slightly louder than a whisper, "There's going to be so much to do."

"Yes," I responded quickly, "there will be a lot to do. But you are going to have a lot of help. I am going to help you, and I think Bernita Bennette will also be interested in assisting you."

"But you have to accept that teaching position at West Chester State," she replied.

"I don't intend to take it," I responded. I had decided years earlier that if something happened to Martin, I would step in and help Coretta. That time had come.

Coretta relaxed her head against the pillows as if a weight had been lifted from her shoulders. She closed her eyes and slid down in the bed. A moment or two later, I crossed the room and quietly slipped out to the hallway.

Later that afternoon, Bernita came to the house. She and Coretta talked for a while. I stayed out of the way and gave them as much privacy as possible. When Bernita was gone, Coretta told me that her friend had agreed to work with her. Bernita had a full-time job with the Atlanta Public School System, but she was certain she could get at least a temporary leave of absence.

She became Coretta's first full-time assistant and served tirelessly with her for many years. A gifted person, Bernita was a trained musician and had worked as a radio disc jockey for a number of years. She was a careful writer who was well informed and a thorough researcher.

Throughout the remainder of the week, people continued to stop by the house. Many brought food and flowers. Others offered to help as we continued to respond to media requests and other details concerning Martin's death and the funeral services, and as we tried to find our way forward. With Martin gone, some no doubt wondered what would happen next with SCLC and the Movement, but not Coretta. She was not one to leave much to happenstance. On Thursday, she met with a group who had been Martin's advisers, one of whom was Harry Belafonte. Uppermost in Coretta's mind was planning a memorial to Martin.

Easter came the following Sunday, April 14. I sat with the King family at Ebenezer's service. Occasionally, Mama King wiped away a tear from her eyes, but other than that there was no display of emotion. Women who attended the service wore their Easter hats, and children had on their Easter clothes. Yolanda, Martin, Dexter, and Bernice wore special outfits, too. They had gone shopping for Easter clothes with Coretta the day Martin was shot. The service was worshipful and reverent, but unlike Easters past no one was in a festive mood.

After the service, we drove out to Southview Cemetery to Martin's gravesite. Coretta placed a floral arrangement on his crypt. The full implications of his death had not yet settled on me, but already I could sense Coretta was slowly and carefully moving forward emotionally.

Early Monday morning, I took a flight back to Philadelphia accompanied this time by my friend Esther Turner. When I met my eight thirty class at Cheyney later that morning, the students looked tense and nervous. I alluded to the assassination only once, in reference to why I had missed class, and launched into the course work.

Back in Pennsylvania, away from the tension and bustle of Atlanta, my own private period of mourning began. What the Civil Rights Movement had lost, what

America had lost, what the world had lost in the assassination of Martin Luther King Jr. became the constant preoccupation of my mind. During the week I was fine, but starting on Friday evening, I grieved throughout the weekend.

In late April, Coretta came to spend a few days with us in order to rest and get away from the barrage of phone calls and details in Atlanta. She left our house only once, to attend the spring concert of the college choir. The Sunday afternoon while Coretta was with us, a radio station in New Jersey was broadcasting Martin's sermons. I noticed that while she was listening to that program, she intermittently wiped away tears. That was the only time since the Montgomery boycott that I had seen her shed a tear.

My feeling of bereavement lasted throughout the summer. I didn't mope around with a glum look on my face, but inside I felt like something of immeasurable worth had been ripped from my life and from the life of our nation.

40

Finishing Martin's Business

As painful as Martin's death was for Coretta and her children, there was work remaining to be done. Coretta had very little time to grieve and reflect. In addition to her own busy schedule, Martin had speaking obligations that needed to be filled. Each one of those scheduled engagements represented an opportunity to raise anew the issues of economic and social justice, both at home and abroad. Now, with him gone, those engagements took on added meaning and significance. They were not merely speeches someone had to give, but opportunities purchased at the cost of his life. Coretta was determined to fill as many of those engagements as she could possibly manage.

On April 27, 1968, Coretta went to New York for another Spring Mobilization Rally against the war in Vietnam. After marching through the streets of Manhattan, she gathered with protesters in an area of Central Park known as the Sheep Meadow. There, Coretta addressed the gathering in a speech that lasted twenty minutes. Once again, she stressed that universal application of nonviolence was a means of confronting injustice without the need for war, that freedom and dignity in America meant freedom and dignity for the people of Southeast Asia, and she reminded the audience that this was the cause for which her husband had died.

As May approached, Coretta's attention turned to the Poor People's Campaign. Conceived by Martin as a nonviolent mass protest, the campaign was to be a larger version of the protests he had been leading in cities across the South and around the nation; this time, however, the attention would focus on broader economic issues as opposed to the racial issues that had been the subject of past marches. What he originally wanted was an invasion of poor people rising up from impoverished obscurity, getting themselves to Washington by any means possible, and staying until Congress acted to address their circumstances. What actually occurred was nothing like what he had envisioned.

The campaign had been scheduled to begin in early April. But even before Martin's death, that date had been pushed back. After the funeral, a discussion ensued among SCLC staff about whether to continue or simply cancel the whole thing. Some had opposed it since the day Martin first broached the idea. They used his death to buttress their argument to forgo the event. Others thought his death would provide a powerful impetus for large-scale participation. Ralph Abernathy, Andrew Young, and the SCLC team that had been with Martin when he died were adamantly in favor of continuing. They forced the others to go along.

On May 2, 1968, groups of volunteers set out from various locations across the nation and headed toward Washington, D.C. In his speeches, Martin had suggested they come on foot, by car, or even by wagon if necessary. Many who participated in the march did what he had said and came in covered wagons drawn by horses and mules. For some, riding in a wagon was an everyday occurrence, but for most it was a caricature. Coretta spoke that day from the balcony of the Lorraine Motel in Memphis, the site where Martin had been killed earlier that spring, as marchers set out from Tennessee toward Washington. There, they were to meet with a group from the town of Marks, Mississippi, a community mired in abject poverty that had been a source of inspiration for the original campaign idea. Martin had visited there earlier that year and had seen children living in squalid conditions. He was determined to do something about the economic system that allowed such circumstances to exist.

In spite of staff differences, organizers had worked hard to recruit volunteers for the campaign. Martin had crisscrossed the nation trying to muster as many as possible for what he hoped would be an overwhelming presence in Washington. As the campaign began without him, Ralph and others at SCLC expected about fifteen hundred to actually reach the nation's capital. Those fifteen hundred had been specifically recruited and trained for lobbying and for nonviolent protest. They were to be sent to Congress and government agencies for direct action. The masses who would arrive on their own would act as reinforcements, conducting protest marches and holding sit-ins in and around agency office buildings.

The first protesters began arriving in Washington on May 12. People of all ethnic backgrounds responded to Martin's call—Appalachian whites, Native Americans, African Americans, and Latinos. SCLC staff and volunteers erected plywood shanties—A-frames with plastic sheeting for fronts—on the mall between the Lincoln and Washington Memorials as places for people to stay. They called the encampment Resurrection City, but it soon became a nightmare. With five times as many volunteers as had been anticipated, sanitary services and meal provisions were inadequate from the first day.

That same day, Coretta and Ethel Kennedy, the wife of Senator Robert F. Kennedy, led a Mother's Day Parade through the streets of Washington, D.C. Composed of five thousand "Welfare Mothers," the parade highlighted the effects of poverty on women and children. Ethel and Coretta had known their share of tragedy, and there would be more to endure, but that day they worked together to focus national attention on issues that involved women and their families, issues that were important to Ethel's and Coretta's husbands and were dear to both women.

Meanwhile, volunteers for the Poor People's Campaign continued to arrive. Filled beyond capacity, Resurrection City overflowed with residents in numbers too large for the kind of activities planned. SCLC staff did their best to make the campaign work, but it was out of control from the beginning. Staff members held training sessions and workshops and sent people out for direct action, but the groups were too unwieldy to be effective and not large enough to be overwhelming. Then, things got worse.

After a late start, Senator Robert Kennedy had mounted a convincing campaign for the Democratic Party's 1968 presidential nomination. Focused on the issues of war, poverty, and the need for greater economic opportunity, his message resonated with the times and with many in the United States. Decisive victories in strategic states helped him gain late momentum. On June 5, he won the California primary, which put him in position to challenge Vice President Hubert Humphrey for the nomination. Those of us associated with the Civil Rights Movement were once again optimistic about the possibility of real change in America.

In Los Angeles that evening, the Kennedy campaign held a victory celebration in the ballroom at the Ambassador Hotel. Senator Kennedy made a brief appearance, addressed the crowd, and then started from the room through the kitchen to leave the building. There, Sirhan Sirhan confronted him and, before anyone could react, emptied a revolver into Senator Kennedy's body. He was rushed to the hospital but was pronounced dead the following day.

Robert Kennedy's death, coming so soon on the heels of Martin's, compounded our misery. Senator Kennedy had offered help to Martin and Coretta at critical junctures and had reached out to Coretta in the hours immediately following Martin's death. He not only provided material assistance, but he and his wife, Ethel, visited Coretta at her home and marched in the funeral procession from the church to Morehouse College. Just a few weeks before her husband was killed, Ethel had been with Coretta in the Mother's Day Parade. We considered them and their family our friends.

Though Coretta was concerned about the success of the Poor People's Campaign, she interrupted her schedule and, accompanied by Bernita Bennette, traveled to California to be with Ethel and her family. Coretta and Bernita remained with the Kennedy family in California and then returned with them to New York for the funeral. Jackie Kennedy joined them aboard the plane for the flight east. Still not beyond their own grief, Coretta and Jackie comforted Ethel and others with a sense of understanding only those who have experienced deep personal pain could know or understand. Following the service in New York, Robert Kennedy's body was transported by train to Washington for burial in Arlington National Cemetery. Upon reaching Washington, one of the stops the funeral procession made along the way to the cemetery was at Resurrection City.

The effect of the Kennedy assassination on the Poor People's Campaign was devastating. Already subdued and confused by Martin's absence, the volunteers found that the death of Senator Kennedy sapped what remained of their energy. Then, to make matters even worse, rainstorms turned Resurrection City into a muddy bog. As with demonstrations gone awry in the past, SCLC needed an exit strategy.

One of the highlights planned for the campaign was a celebration scheduled for June 19 called Solidarity Day. Martin had been slated to give an address from the steps of the Lincoln Memorial, the site of two earlier speeches by him, most notably the "I Have a Dream" speech in 1963. Coretta was to speak in his place. My husband and I brought our young son to see her deliver that speech. We joined her in her room at the Willard Hotel. Later that day, Ralph gave us a tour of Resurrection City.

In the afternoon we rode with Coretta to the Lincoln Memorial where she would speak. Sitting beside her in the car on the way over, I could tell she was excited and enthusiastic about the event. When we arrived, we found a crowd of fifty thousand people gathered in and around the reflecting pool.

A number of leaders preceded Coretta with long and uninspiring speeches. The crowd grew restless and wandered about, splashing in the pool. Coretta gave an outstanding address, but no one could match Martin's eloquent oratory.

In the end, the day, like the campaign as a whole, left little impression. I was glad when, on June 23, Ralph Abernathy and Andrew Young brought the campaign to a close.

The Poor People's Campaign and the march with striking Memphis sanitation workers were the last efforts Martin had planned in a long and arduous struggle for social and economic freedom. In the weeks following his death, President Johnson convinced both sides of the Memphis strike to accept a settlement. Memphis was restored to peace, and the union gained the recognition it had sought. Unfortunately, the Poor People's Campaign did not accomplish as much. The campaign brought thousands of people to the nation's capital in dramatic fashion, but it did little more than dramatize the plight of the nation's poor.

In the weeks that followed, Coretta was placed on the SCLC board of directors. She was happy to participate in the organization's ongoing efforts, but her primary focus was on seeing her husband's legacy preserved in proper fashion. No one knew his thoughts and dreams, his hopes and aspirations, better than she.

In 1959, when Coretta and Martin had traveled to India, they had worked with the Gandhi National Memorial Fund. She had seen how that organization had not only preserved and memorialized the image and work of Gandhi, but also was an organization that sought to continue his work and spread his commitment to nonviolence. That was what Coretta wanted, an organization that would propagate Martin's belief in the use of nonviolent methods to promote change—deep, systemic, fundamental changes to America's social and economic structure. SCLC had been Martin's vehicle for exercising his calling. It had worked well with large events that required recruitment, training, and mobilization of the masses for specific, limited tasks. But that was not Coretta's calling. The organization she envisioned was one that sought to explain the efficacy of nonviolence as a method, philosophy, and lifestyle. It would teach principles but leave much of the specific application to individuals and grassroots organizations acting on their own. Such an organization would also incorporate her love of the arts, which she felt were a vehicle for effecting change.

Through the summer of 1968, Coretta continued to fill as many of Martin's speaking engagements as she could. In June she spoke at Harvard University's Class Day exercises,[1] becoming the first woman to deliver a Class Day address at that institution. In her remarks to the senior class, she focused again on opposition to the war in Vietnam, calling for an end to aerial bombing. She also voiced what she saw as inadequacies in the investigation into the deaths of Martin and Senator Kennedy.

Following Martin's death, publishers wasted little time in seeking a book deal from Coretta. Martin's demise, while devastating to many, presented a marketing opportunity few in the book industry could resist. She reached an agreement for her first book by the end of June.

On July 10, Coretta and the children traveled to New Hampshire for a peaceful summer retreat. With the help of Walter Dunfrey, Coretta and the children obtained the use of a house on the estate of William Russell Burwell. Situated along the shore of Lake Winnipesaukee, near Wolfeboro, the house offered them an idyllic environment in which to rest, heal, and renew their spirits.

Tucked away in the lakeside cottage, Coretta spent her days working on her book. The children played on the lake and romped through the countryside with the Dunfrey children and the children of Gary and Nancy Hirshberg, who were also staying on the property.

While she rested, Coretta quietly laid the groundwork for establishing the new organization to preserve Martin's legacy and continue his work, one that would be separate from SCLC and more directly under her control. As an initial step, she formed the Martin Luther King Jr. Foundation to handle the many contributions that were still arriving.

Later that summer, she took a break from work on her book to hold a press conference in which she announced her intention to form the King Memorial Center. She also traveled to New York, where she spoke at the Conference on Women sponsored by Norman Cousins.

After Martin's assassination, SCLC moved its 1968 convention to Memphis. It was held there in August. Again, my friend Edith Savage and I flew there together. My son, Arturo, who was three years old, went along with me. Like many other events that summer, the convention and the experience of being in that city was bittersweet. Being there made us feel closer to Martin. It was the last place where he had been alive and active, but it also was the place where many of our hopes and dreams came to an end.

The tone of the convention was one of melancholy. Aretha Franklin, who had been close to Martin, performed for us, but even her singing, normally robust and full of power, reflected pain and despair. We all bore our grief with tender smiles.

While we were in Memphis, we visited the Lorraine Motel and climbed the stairway to the walkway that led to Martin's room on the second floor. A stone marker had been placed in front of the room, and I was told that local churchwomen brought fresh flowers to it every day. An inscription from the book of Genesis was inscribed on the marker. "Here comes the dreamer. Come, let us slay him and we shall see what becomes of his dreams."[2]

On Labor Day weekend of 1968, I went to Atlanta to work with Coretta full-time. Arthur, my husband, was away finishing course work for his doctorate. When I met with Coretta's staff for the first time, I told them, "I am here in the interest of harmony," and that is what the experience turned out to be. There were no fights, no bad attitudes, and no instances of malicious gossip. It was an amazingly harmonious situation for which I was grateful.

During the summer, construction crews built out the basement beneath the house to add a playroom, kitchen, and office space. When Coretta officially opened her office that September, she had a staff of ten people. Despite the need for a large number of employees, Coretta was determined to maintain her offices at home. Having her offices there allowed her to structure her schedule around her children's schedules and afforded them immediate access to her.

From the beginning, one of our biggest issues was sorting and responding to the mail. In addition to letters of condolence and appreciation, there were requests for appearances, messages from school children, publishing offers, theatrical scripts, and poems. Some sent paintings and other images of Martin, including his likeness created with flowers from a garden in Scandinavia. It was, as Fran Thomas once said, "like pulling down a mountain with a toothpick."

Frances Lucas, Coretta's friend from their college days, came to help us for a semester. Frances Thomas, our Lincoln School mentor and teacher, also worked with us as a volunteer along with Jessie Treichler, who had retired from Antioch. The volume of work served us well; it allowed us to process our grief while remaining busy.[3] There was little time to grow maudlin or morose. Instead, we were doing precisely what I had heard on the day of the funeral as those words of Martin echoed through my head, "Do something, Edythe."

One of the big events that year was the premier of the documentary film *King: A Filmed Record . . . Montgomery to Memphis.* It was produced by Ely Landau and Richard Kaplan. I had known Richard when we were students at Antioch College. The film used actual newsreel footage with narration by a number of celebrities including Harry Belafonte, Paul Newman, Joanne Woodward, Burt Lancaster, Charlton Heston, and James Earl Jones.

As the heat of summer turned to autumn, we braced ourselves for the coming presidential election that November. With Robert Kennedy gone from the campaign, the Democratic Party was fragmented over a number of issues. Supporters of Hubert Humphrey and George Wallace divided the loyalty of usual party supporters over the issue of civil rights, with American Independent Party–nominee Wallace taking conservative white Southern Democrats and Humphrey receiving most of the liberal support. Antiwar activists found it difficult to support Humphrey, who had been tainted by a term as Lyndon Johnson's vice president. They were even more repulsed by Wallace, who still favored winning the war. Some Democrats stayed home while others crossed over and voted for the Republican, Richard Nixon. Those deep divisions handed the election to Nixon.[4]

On the day following the election, Coretta's house was very quiet. No one talked much, and when we did, we spoke in hushed tones. Martin and Robert Kennedy were gone. Johnson was on his way out, and Richard Nixon was set to occupy the Oval Office. Depression seemed to hang over us like a thick blanket. We were feeling low, but Coretta never missed a beat.

Ten days after the election, she was back in Washington, D.C., leading an antiwar rally. One week later, she attended a banquet in Chicago at which the Governor of Illinois, Otto Kerner, was honored with the John F. Kennedy Award from the Catholic Interracial Council of Chicago. In spite of the setbacks we had experienced that year, Coretta had not stopped. We on her staff could not slow down, either.

In December, I accompanied Coretta to Kingston, Jamaica, where Martin posthumously received the Marcus Garvey Prize for Human Rights. Awarded by the Jamaican government, the prize was named in honor of the Jamaica native, who had spent his life advocating black pride and the return of all Africans to the continent of Africa. By that repatriation he sought to redeem the African continent from European colonial control.

We arrived in Jamaica under the most perfect weather, with mild days and cool nights. The entire island was alive with festivities surrounding the prize and its award to Martin. As guests of the Jamaican government, we were treated like royalty, but our stay was too short to enjoy much of the culture. We returned to Atlanta feeling refreshed and with Coretta thinking she might return to Jamaica some day for an island vacation.

41

1969

As 1969 began, there were obligations from Martin's schedule yet to be met. Coretta was also active in opposing the war in Vietnam and in promoting international peace. While she worked hard to complete Martin's schedule and to continue advocacy for her own causes, she was also a mother. And, like all good mothers, she always had her children first in her heart.

Though Martin's absence from her life left her to carry on alone, rearing four children by herself was nothing new for her. She had been caring for them on her own most of their lives. Martin was gone from home much of the time. Coretta had long since learned to juggle the children's schedules and her own without relying on him to get them to school or tend to household chores. Still, his death was a devastating blow to their lives and left a void still felt by the children even today.

Several of us stepped forward immediately to help fill that void. I took a leave of absence from teaching and came to Atlanta. For the first two years following Martin's death, my son and I lived with Coretta and her children. During that time, Coretta and I cared for the children together. One of us was there all the time and made certain they had a stable home life. Daddy and Mama King, who were around much of the time, kept a watchful eye on the children also, as they did on all their grandchildren.

Martin's sister, Christine, and her husband, Isaac, joined in the effort, too. Though she had a full-time job as a professor at Spelman College, Christine became Coretta's bookkeeper. She came to the house two or three nights each week to work on Coretta's financial records. Christine's children came with her and spent the evening studying and playing with Yolanda, Martin, Dexter, and Bernice.

Martin's brother A.D. relocated his family to Atlanta where A.D. became co-pastor with his father at Ebenezer. He and his wife, Naomi, became deeply involved in the lives of Coretta's children. A.D. became a surrogate father for them during that first year following the assassination.

Throughout our lives, Coretta and I were privileged to have adult mentors; people who, on their own initiative, took an interest in us and helped us through difficult and confusing times. In the years following Martin's death, several people stepped forward to extend that same assistance to Coretta and her children. Among them were Cecil and Frances Thomas, and Robert and Lettie Green.

Cecil and Frances Thomas had been mentors to us since our days at Lincoln School. They had continued to support us when we left Marion and made our way north to Antioch. Indeed, they were the ones who pointed us in that direction. After Martin's death, they continued that relationship by calling, writing, and dropping by Atlanta at every opportunity, especially during the year immediately following the assassination. By then, Cecil was executive director of the National Committee on US-China Relations, working to reestablish ties between the two nations. His hectic schedule kept him busy much of the time, but he and Fran maintained their involvement with Coretta and the children. Cecil usually traveled to Atlanta once a month to engage in activities with the boys, while Fran assisted with the children and office work. Sadly, Cecil died in 1969 as the result of an automobile accident in Kenya. Fran, however, continued to assist Coretta.

Bob and Lettie Green had been friends of Coretta and Martin since the early 1960s. Bob was a professor of psychology at Michigan State University. His leadership of civil rights protests in and around Detroit caught Martin's attention. Later, Bob's lifelong friend, Edwina Moss, worked as one of Martin's secretaries. She helped Bob schedule Martin to speak at Michigan State to raise money for a summer educational program. In the fall of 1965, at Martin's invitation, Bob took a one-year leave of absence from Michigan State to accept a position as education director for SCLC.

The year Bob and Lettie lived in Atlanta, Coretta and Martin's children often played at their house. The Greens had three children who were roughly the ages of Martin, Dexter, and Bernice. They swam in the pool at the Green home and played basketball in their backyard. After Martin died, Bob and Lettie made a concerted effort to continue their involvement with the King children. For the next six or seven years, they had them up to their home in Michigan for extended vacations. During those years, they took the children to tennis camp on the north shore of Lake Tahoe, horseback riding in California, and snow skiing multiple times in Michigan.

To the King children, they became Uncle Bob and Aunt Lettie and provided experiences that helped validate the children's growing self-awareness.

Another person who took an interest in the welfare of the children, both before and after Martin's death, was Harry Belafonte. Following the birth of Bernice, Coretta and Martin's youngest child, Harry realized the toll the Civil Rights Movement was taking on Coretta's time and energy. To help alleviate that situation, he offered to pay for a nurse to assist Coretta with the children. Coretta and Martin gladly accepted his offer and hired a person who held that position for five or six years.

❦

In January 1969, Coretta and Bernita Bennette left for a trip to India. En route, they stopped over in Verona, Italy, where the Italian government bestowed upon Coretta the Universal Love Award. It was the first time the Italian government had granted the award to a non-Italian. From Verona, Coretta and Bernita traveled to Rome where Coretta had an audience with Pope Paul VI at Vatican City.

In New Delhi, Coretta accepted the Jawaharlal Nehru Award, which was posthumously bestowed on Martin in a ceremony conducted at New Delhi University. As Coretta accepted the award, students who had gathered to watch the event spontaneously began to sing, "We Shall Overcome." Coretta joined in with them. Prime Minister Indira Gandhi, who was standing with her, joined in as well, the two of them singing through tears.

The following month, Clergy and Laymen Concerned about Vietnam held a conference at the Metropolitan AME Church in Washington, D.C. Coretta attended the event, then led a delegation to the White House for a meeting with Henry Kissinger. At the time, Kissinger was serving as President Nixon's special assistant for national security affairs. Accompanying Coretta that day was the Reverend William Sloan Coffin, chaplain of Yale University. They presented Kissinger with a proposal to grant amnesty to those who had been imprisoned for refusing to accept deployment to Vietnam as well as those who had fled to Canada to avoid the military draft.

On March 16, 1969, Christine, Bernita, several others, and I accompanied Coretta to London where she was set to preach at St. Paul's Cathedral. No woman had ever delivered a sermon in the cathedral at a regularly appointed service. The text for the sermon was from the Gospel of Luke, a quote from the prophet Isaiah, "The Spirit of the Lord is on me, because he has anointed me to preach good news to the poor.

He has sent me to proclaim freedom for the prisoners, and recovery of sight for the blind, to release the oppressed, to proclaim the year of the Lord's favor."[1]

No text could have been more appropriate. Bernita, Christine, and I sat up most of the night helping Coretta polish and hone her sermon for that special occasion.

As our motorcade moved from our hotel to the cathedral, throngs of people lined the streets, hoping to get a glimpse of Coretta. Her performance on that historic occasion was impressive.

The next morning, Monday, we had tea with the wife of Prime Minister Harold Wilson at 10 Downing Street. While we were there, the prime minister stopped in briefly to greet us.

When we returned to Atlanta, Coretta's schedule continued to fill, so much so that even I was pressed into service, standing in for her at Crozer Seminary's graduation exercises. Martin had studied for three years there, receiving a Master of Divinity degree. His experience at Crozer helped shape his views of nonviolence and gave his preaching the deep theological content that later served the Movement well. I delivered the major address that day. After the address, the president announced that Martin's sons, Martin III and Dexter, were being offered scholarships to attend Crozer and that its Upland School of Social Change was being renamed the Martin Luther King Jr. School for Social Change.[2]

In July of 1969, I joined Coretta and her children along with A.D., Naomi, and their two younger children for a two-week vacation in Jamaica. We stayed at a house in the hills away from the tourists and the crowds that often came out to see Coretta. The house had a swimming pool and was staffed with a caretaker, housekeeper, and cook. Coretta thought it would be a restful trip and afford a chance to escape temporarily from her many responsibilities. However, it was not the experience we expected and was one that would have a tragic ending.

The climate in Jamaica in July and August was tropical, unlike during our previous trip in December. Coretta found the heat and humidity unbearable and was unable to function at all during the day. I developed a headache in the morning that lasted throughout the day. While the heat was debilitating for the adults, the children enjoyed the pool. A.D. entertained them and made sure they had a wonderful time. In the evenings, after the sun went down and the air cooled, we all enjoyed relaxing by the pool.

There was a tenderness about A.D. that endeared him to everyone, and we loved being in his presence. He and the children went to the pool early in the morning, and as we listened from our bedroom, his voice sounded exactly like Martin's. A.D.

stayed with us for only a week, then returned to Atlanta to attend a Women's Day Celebration at Ebenezer.

On the day we were scheduled to return to Atlanta, we arose early and began packing. As we were busy packing our suitcases, the telephone rang. Coretta answered the call. From what I overheard, it was clear that something had happened to A.D. Coretta seemed upset. After hanging up the phone, she said, "A.D. was found dead in his swimming pool this morning. Will you go tell Naomi?"

The thought of breaking the news to his wife was more than I could bear. "I just can't," I stammered.

Reluctantly, Coretta went to tell Naomi. Then we had to tell the children. The shock of A.D.'s death left us all dismayed. When we landed at the airport in Atlanta, the now all too familiar mood of tragedy enveloped us.

42

Coretta's Agenda

During the first part of 1970, Coretta was busy helping members of the King family cope with the loss of A.D. and dealing with her own grief. Martin and A.D. had been close and losing him so soon after Martin's death reopened wounds for Coretta that had only just begun to heal. Beginning in the spring, however, she resumed her usual activities.

In March, she spoke at an antidraft rally held in Pittsburgh. The event was sponsored by a hastily assembled Pittsburgh Peace Coalition. Coretta emphasized again her opposition to the Vietnam War and the effectiveness of nonviolent protest. Two months later, she showed up as a surprise speaker at an antiwar demonstration in Washington, D.C.

Later that year, we became involved in saving Lincoln School, which we had attended back in Marion, Alabama. Over the years since we had graduated, the American Missionary Association had phased out its funding for secondary education. When it ceased funding Lincoln School, the property was transferred to the county school board. At the time, rumors circulated that Lincoln was in financial trouble and its future uncertain.

In 1970, with integration at last coming to public schools in Alabama, Lincoln was closed. Students in the area, both black and white, attended Francis Marion High School, a new facility constructed for the purpose of combining the previously segregated schools.

The issue of what would happen to the buildings and the student records weighed on our minds. My friend Ritten Lee drafted a letter to the superintendent of schools,

Fred Hubbard, raising these issues. Ritten was especially concerned about the student records. Following up on this letter, in July, I called Superintendent Hubbard and asked for a conference. Idella Childs, a prominent woman in the local community, accompanied me to the meeting.

Superintendent Hubbard greeted us in a friendly, southern style. He was cordial and listened attentively to our concerns but had no answers to our questions. Particularly troubling to us were rumors that nearby Marion Military Institute might annex Lincoln's campus.

Coretta and I sought help from Movement leaders to salvage as much of Lincoln as possible. Randolph Blackwell, who had worked with Martin and had founded an organization called Southern Rural Action, was a strong supporter of the project. He suggested that Lincoln alumni develop a corporation, which would give us legitimacy and enable us to file a lawsuit if that became necessary. There was substantial evidence that at least part of the campus had been deeded to the AMA as a gift from a black man in the community with the stipulation that it was to be used for the education of blacks. Assuming that proved correct, we might be able to argue that legally the campus belonged to Marion's black community and consequently should be given back to us. Coretta and I sent letters to alumni informing them about the status of Lincoln. Many responded, sending financial contributions.

In an attempt to mobilize the black community in Perry County around the issue of saving Lincoln, Coretta and I held several meetings at which we distributed information regarding Lincoln's history. Even those who had not attended Lincoln School needed to know how important the school had been in the lives of black people, both in the state and nationwide. One of those meetings was held at Marion Baptist Academy. Another was conducted at Mt. Tabor Church. The meetings were well attended.

Albert Turner, president of Perry County Civic League, and Hampton D. Lee, a mortician, were both Lincoln graduates. They joined the struggle to save the school. Others did as well. We succeeded in raising sufficient funds to incorporate, and we established the Lincoln School Alumni Association. Though at that time it was little more than a file in our attorney's office, we were making progress.

As we continued in our search for ideas to save Lincoln, Randy Blackwell discovered that Daniel Payne College in Birmingham was interested in purchasing or renting the Lincoln property. If they could buy the property, they would relocate to Marion. For several reasons, we felt this was an idea we should pursue. Consequently, we requested a meeting with the Perry County Board of Education for the purpose of discussing this issue. Members of our group included Idella Childs, Albert

Turner, and Andrew Hayden. At the time, Hayden was serving as mayor of Union-town, a prominent Perry County community.

Fred Hubbard conducted the meeting in a professional manner, but the other members of the all-white board seemed smug and disinterested in our concerns. The session closed with the board taking our request under consideration. As we expected, the board later issued a statement refusing our request. But support for saving Lincoln continued to grow.

During the summer of 1971, approximately four hundred Lincoln alumni met in Fort Wayne, Indiana. Raising money to save Lincoln was our chief aim. Following that gathering, we had enough money to purchase the twenty-two acre square on which the campus had been built, saving Phillips Memorial Auditorium and the gymnasium. Many of us felt that when the county ceased to use the property as a school, it lost legal claim to it. However, pressing that point meant filing a lawsuit. Rather than litigate, we decided to negotiate and reached an agreement to purchase the property. Phillips Auditorium and the nearby Congregational church are now listed on the National Registry of Historic Places.

As a result of the rescue effort, alumni chapters were formed in a number of locations throughout the country. Ritten Lee and I compiled an alumni directory listing members of all graduating classes from 1880 to 1970, along with other pertinent information.

With the building and grounds safely preserved, the alumni raised funds to create a museum. The facility was opened to the general public on April 30, 2002. Local alumni along with faculty members from Judson College worked diligently to bring this project to fruition. Coretta raised a considerable sum of money for its construction. One of the donors she secured was Bishop T. D. Jakes, the son of Odith Patton, a member of the class of 1944.

In February 1971, Coretta embarked on a seven-country European trip promoting the international release of her book *My Life with Martin Luther King, Jr.* She took me and several others with her. During that tour, we traveled to England, Sweden, Germany, the Netherlands, Italy, Spain, and France. Coretta's schedule was filled with press conferences, radio interviews, and television appearances.

In Amsterdam, Coretta gave a Freedom Concert, her first in several years. Christine, Martin's sister, and I spoke at a school in Amsterdam that had been named for him. Students there were eager to hear firsthand accounts of Martin, the Movement, and all that he had accomplished. One of the greatest highlights of the trip came in Milan, Italy, where we enjoyed a production of Verdi's opera *Manon* from the Royal box at the La Scala Opera House.

On the last leg of the trip, we stopped in Paris where we visited Eunice Kennedy Shriver at the American Embassy. Her husband, Robert Sargent Shriver, was the American ambassador to France. He accompanied us back to the United States, sitting with Coretta on the plane.

That spring, SCLC joined with the National Peace Coalition and the People's Coalition for Peace and Justice in conducting a series of protest marches in Washington, D.C. Coretta attended a march there on May 9, and spoke at a rally on May 30, 1971.

Coretta remained on SCLC's board of directors, but most of her time was devoted to soliciting funds for the King Memorial Center and in her work with the Peace Movement and human rights organizations. In August, she attended the SCLC convention and spoke at the gathering. That year, the convention was held in New Orleans, the site where SCLC had been founded in 1957.

Coretta had spent much of the three years since Martin's death finishing his work and completing projects he had set in motion. She did that as an honor to him and the dream they shared together. As she worked through the remainder of his schedule, she also continued to address issues that she had cultivated on her own: international peace, the use of nonviolent protest for social change in other countries, and women's rights issues.

As she made her way forward, three issues came to occupy more and more of Coretta's attention. Of primary importance was the establishment of the Martin Luther King Jr. Center for Nonviolent Social Change. Almost as important was the creation of a national holiday honoring Martin's memory and the legacy of racial, economic, and social justice he had set in motion through nonviolent protest. Underlying both of those concerns was her continuing interest in international peace and the broader implications of the Civil Rights Movement. Those three issues would dominate the remainder of her life.

43

Building the King Center

Among the initial issues Coretta faced in establishing the King Center was the gathering of Martin's papers. At the time of his death, those papers were housed in several locations. Some were at Boston University where he had obtained his PhD. Others were in the archives at Crozer Theological Seminary, where he had attended seminary, and at Morehouse College, where he had received his undergraduate degree. He also had papers at his first pastorate, Dexter Avenue Baptist Church, in Montgomery. A large number were at Ebenezer Baptist Church in Atlanta and still others, collections of sermons and private papers, were in his study at home. Much of his correspondence after 1960 was included in the records of SCLC and a few significant documents were in the hands of private individuals and collectors.

As early as 1967, Coretta had convened a group of supporters to begin gathering Martin's papers for preservation at a central site in Atlanta. Once the center had obtained a permanent location, she expected to make those papers available for research as a historic archive of Martin's work, the Movement's development, and the effectiveness of nonviolence as a means of promoting social change.

The Martin Luther King Jr. Memorial Center was incorporated on June 26, 1968. Later, the name was changed to the Martin Luther King Jr. Center for Social Change and finally to the name it has today, the Martin Luther King Jr. Center for Nonviolent Social Change. Coretta served as its inaugural president and chief executive officer. The center began operations in the basement of her home. As fund-raising and other work expanded, the offices were relocated to the Interdenominational Theological Center, part of the Atlanta University Center.[1]

Ongoing efforts to collect Martin's papers became known as the Library Documentation Project. A grant from the Ford Foundation helped make that possible. The grant also provided funds for an oral history project, which was developed in conjunction with the library. We were able to begin recording and electronically preserving the memories of many who had been on the frontlines of civil rights protests in the 1950s and 1960s.

In 1974, while still housed in temporary offices, the center began a Scholars-Internship Program aimed at attracting students interested in studying the Civil Rights Movement. Coretta saw it as a way of furthering their education while teaching them the history of the Movement. She was determined that subsequent generations know and appreciate the sacrifices that had been made to give the rising generation of African Americans new and better opportunities. The program was initially directed by Sister Ann Brotherton, a Catholic nun with a keen interest in continuing the work of the Civil Rights Movement and a passion for conveying to others the Movement's teachings. Through her work, college students spent the summer studying at the center where they participated in a fully accredited college program. They learned about the history of the Civil Rights Movement and the use of nonviolence from Coretta and others who had been close associates of Martin. The internship program became one of the center's most popular programs.

Two years later, the center established a learning center for preschool children. Modeled after programs that had been successful in other urban environments, it provided meals, education, recreation, family counseling, and nonviolence education for thousands of preschool children. That same year, a reading academy opened to help Atlanta citizens of all ages learn to read. Literacy programs would become a key component in the center's overall work. Several years earlier, the American Library Association had established the Coretta Scott King Award for African American writers and illustrators. At every opportunity, Coretta continued to promote the arts as a means of changing lives by changing the hearts of individuals.

In August 1976, the center conducted its first Institute on Nonviolence. Offered to a limited audience of one hundred carefully selected African American leaders, the five-day event included workshops and classes on nonviolent social reform. Participants came from diverse organizations like the United Farm Workers, the Southern Rural Action Project, and the National Education Association. Noted activists Fannie Lou Hamer and the Reverend C. T. Vivian were also in attendance.

Institutes of this nature were not uncommon. A number of organizations had conducted similar programs. Martin and the Montgomery Improvement Association had held their first institute in 1956. The MIA continued that tradition long after Coretta and Martin moved to Atlanta.

SCLC had held its own institutes as well. As early as 1971, the center had held similar conferences on an occasional basis. However, as Coretta continued to develop and expand the King Center and its programs, she expanded the institute concept to include inner-city gang leaders and used the gathering to educate leaders from the street in ways to effect change without resorting to violence. Veteran civil rights activists like James Orange and Dorothy Cotton trained alongside Coretta and Christine King Farris in workshops designed to provide practical, hands-on experience. The institute became a highly successful annual event, training leaders of recognized social organizations, educators, and gang leaders in effective ways of protest that offered the potential for real and lasting change.

The following year, 1977, Martin's permanent crypt, the reflecting pool, the Freedom Walkway, and the chapel building were completed on a twenty-three acre site in the Sweet Auburn section of Atlanta, an area that included Ebenezer Baptist Church and the surrounding neighborhood. That same year, the center launched its Cultural Affairs Program.

In many ways an extension of Coretta's commitment to the use of the arts as a means of change, the center's cultural program included a Nonviolent Film Festival, original theatre productions, a children's theatre, King Week, and Kingfest—a series of summer musical and cultural performances offered free to the public. The Trumpet of Conscience Award was established to recognize artists who consistently demonstrated personal and professional commitments to the goals Martin espoused. Subsequent winners included Stevie Wonder, Harry Belafonte, Tony Bennett, and Dick Gregory, among others. Benefit concerts were held during King Week, the week of the Martin Luther King Jr. Holiday. Guest artists included Marvin Gaye, a long list of Motown stars, the Neville Brothers, and later U-2, to mention a few.[2]

President Jimmy Carter hosted a White House event in 1978, kicking off the center's campaign to raise money for construction of the Freedom Hall Complex. The Carter administration's support proved vital to the success of that venture. In conjunction with the kickoff event, Coretta sang a Freedom Concert at the White House.

Construction was completed in 1981 on the final buildings of the center's original design. Design, fund-raising, and construction had been a monumental task, but with the assistance of her staff, Coretta put all the pieces together in exemplary fashion. With the buildings in place, Martin's papers were transferred to the center. The library and archives opened to the public that year. As a result of Coretta's efforts to gather Martin's papers, the center holds the world's largest collection of primary source materials relating to his life and the Civil Rights Movement.

The following year, Coretta began preparation for a celebration of the twentieth anniversary of the 1963 March on Washington. That event was held on August 27, 1983. With the help of the Coalition of Conscience—a cooperative group of human rights organizations—the celebration marked the largest gathering of nonviolent organizations in history.

To make Martin's papers accessible to the broadest audience possible, Coretta asked Stanford University history professor Clayborne Carson to edit and compile them into publishable volumes. In conjunction with that, Stanford created the Martin Luther King Jr. Research and Education Institute. Work on the papers began in 1984.

With the establishment of the King Center, Coretta succeeded in creating an institution that preserved the record of Martin's work and defined for future generations his stance on social and economic justice. Not content with merely establishing a record of distant memories, the center's nonviolence programs provided the next generation access to an effective means of continuing the momentum for change Martin set in motion. Many of those programs have spun off to other organizations, and some, like the programs on nonviolence, have been effective in locations around the world.

44

Sweet Auburn and the Historic Site

At the end of the Civil War, the section of Atlanta that lay east of downtown, between Peachtree Street and what is now the Old Fourth Ward, was home to a thriving community of African Americans. During Reconstruction, the community continued to expand as newly freed blacks established homes there. By 1900, Auburn Avenue, which traversed the community, had become the heart of an upwardly mobile black neighborhood. Known in its heyday as Sweet Auburn, it extended from Irwin Street on the east side almost to Peachtree Street on the west and was home to a diverse community that included laborers, professionals, and some of the nation's most prosperous African Americans. It was home to a vast array of successful black leaders and black-owned businesses. Men like John Wesley Dobbs, Alonzo Herndon, and A. D. Williams, Martin's maternal grandfather, ruled the street with benevolence, pride, and dignity. At the time Martin was born, in 1929, Auburn Avenue was known as the "wealthiest black street in America."[1]

Auburn was home to a community as diverse as any in the nation. Atlanta Life Insurance Company, one of the largest black-owned businesses in the nation, had its headquarters there. The Top Hat, which later became the Royal Peacock Club, offered shows featuring the best African American entertainers in the nation. The *Atlanta Daily World,* the world's first black daily newspaper, was published there. Big Bethel AME Church, First Congregational Church, Wheat Street Baptist Church, and Ebenezer Baptist Church anchored the community. For blacks in Atlanta, it was the place to be, and it was one of the strongest black communities in America.

Even after Coretta and Martin moved to Atlanta in 1960, Auburn remained a strong and vibrant center of black life. Ebenezer Baptist Church had a large and active congregation as did other churches up and down the avenue. Businesses were viable. A strong middle class still occupied the surrounding homes. But as time moved on, the community began to deteriorate. By the 1970s, the Civil Rights Movement had successfully put an end to housing discrimination. Upwardly mobile blacks moved out of the old neighborhood to find homes in other sections of Atlanta. As a result, houses along Auburn Avenue stood empty. Businesses closed, and buildings were boarded up. As Coretta began working to establish the King Center, many of the older buildings along Auburn Avenue had been demolished, and more were scheduled for destruction. Even the home where Martin had been born had fallen into disrepair.

There was never any doubt Coretta would locate the King Center in the Auburn community, but the center she envisioned would stand in stark contrast to what the neighborhood had become. If her dreams for the center were realized, international leaders and serious-minded scholars would come there to attend functions, conduct research, and teach the next generation about the use of nonviolent protest in the fight for freedom. Thousands of visitors would flock to the area to see the community that had produced Martin Luther King Jr., but the community along Auburn Avenue in the 1970s was nothing like the community in which Martin had grown up. For the King Center to be the kind of place Coretta envisioned, the surrounding community would have to recapture some of its illustrious image.

Coretta took the first step toward revitalizing Sweet Auburn when she lobbied to have it placed on the National Register of Historic Places. She achieved that goal in 1974 when the area immediately adjacent to the center, including Ebenezer Baptist Church and Martin's birthplace, was added to the register. Later, in 1976, a larger portion of the Auburn community was included. Doing that established control over redevelopment efforts and halted further demolition.

For the next six years, Coretta worked to find funding to redevelop the community. In conjunction with that, she lobbied Congress for a bill establishing the area as a national historic site. When Jimmy Carter, a native Georgian, was elected president, Coretta sought his assistance for the effort.

In 1980, with President Carter's help and Coretta's tireless lobbying efforts, Congress passed legislation establishing the Martin Luther King Jr. Historic District, which encompassed a larger area, and the Martin Luther King Jr. National Historic Site, which included a smaller area in and around the King Center. With that legislation, the National Park Service took control of the Ebenezer Church site, the house where Martin was born, and the area immediately surrounding the King Center. In the ensuing years, federal funds were allocated to renovate the church.

Working outward from the King Historic Site, community leaders and other interested citizens made plans for renovation of the area along Auburn Avenue. Coretta's work to save the core buildings there—Ebenezer, the King home, the building that once housed SCLC's offices and the *Atlanta Daily World*—became the catalyst for revitalization of the entire community. With the help of President Carter, Christine Farris, and Representative John Lewis, the community began to regain some of the luster it had once known.

45

The United Nations and Apartheid

Since her days at Lincoln School, and even before then, Coretta's ideas and convictions about social responsibility had been steadily growing. Issues regarding basic human rights—the notion that each of us has been created by God and endowed with value as limitless as the Creator himself—slowly developed in her mind, forming first a social conscience, then a calling, and finally maturing into a life's work. As that social conscience developed, she became painfully aware of the pervasive civil and economic injustice in the United States and abroad. Protecting and ensuring the personal worth and dignity of every human being, regardless of race, occupied more and more of her thoughts, time, and energy.

Working alongside Martin in the Civil Rights Movement then with Women Strike for Peace and the antiwar movement, as well as traveling abroad, opened Coretta's eyes to the full implications of what she and Martin had experienced in Montgomery, Birmingham, Selma, and the other cities where they had worked. After Martin's death, the international implications of the basic tenets they had embraced in the Civil Rights Movement became increasingly important to her. Apartheid in South Africa and economic injustice across the African continent troubled her deeply. Her concern over the treatment of women, always an issue for her regarding the United States, developed an international dimension. In 1977, after a lifetime of addressing those issues as a private citizen and social activist, she had the opportunity to turn the spotlight on those issues in the world's largest international forum.

In September of that year, President Carter appointed Coretta as one of the United States' four representatives to the thirty-second session of the United Nations General Assembly.[1] The session lasted the final three months of the year. Coretta was delighted by the opportunity and was determined to make the most of her position. To do that, she stepped away from the daily work of developing the King Center and devoted her attention to her duties at the UN. She rented an apartment in New York for the fall and moved there to work full-time.

From opening day in September until the end of the general session in December, Coretta worked hard, pursuing the broader ramifications of issues to which she had devoted her life. She participated in international negotiations on those issues and attended General Assembly sessions at which those topics were addressed.[2] In addition, her position at the UN gave her unique access to some of the world's leading figures and allowed her to participate in historic international decisions and events.

On September 20, she witnessed the passage of a resolution admitting the Socialist Republic of Vietnam to membership in the United Nations. Since the time of her first involvement with Women Strike for Peace in 1962, international peace had been an issue close to Coretta's heart. Involvement with that issue had led her to oppose the war in Vietnam, a cause to which both she and Martin devoted considerable attention during the last two years of Martin's life. With the war now over, seeing Vietnam admitted to the United Nations brought her full circle and was vindication of her work for justice in Southeast Asia.

On November 7, the General Assembly turned its attention to Africa and adopted multiple resolutions reaffirming its earlier commitment to end "racism, racial discrimination and apartheid."[3] At the same time, the UN Security Council passed a resolution imposing an arms embargo on South Africa in a further effort to pressure South Africa to end its oppressive racial policies. For Coretta, opposition to apartheid was a logical extension of her opposition to racism and government-enforced segregation in the United States. She spent much of that General Session lobbying for tougher sanctions against South Africa, including a full economic boycott.[4]

In addition to official assembly sessions and negotiations, working at the UN afforded Coretta an opportunity to meet international leaders at numerous social events. One of those was a dinner at the Waldorf-Astoria Hotel hosted by Andrew Young, the US ambassador to the UN. The event was held in honor of Olusegun Obasanjo, president of Nigeria. In his address that evening, Obasanjo announced that his country would no longer conduct business with companies that maintained ties with South Africa. Coretta supported the position and encouraged other nations to follow suit. Establishing ties between African American business leaders and their African counterparts would be an issue to which she would return several years later. That social event and others like it also enabled Coretta to establish relationships with African leaders that would open doors for expansion of the King

Center's work, taking it to an international level and placing her in the forefront of developments on the African continent.

Addressing issues that pertained to Africa brought Coretta in contact with Ruth Schachter Morgenthau, the US representative to the UN Commission for Social Development.[5] Ruth was born in Vienna, Austria, and immigrated to the United States during World War II. In 1977 she was the Adlai Stevenson Professor of International Politics at Brandeis University. During the Carter Administration, she helped shape US policy on Africa. Through her, Coretta gained invaluable insights into the nature of the difficulties confronting African nations. Coretta formed a friendship with Morgenthau that lasted the remainder of their lives.

Later that month, from November 18 to 21, Coretta traveled to Houston, Texas, where she participated in the National Women's Conference, which was part of the International Women's Year proceedings. Rosalynn Carter, Betty Ford, and Lady Bird Johnson also attended. The conference was chaired by Bella Abzug. Women's issues had been a key component in Coretta's drive to extend the Civil Rights Movement's quest for justice and freedom to all people.

Following the conference in Houston, Coretta returned to New York. My son, Arturo, and I visited her there for Thanksgiving weekend. On Thanksgiving Day, we accompanied her to Hyde Park, New York, where we were dinner guests of Ruth Morgenthau and her family.

In December, the UN's attention turned to nuclear arms, disarmament, and efforts to halt proliferation of nuclear weapons. Coretta's first involvement in the peace movement had been as a delegate from Women Strike for Peace to the 1962 disarmament conference in Geneva, Switzerland. At that conference she had lobbied both US and Soviet representatives to reach agreement on what became known as the Limited Test Ban Treaty. Returning to that issue once again, some fifteen years later, brought her back to an issue that had marked her first public acknowledgement of the broader implications of the Civil Rights Movement's quest for justice and freedom through the use of nonviolent protest.

After completion of her term at the United Nations, Coretta continued to press for an end to South African apartheid. In 1985, she lobbied Congress for passage of the Anti-Apartheid Act and added her feet to her voice by protesting against apartheid outside the South African Embassy. Joined by two of her children, Martin and Bernice, she was arrested during that protest.

The following year, Coretta hosted Bishop Desmond Tutu at Ebenezer Baptist Church. Later, she took members of the King Center board of directors on a fact-finding mission to South Africa to determine practical ways the King Center could be helpful in the struggle against apartheid. They were present when the Reverend Tutu was installed as archbishop of Cape Town. During that trip, Coretta met with Winnie Mandela, wife of imprisoned antiapartheid leader Nelson Mandela. Both women had joined their husbands in a struggle against racial prejudice and hatred and had endured the hardships associated with that fight. Their mutual experiences helped form the basis of a lasting friendship, one that endured many more challenges.

In 1991, as international pressure mounted, Nelson Mandela was released from prison. A few months later, he and Winnie toured the United States. Coretta and the King Center hosted them for a stop in Atlanta where they toured the center and greeted a crowd of well-wishers at Martin's crypt. Later, after apartheid was abolished, the King Center received a USAID grant to conduct training in South Africa on the use of nonviolence as a catalyst for change. The center also conducted voter registration and voter education drives prior to South Africa's first free democratic election. That election brought Nelson Mandela to office as president. Coretta watched the results with great anticipation, then traveled to Pretoria where she attended the presidential inauguration.

Coretta continued to devote considerable energy to cause of Africa. While she worked to help end apartheid in South Africa, she also participated in much broader efforts to assist the entire continent. In 1991, that effort took her to the inaugural African–African American Summit held in Ivory Coast. Conceived by Leon Sullivan, a Baptist minister and civil rights activist from Philadelphia, the summit was designed to facilitate business and cultural relationships between African Americans and Africans.[6] Through that, Sullivan hoped to assist African companies in establishing businesses, while encouraging awareness among African Americans of the true nature and responsibilities of their African heritage. A second summit, which Coretta also attended, was held in 1993 at Libreville, Gabon.

46

The Holiday

While Coretta worked to fund and build the King Center, she also lobbied hard for a national day honoring Martin and his work. Doing that required special legislation from Congress. Either of those projects—establishing the center or obtaining a federal holiday designation—would have marked a lifetime achievement. Coretta tackled both at the same time.

To some in America, the notion of designating a federal holiday in Martin's honor seemed pretentious and unwarranted. For Coretta it was essential, not just as an acknowledgement of Martin and his life's work, but as validation of the claims raised by the Movement and those who had marched, protested, and died for the cause of civil rights. Until then, the only official national holiday honoring an individual was the one marking George Washington's birthday. At the time it was established, a day in honor of the father of our country seemed necessary and appropriate. Washington had been an essential figure in creating a nation dedicated to freedom and equality. Yet, from the beginning of the nation's founding, it had fallen short of those ideals in its treatment of nonwhites. Washington, a slaveholder, recognized the inhumanity of slavery, providing for his slaves to be freed upon his wife's death, but he had not moved to end the institution when he helped create the nation. Establishing a day to remember the man and the Movement that brought an end to the legal segregation that had emerged as a part of slavery's legacy, thus bringing America closer to achieving its most cherished ideals, seemed not only fitting, but an honor demanded by the very nature of his cause.

Four days after Martin was assassinated, Representative John Conyers, a Democrat from Michigan, introduced a bill in Congress to establish a Martin Luther King

Jr. federal holiday. Later, in 1970, Conyers and Shirley Chisholm, a Democratic representative from New York, presented a petition to Congress bearing six million signatures in support of the legislation. The following year, three million additional names were gathered by SCLC. Despite overwhelming public support, Conyer's bill failed to survive the committee process.

Although Congress was reluctant to act, individual states proved more responsive. Between 1973 and 1975 four states—Illinois, Massachusetts, New Jersey, and Connecticut—established holidays honoring Martin. Religious and civic organizations came forward with their support, also. In November 1978, the National Council of Churches added its voice in favor of the holiday.

To gain renewed congressional attention, Coretta organized a nationwide citizen's lobby in support of a King holiday designation. In conjunction with that effort, the King Center launched a petition campaign that collected more than three hundred thousand signatures. Finally, with President Carter urging Congress to act, legislation began to move through the committee process.

Once more, public attention was focused on the issue. To maintain the growing momentum, Coretta wrote to governors, mayors, and city councils across the country asking them to pass resolutions and issue proclamations commemorating Martin's birthday. She also encouraged them to organize celebrations and programs in his honor.

Coretta worked tirelessly and used every means possible to keep the holiday issue alive and moving forward. She gave speeches, wrote letters, and made phone calls. She wined, dined, and cajoled anyone she thought could help. In 1982, she reached beyond requests for individual support and mobilized a coalition of one hundred organizations that lobbied Congress for the holiday designation. Stevie Wonder funded an office for that purpose in Washington, D.C., and provided a staff at his own expense.

Finally, in August 1983, the House of Representatives passed the King Holiday Bill, establishing a holiday in Martin's honor to be observed on the third Monday of each January. The bill was sponsored by Representatives Katie Hall, a Democrat from Indiana, and Jack Kemp, a Republican from New York. Senator Ted Kennedy of Massachusetts was the sponsor in the Senate. Senate approval was obtained on August 19. That November, with Coretta looking on, President Ronald Reagan signed the legislation into law. Arthur and I, Coretta's children, and other members of the King family joined them for that ceremony. Vice President and Mrs. George H. W. Bush were there as well and gave us a genuinely gracious and warm reception.

The following April, in anticipation of the first Martin Luther King Jr. federal holiday, Coretta asked Congress to establish a holiday commission that would work to promote observance of the day. With little opposition, the necessary legislation passed both houses on a voice vote. President Reagan signed the legislation into law on August 27, 1984.

In November 1984, the holiday commission held its first meeting at which Coretta was elected chairwoman. Lloyd Davis, a HUD senior executive, served as executive director. The commission began its work with private money secured through the efforts of Senate Majority Leader Robert Dole and Edward Jefferson, Chairman of the Board of Directors of the DuPont Company. Congress later authorized an annual appropriation for its support.

On January 20, 1986, after two years of planning and almost twenty years of waiting, the first Martin Luther King Jr. Holiday was officially celebrated. The holiday theme that year was "Living the Dream: Let Freedom Ring."

Subsequent presidents have supported continuing growth and development of the King Holiday with a much larger emphasis than merely the celebration of Martin's life or the cause of civil rights. President George H. W. Bush insured that development by extending the life of the Martin Luther King Jr. Federal Holiday Commission beyond its original expiration date.

President Clinton later signed legislation expanding the mission of the holiday to include a day of community service, interracial cooperation, and youth antiviolence initiatives. That bill was signed in a special White House ceremony that included Senator Harris Wofford of Pennsylvania and Representative John Lewis of Georgia. Both men had played major roles in the Civil Rights Movement. Clinton's expansion of the holiday's purposes created an official working relationship between the King Holiday Commission and the Corporation for National Service, the nation's volunteer service organization. With that authorization, the corporation was permitted to make planning and implementation grants for community service activities in conjunction with the King Holiday.

Writing about the meaning of the Martin Luther King Jr. Holiday, Coretta said, "The Martin Luther King Jr. Holiday celebrates the life and legacy of a man who brought hope and healing to America. We commemorate as well the timeless values he taught us through his example—the values of courage, truth, justice, compassion, dignity, humility and service that so radiantly defined [his] character and empowered his leadership. On this holiday, we commemorate the universal, unconditional love, forgiveness and nonviolence that empowered his revolutionary spirit."[1]

47

Coretta and Atlanta's Creative Community

Two of the most distinguished awards Coretta received during her lifetime honored her contributions to the enrichment of American life and culture. The first of those came from Antioch College.

On Friday, June 21, 2004, the Antioch College Alumni Association presented Coretta with the Horace Mann Award, which honors individuals who have won victories for humanity. The citation read, "As one of the most influential women leaders in the world, you have become an international icon for your determination to promote nonviolent social change. In doing so, you have brought distinction to yourself and to your alma mater. Horace Mann would be extremely proud of you for your victories for humanity."[1]

The following year, Coretta was the recipient of the Heroes Award, presented by the Atlanta Chapter of the National Academy of Recording Arts and Sciences. That award honored her for work to improve Atlanta's creative community.

During segregation, when the Metropolitan Opera toured southern cities, tickets were not available to black patrons unless they obtained them from their white friends. This was the practice throughout the South. Shortly after Coretta and Martin moved to Atlanta in 1960, Coretta worked to change that practice. Through Rudolph Bing, tour manager for the Met, distribution of tickets for the Metropolitan Opera's appearances in Atlanta became available to all races. The operas were held at the historic Fox Theatre.

The Fox Theatre had an illustrious history as a film and performing arts center. However, as an arts institution, it often teetered on the edge of financial collapse.

By the 1970s, it had fallen on hard times. Developers wanted to demolish it, along with the hotel across the street, to make room for a high-rise office complex.

The original building was constructed as a Yaarab Temple Shrine. Designed in the late 1920s, it served as headquarters for the Shriners organization. When the Great Depression reached Atlanta, the Shriners struggled to survive. Consequently, they could no longer afford the upkeep on the building. To generate income for their organization, they transferred the building to movie mogul William Fox, who was building motion picture theaters in major cities around the country. With a few alterations, the Shriners temple became one of Fox's jewels.

In the summer of 1973, two ladies came to Coretta's office to ask for her help in saving the Fox. Coretta was upstairs resting, so they were sent to see me. Listening to an explanation of the potential fate for that historic landmark and seeing the excitement on the faces of the ladies as they explained it to me, I became enthralled with the idea of rescuing the theatre. I left them seated in the office and went upstairs to see Coretta.

At first, Coretta was reluctant to get involved in the theatre's restoration. That year, 1973, was a busy time for her. She was heavily involved with establishing the King Center and in lobbying Congress and individual states to create a Martin Luther King Jr. holiday. As I explained to her how preserving historic theatres was as crucial to American culture as preserving Lincoln School, she graciously agreed to lend her name to the Fox Theatre restoration effort. I returned to my desk downstairs and composed a letter expressing Coretta's support.

A few days later, the letter was published in Celestine Sibley's column in the *Atlanta Journal-Constitution*. The newspaper was widely circulated and Sibley's column was quite popular. Coretta's letter caught the public's attention and lifted the project from a local issue to one that sparked interest across the region.

In 1976, Landmarks, Inc., was formed as a nonprofit organization for the purpose of acquiring the Fox Theatre. With the help of local residents, Landmarks launched a successful four-year campaign to "Save the Fox." Individual and corporate donors made substantial contributions. Their efforts enabled Landmarks to save the building and put the Fox on sound financial footing as a multipurpose performing arts center. A subsequent campaign in 1987 restored it to its original grandeur.

✿

Coretta was also involved in the development of the Atlanta Children's Theatre. In the 1960s, Walter and Betty Roberts moved to Atlanta and founded Atlanta's first children's theatre.[2] Soon after their arrival, they paid Coretta a visit to discuss their mission. Their timing could not have been better.

Before the Robertses arrived in Atlanta, Coretta had taken her oldest daughter, Yolanda, to see an opera. After watching the performance, Yolanda announced that she wanted to work onstage. When Coretta responded with comments about doing that when she grew up, Yolanda insisted, "I want to do it *now*."

Not long after that, the Roberts came to Atlanta with the idea of organizing a children's theatre. Coretta was more than ready to help and quickly became their chief benefactor. Working with Atlanta Children's Theatre, Yolanda performed on stage from childhood through her high school years. Though often operating on a meager budget, the group's productions were of exceptional quality.[3]

Yolanda's experiences with Atlanta Children's Theatre formed the foundation of her theatre training. She learned much during those years and went on to make theatre her career. She performed in many locations and venues throughout the country, including the John F. Kennedy Center for Performing Arts, and around the world. Her one-woman show was a poignant, compelling piece of social and political drama. What she did in that show began with the training she received as a young girl.

48

Coretta

Traditional African thought made no distinction between secular and sacred. Because God created everything, everything was sacred. It was a culture and worldview that incorporated all aspects of life—pain and ecstasy, suffering and joy—without the sacred/secular dichotomy prevalent in Western thought. That perspective gave African culture what Lerone Bennett once described as, "a certain dark joy."[1]

When Africans were brought to this country against their will, chained together and packed in ships under miserable conditions, they did as they had done in the past. They folded the pain and sorrow of their experience into the fabric of their culture. The sacrilege of enslavement melded with the sacredness of their lives.

As Africans in America struggled against slavery and segregation, that blend of misery and beauty, sacred and secular, Saturday night and Sunday morning, became a seedbed for new and vibrant art forms: haunting and melodic blues, complex and unassimilated jazz, searching and mystical spirituals. African Americans found release from pain and suffering through music, dance, and worship, one moment crying out, "I'm so glad trouble don't last always," and the next swinging across the floor to a lively beat. The sacred and secular were intertwined, with hardly a note between them. Coretta was very much a child of that culture.

Although in public she often appeared serious and cerebral, Coretta had a lighter side that she readily shared with relatives and close friends. She enjoyed giving parties and took particular delight in bringing people together in a relaxed atmosphere. Often those parties were the means by which her friends established new relationships that opened doors of opportunity in their lives.

Coretta had many friends, cultivated over many years, and she worked hard to keep those friendships alive. Some of her best friends were also mentors with whom she enjoyed relationships that spanned most of her life. Among them were Olive Williams, Frances Thomas, Jessie Treichler, Walter Anderson, Christina Lawson, and Bertha Wormley.[2] She shared a common bond with Myrlie Evers-Williams and Betty Shabazz, who were also widows of civil rights martyrs.[3] And she enjoyed a particularly fun relationship with Maya Angelou, playing word games and laughing on the phone until late into the night. More than mere friends, these were Coretta's extended family. The strength she received from them enabled her to endure the many trials she faced.

Aside from being a devoted friend, Coretta was an attentive daughter, daughter-in-law, sister, and aunt. She was as diligent in maintaining family relationships as she was with friendships. Her door was always open to cousins and other relatives who might stop by, and many did.[4]

Throughout much of her adult life, Coretta was defined by the public through her marriage to Martin. However, she lived thirty-eight years after he died. During the years following his death, she poured her heart and soul into pursuing the cause of economic and social justice and the promotion of nonviolent means to achieve that end. Some have seen that merely as a continuation of Martin's mission and Martin's ideals. It was much more than that.

The ideals to which Coretta devoted her life were handed down to her through the sermons we heard on Sunday and the lives we saw around us every day of our childhood. Those ideals were modeled through the lifestyle of our parents and other African Americans in the corner of Perry County where we lived as children. Later, she encountered those same ideals in our teachers at Lincoln School and saw them lived by our professors at Antioch College. Martin's life was but a greater example of the principles and ideals with which she had long been acquainted. In building the King Center and promoting the King Holiday, she was not simply building a monument to a man. She was promoting the ideas to which they both had given their lives.

Coretta's commitment to the cause of economic and social justice was made long before she met Martin. Her devotion to that cause was forged in the fire that burned our father's sawmill to the ground and was tempered by teachers and professors at Lincoln School and Antioch College who themselves were steeped in the ethos of the American Missionary Movement.

In many ways, Coretta was ahead of Martin. While he concentrated on the details necessary for conducting protests in cities like Birmingham and Selma, she had already recognized the inherent incongruity between supporting nonviolent change in the United States and supporting the US government's use of military force to impose change on foreign countries. And, while Martin and others were focused on using politics to win control of the government to effect change, she realized that real and lasting change required a conversion of individual hearts and minds. For that, one needed to utilize the arts.

Coretta's interest in using the arts to convey the message of the Civil Rights Movement was a timely one. The Civil Rights Movement coincided with other upheavals of American culture. One of those was the protest against the war in Vietnam. That antiwar protest movement was enmeshed in music. Leaders of the antiwar movement used music to convey a powerful message, one that was emotionally evocative and life changing. Coretta, in emphasizing the music of the Civil Rights Movement, showcased artistic expression that came from the souls of African Americans and spoke to the soul of the entire nation.

When she died on January 30, 2006, Coretta was a few months shy of her seventy-ninth birthday. Her last years had been a physical struggle. Though many in our family lived much longer, her body was used up and spent after years of travel and service to others. Some people live their lives constantly reinventing themselves, changing from one thing to the next, reaching the end of their lives as beings completely different from the people they were in the beginning. Coretta was pretty much the same all her life.

Sometimes when I think of her, I see her as a little girl singing and reciting poetry at a function back at Crossroads School. She would stand up before a packed audience and recite a poem or give a dramatic reading as if she had written the piece herself, confident and filled with assurance. Then a few minutes later she would sing a song with the composure of someone many times her age. The Freedom Concerts she gave as an adult followed that same pattern.

Other times I think of the afternoon when she stood up for me, defending me against the Tubbs boys on our way home from school. She was not even half their size, but she never thought twice about stepping in front of me and demanding that they leave me alone. It was a pattern that she followed all her life. She never hesitated to stand up for those in need, even if doing so meant risking her own safety.

As children, we regularly attended church services on Sunday. We heard sermons on almost every text in the Bible. On more than one occasion we heard the words of Jesus when He said, "Those of you who aspire to greatness must be the servant of all." Those words found fertile soil in Coretta's heart, a soil that had been tilled and prepared by a rich heritage handed down by our forebears from generation to generation. Nurtured and watered, those words took root in Coretta and grew into a life spent delivering good news to the poor, liberty to the captives, release to the oppressed, and sight to the blind. I have no doubt that as breath slipped from her lungs for the last time, she heard the voice of God once more, whispering to her those words we all long to hear, "Well done, my good and faithful servant."

Afterword

It was around 8 a.m. on Saturday June 11, 2011, my phone rang, waking me. I turned to look at the caller ID. It was my cousin Arturo calling with the dreaded news I had been expecting to receive any day. I wasn't quite alert enough to receive the news, so I didn't answer the call but let it go to the voicemail. I knew he was calling to tell me that his mom, my aunt Edythe, had passed. I pulled myself together and braced myself to hear those words. I called my best friend, DeLeice Drane, who connected Pat Latimore—my mother's personal assistant for many years who now works with me and is like family—for support. I then added Arturo on to the call, and he stated, "My mom died this morning around 7:00 a.m." I remember being silent for a moment while I took in the reality that my aunt Edythe was gone and that I would no longer have those periodic calls where she would share her wealth of wisdom, encouragement, assessment of things in the world and knowledge of our family history with me. She was my one and only aunt on my mother's side of the family, and I had come to rely on her presence. The very anticipation of the void her death would leave in my life weighed heavily on my heart. However, I was comforted by the fact that just a few weeks prior, I was able to help her achieve her forty-five-year mission to complete her biography on the life and legacy of my mother, Coretta Scott King. It was shortly after my sister, Yolanda, passed in 2007 that Aunt Edythe mentioned to me that she started working on a book about my mother's life in the late sixties that was interrupted due to my dad's assassination in 1968. She was encouraged by my mother in the spring of 2004 to finish writing the book. After sharing with me that she was close to completing the manuscript but needed some additional information about mother and her work with the King Center, I encouraged her to reach out to

Steve Klein at the King Center. I soon realized simply aiding her in information gathering wasn't enough. After reading the initial manuscript, I was moved by how my aunt captured the essence of my mother. She provided an insightful look into the life of the woman who walked with my father. I knew the world needed to see Coretta Scott King through the eyes of her sister; therefore, I offered to assist her in getting her book published. She was ecstatic about the offer, so I immediately went to work.

In 2008, I reached out to an agent I knew and had previously worked with and sent him a copy of the manuscript. Being a drama/theatre professor, I knew that Aunt Edythe had written an exemplary manuscript, and I had every confidence it would ultimately get published. The agent agreed to work with me to get it published, but he suggested that the manuscript needed a few finishing touches from a bestselling author to enhance what Aunt Edythe had written. When I presented the idea to my aunt she was open to working with someone, but she initially felt that it needed to be someone black who understood the history and background of the Modern Civil Rights Movement. When I discovered that the person chosen by the agent was white, I knew I would have to make my case to Aunt Edythe. Fortunately, Joe Hilley was from Alabama where many of the milestones of the Movement occurred, and he grew up in the fifties and sixties when segregation was the law in the South. After giving Aunt Edythe information on Hilley's background, she requested that Mr. Hilley call her at 7 a.m. Eastern Standard Time, which was 6 a.m. his time, for their initial conversation. All went well. I sent an electronic copy of the manuscript to Hilley, and they soon began their journey together to enhance the manuscript. Aunt Edythe shared with me that it initially took several conversations with Joe to get him properly oriented to her and Coretta's upbringing as blacks in Perry County as well as the King legacy. She felt this knowledge was essential if Hilley was going to enhance the manuscript and to keep the story organic and authentic. Once their rapport was established, it took a few months for Hilley to add his enhancements to what was already a classic from my perspective.

With a completed manuscript in hand by the end of 2008, finding a publisher proved more challenging because of the economy and, to my dismay, the inclination of publishers to favor sensationalism over substance. Aunt Edythe kept reminding me how imperative it was to get the manuscript published. In fact, there was such urgency on her part that she reached out to family friend Bob Green, who was a former college dean, to assist us in finding a publisher. She felt that maybe a university press would publish it since it was more of a historical document. Uncle Bob, as I called him, recommended me to a friend of his who had been in the publishing industry for over thirty years. After reviewing the manuscript, he, too, suggested adding some type of sensationalism to make the manuscript more appealing. I finally mentioned to Aunt Edythe the type of responses I continued to get, and she agreed with me that one way or another it would get published because her manuscript told an important story that needed to be shared. We put it in the hands of God, and I stopped actively pursuing a publishing deal. This was around the spring of 2010, which was followed by a seemingly long summer, fall, and winter. From time to time, though, Aunt Edythe would remind me of the importance of getting the book published. The urgency in her voice resonated with me, especially as her health began to decline in the fall of 2010. I remained restless in my spirit, hoping and praying that a way would be found to get her book on my mother's life published. I was also conscious of the fact that there had been no biography of this caliber on my mother, and I felt it apropos that her sister's book be the first official biography.

As spring 2011 emerged from a desolate winter, a bright light shone forth in my mind: The University of Alabama Press. I happened to be driving down the highway when the thought first entered my mind. I soon realized that it was more than a thought: it was a revelation and the long-awaited answer to our prayer. I reached out to a long-time family friend in Montgomery, Alabama, Doris Crenshaw, and asked her if she knew anyone with the press. She did and made the initial contact with Dan Waterman, editor-in-chief, on my behalf. I was happy to hear that Dan would be willing to talk with me about the manuscript. When I finally spoke with Dan, I shared how I had come to bring the project to The University of Alabama Press and how I felt this was the appropriate home for the book because of my mother's and Aunt Edythe's deep roots in Alabama and the wealth of Alabama history contained within the book. After explaining the process to me, Dan agreed to read the manuscript over the weekend and get back with me by the following Monday. After that call I felt extremely hopeful, believing we had found our publisher.

I received a very touching and affirmative email from Dan on Monday, April 25, 2011, accepting the manuscript for publication. Although we still had to go through their editorial review process, it was practically a done deal. Before I shared the news with Aunt Edythe, I wanted to ensure we had indeed worked out all of the details My aunt wasn't doing well, and I didn't want to offer her false hope. By the time we worked out the details, Aunt Edythe's health had taken a turn for the worse. I shared the news with her, hoping to boost her spirit. She was elated to hear the news and especially that it would be with The University of Alabama Press, the scholarly press of the state of her birth. She sent me some additional items she wanted included in the book before she soon became too weak to respond. I sent Dan's moving email to Aunt Edythe's son, Arturo, and he shared it with her. He conveyed to me that she was happy to hear the thoughts and sentiments expressed by Dan in the email.

It was about two weeks prior to Aunt Edythe's passing that we finally signed a publishing contract. Although she didn't live to see the publication of a work that began forty-six years ago, she died knowing that her story about her sister's life was on its way to the world stage. She rests in peace with the confidence that, "I fought the good fight, I finished the course, I kept the faith..." Although I will miss her dearly, I know her love, her lessons, and her legacy will continue to live in my heart.

Acknowledgments

This has been one of the most fulfilling and rewarding journeys in my life thus far. And first and foremost, I want to thank Aunt Edythe for entrusting me with the responsibility of finding a publisher for her book on the life and legacy of my mother. I enjoyed learning from Aunt Edythe and laughing with her, and most especially, seeing my mother through her eyes. However, I would be remiss if I did not acknowledge those who shared this journey with me and whose efforts contributed to the fruition and materialization of this work.

I truly have to acknowledge a woman who proved invaluable to me throughout this entire process, Bonita Hampton. When I shared my aunt's book with her and asked her to assist me, she read the manuscript and without hesitation agreed to join me in what turned out to be a three year endeavor. Through negotiations, long nights of reading and editing, deadlines, skepticism from publishers, and finally the ultimate yes, we shared every step of this journey. I am extremely grateful for her dedication, hard work, and commitment to this project, but most of all her belief in my aunt's work. There are others whose efforts and input I will never take for granted, especially Pat Latimore, who was always there whenever my aunt or I needed her, and Donald Bermudez for assisting with photo acknowledgments and credits. I also want to thank Tom Winters, who connected my aunt and me with Joe Hilley, to whom I owe special thanks. I am truly grateful for Joe's dedication and patience in helping my aunt craft a manuscript that I believe will become a bestselling book.

Before I penned the words for this next individual, I searched my mind to find the most profound way to capture just how grateful I am to Dan Waterman. "Thank you" somehow seems simply inadequate at times when your heart is filled with so much gratitude. From the very beginning, Dan saw the value in my aunt's work. His immediate response was timely, and I now believe it was a divine connection. Dan and the team at The University of Alabama Press have worked patiently with me and my team throughout this process and for that I am truly appreciative. I am eternally grateful that my Aunt Edythe passed in peace knowing her book, *Desert Rose*, had finally found a publishing home.

Last, but certainly not least, I want to acknowledge my cousin Arturo for all of his valuable contributions to this project and helping me meet critical and important deadlines to insure the fruition of one of his mother's most important works. Arturo's knowledge and strength came at a time when I needed it most. His assistance in the editing process gave me peace in knowing that Aunt Edythe's work would remain true to her voice. I am glad we shared this experience together, and I know Aunt Edythe is proud of him.

Thank you, God. This has been a wonderful and rewarding journey.

Bernice A. King

Notes

Preface

1. Name has been changed.

2. Schomburg Center for Research in Black Culture, New York Public Library, *Standing in the Need of Prayer: A Celebration of Black Prayer,* with a foreword by Coretta Scott King (New York: Free Press, 2003), xiii.

Chapter 1

1. In spite of laws against teaching slaves to read and write, many found ways to learn both. Our great-grandfather Willis Scott could read, though no one knows where or how he learned. See John Hope Franklin and Loren B. Schweninger, *In Search of the Promised Land: A Slave Family in the Old South* (New York: Oxford University Press, 2006), 26.

2. Not much is known about the slavery life of Willis Scott, but quite a bit is known about the general nature of plantation life in the South. Willis's experiences would have been typical of those encountered by other slaves. See John Hope Franklin and Alfred A. Moss Jr., *From Slavery to Freedom: A History of African Americans* (New York: Alfred A. Knopf, 2000), 138–66.

Chapter 2

1. At the time this book was written, Grandfather Scott's youngest child, Jasper Scott, was still alive.

Chapter 3

1. According to the 1960 census, Perry County had a population of 17,358 persons, 11,401 of whom were African American (65.7 percent of the total). In 1940, when Coretta was a seventh grader, blacks outnumbered whites in Perry County 3 to 1.

2. See "Delegates to the Constitutional Convention," Alabama Legislature, accessed May 15, 2011, http://www.legislature.state.al.us/misc/history/constitutions/1875/1875delegates.html.

3. See opening remarks of the Honorable John B. Knox, president of the convention, made on May 22, 1901, the second day of convention proceedings. "Official Proceedings of the Constitutional Convention of the State of Alabama: Day Two, May 22nd," Alabama Legislature, accessed May 15, 2011, http://www.legislature.state.al.us/misc/history/constitutions/1901/proceedings/1901_proceedings_v011/day2.html.

4. John Tubbs owned a thousand acres of farmland and timberland when he died, holdings that remained in the Tubbs family long after he was gone.

5. Uniontown, located about twenty miles southwest of Marion, was another location in

Perry County where blacks owned significant amounts of real property. It also was the childhood home of Juanita Jones, who later became the wife of the Reverend Ralph Abernathy. Martin referred to Ralph as his "closest friend and perennial cell mate" for the many hours they spent in jail together as a result of their numerous marches and protests.

Chapter 4

1. Perry County Training School was later renamed Robert C. Hatch High School.

2. In addition to transportation issues, most black children lived on farms. They were needed at home to help with daily chores and seasonal work in the fields. Even if a family could get along without the labor of one or more of their younger members, they still had the problem of providing transportation to and from school.

3. According to a 1916 United States Department of the Interior's Bureau of Education *Bulletin,* Lincoln Normal School had sixteen teachers in the year 1914, about the time our father was in attendance there. Only one teacher was African American, and only one was male. The official head of the school was Mary E. Phillips, a woman who was an inspiration to all. Department of the Interior Bureau of Education, *Bulletin: Negro Education: A Study of the Private and Higher Schools for Colored People in the United States,* 2 vols. (Washington, D.C., 1916), No. 38 and 39.

Chapter 5

1. Bessie Smith was an African American blues and jazz vocalist. She lived from 1892 to 1937. Born in Tennessee, she began performing as a child on the streets of Chattanooga, doing song and dance routines with her brother. She went on to become one of the greatest vocalists of the 1920s and 1930s. She died as the result of injuries received in an automobile accident on Route 61 between Memphis and Clarksdale, Mississippi.

2. The Baby Overland was a smaller version of the Overland Touring Car produced first by Overland Automotive and then by Willis-Overland Motor Company. Production of the car in various styles ran from 1908 to 1926.

3. Mr. Belknap's name has been changed.

Chapter 7

1. "Paul Revere's Ride" by Henry Wadsworth Longfellow first appeared in the December 18, 1860, edition of the *Boston Transcript* and was the first poem in his collection *Tales of a Wayside Inn.* I found excerpts in Norman Foerster, *American Poetry and Prose,* 4th ed. (Boston: Houghton Mifflin Company, 1957), 790ff.

2. Bob Hatch's father, Robert C. Hatch Sr., was a well-respected African American educator in Alabama. During the years in which the state operated a segregated school system, he supervised the state's education programs for African Americans. Robert C. Hatch High School in Uniontown, Alabama, is named for him.

Chapter 8

1. Adams, who argued the case before the Supreme Court, took the position that in attempting to liberate themselves from illegal captivity, the Africans had only followed the dictates of self-defense. See United States v. The Libellants and Claimants of the Schooner *Amistad*, 40 US 518 (1841).

2. See Augustus Field Beard, *A Crusade of Brotherhood: A History of the American Missionary Association* (Boston: The Pilgrim Press, 1909), 27–48.

3. The AMA's records and archives are located at the Amistad Research Center, Tulane University, New Orleans, Louisiana. See also, Amistad America's official website www.amistadamerica.net.

4. Though formed by an independent group, the AMA very early became part of the Congregational Christian Church. It has now been merged into the Justice and Witness Ministries division of the United Church of Christ. See United Church of Christ official website www.ucc.org.

5. While primarily concerned with educating blacks, from the outset AMA schools were open to all races. At the time, illiteracy in the South was almost as high among whites as it was for blacks. The AMA felt the entire region would benefit from an integrated educational system.

6. See Augustus Field Beard, *A Crusade of Brotherhood: A History of the American Missionary Association* (Boston: The Pilgrim Press, 1909), 146–47. See also, Addie Louise Joyner Butler, *The Distinctive Black College: Talladega, Tuskegee and Morehouse* (London: The Scarecrow Press, 1977), 18–20.

7. In 1926, when Lincoln School was in its golden age, it had 596 students and 26 teachers. One year of college work was offered. The physical plant comprised five large brick buildings, two large frame buildings, and two smaller structures. The school owned forty acres, ten of which were used for its campus and thirty were under cultivation.

8. Educating blacks ran counter to the philosophy of plantation culture. Slave owners wanted their slaves ignorant, illiterate, and unmotivated. Otherwise, they argued, slaves would realize the enormous power they held and revolt against white authority.

9. The Congregational Church was located near the school campus. Lincoln teachers worshipped there, integrating its congregation.

10. Phillips Memorial Auditorium is the only building of that period still standing on the school's campus today. The others were demolished in the wake of the county's integration efforts.

11. According to a history of the school written by Grace Newell, who taught at Lincoln from 1908 to 1943, in 1935 tuition was reduced from twenty-five dollars a year to nine dollars.

12. From the author's personal recollection.

13. Buell G. Gallagher was a white educator who served for ten years as president of Talla-

dega College. A courageous and progressive leader, he was at the center of much of the controversy of the 1960s. For an overview, see "Education: Retreat of a Reconciler," *Time,* May 16, 1969, accessed May 15, 2011, http://www.time.com/time/magazine/article/0,9171,902571,00 .html.

14. Though he worked primarily behind the scenes in the 1960s, Bayard Rustin's involvement in the struggle for civil rights began in 1937 when he assisted in the defense of the Scottsboro Boys, nine young black men who were charged with rape in Scottsboro, Alabama. In 1947 he organized the Journey of Reconciliation, one of the early Freedom Rides, in an effort to test Supreme Court rulings banning segregation in interstate commerce. For a vivid description of those rides, see James Peck, "Not So Deep Are the Roots," in *Reporting Civil Rights Part One: American Journalism 1941–1963* (New York: Literary Classics of the United States, 2003), 92–98.

15. From the author's personal recollection.

16. Coretta was not part of the chorus group that went on tour that first year with the Thomases. She learned about Antioch from my report of that initial trip and from my first two years there.

17. When Coretta graduated from Lincoln and was ready to leave for college, the choir expressed their appreciation by surprising her with a gift of bedroom slippers and eight dollars.

Chapter 9

1. See Antioch College's official website: http://antiochcollege.org.

2. As a student at Oberlin College, Jane Alice Browne became friends with Horace Mann's widow who told her that while Horace Mann was president, two black girls from Louisiana enrolled at Antioch. In response, the white students threatened to strike rather than eat with them in the common dining hall. Firm and uncompromising in his position on race, Mann told the students that if they were to eat on campus, they would do so with the black girls.

Browne was so taken by the story of Mann's courage that later, when she was married to James Bond, she named her son after Mann—Horace Mann Bond. Like his namesake, Horace Mann Bond had a long and productive career in education. Joy Elmer Morgan, *Horace Mann at Antioch: Studies in Personality and Higher Education* (The Horace Mann Centennial Fund, 1938).

3. In addition to changes in core curriculum and course structure, Mann introduced a system of electives—an idea so novel at the time the Antioch course catalog included a footnote to explain the term.

4. See Antioch College's official website: http://antiochcollege.org.

5. Explaining the need for a new direction at Antioch College and in American education, Morgan said, "America's educational system is preparing men and women to do as they are told. For eight years of common school, for four years of high school, and for four years of college, the student prepares his next day's lessons, taking orders and filling them without further responsibility. We are becoming a nation of employees working under orders; and

our colleges are hastening that result." Hawthorne Daniel, "Arthur E. Morgan's New Type of College," *The World's Work: A History of Our Time* 41, no. 4 (Feb. 1921), 408–409.

6. Burton R. Clark, *The Distinctive College* (New Brunswick: Transaction Publishers, 1992), http://books.google.com/, 22.

7. By way of example, the total 1967–1968 budget for Antioch was approximately four million dollars. Tuition provided 83 percent of the income. See *The Antiochian,* March 1967.

8. Coretta expressed her feelings about attending Antioch in a 1948 article for the Urban League. See Susie Bright, "Wise After the Fact: Coretta Scott King's Memorial," *Susie Bright's Journal* (blog), February 10, 2006, http://susiebright.blogs.com/.

Chapter 10

1. Coretta Scott, "Life Aims" (unpublished paper, Antioch College Archives, 1946).

2. Founded in 1915, Karamu House is the oldest African American theatre in the United States. It is located in Cleveland, Ohio. See www.karamu.com.

3. Part of the Settlement Movement, Friendly Settlement House was established to provide urban residents a safe place to gather for entertainment and cultural enrichment. Modeled after similar programs in Europe, settlement houses in the United States sought to address urban problems, particularly among recent immigrants and minorities. Summer camps, music, and theatre were integral parts of the programs offered.

4. Coretta Scott, "Evaluation of Work at Friendly Inn Settlement" (unpublished paper, Antioch College Archives, 1947).

Chapter 11

1. Coretta Scott, "Senior Paper" (unpublished paper, Antioch College Archives, 1951).

2. Coretta Scott, "Why I Came to College," *Opportunity: Journal of Negro Life,* 26 (April–June 1948): 42.

3. Coretta Scott, "Senior Paper."

4. No political lightweight, Henry Wallace had served as Franklin Roosevelt's vice president and as a cabinet official under Harry Truman.

5. Mary McLeod Bethune was an American educator. Born in South Carolina to parents who were former slaves, she went on to establish a school for African American children in Daytona Beach, Florida. That school later became Bethune-Cookman College. An adviser to presidents from Calvin Coolidge to Harry Truman, her life was marked by a winsome brand of diligent, persistent, and innovative activism that won the hearts of blacks and whites alike.

6. Paul Robeson was a world renowned singer, actor, athlete, and activist known as much for his advocacy for civil rights as for his deep bass voice. He was particularly famous for popularizing the performance of spirituals. On Broadway, his performance in *Othello* played for over three hundred shows. Born in New Jersey in 1898, he was by far the leading black star of his era. He died in 1976.

7. "Coretta Scott, a resident of the North Perry Community, and a student at Antioch

College, Ohio, will give a benefit concert at 4:30 p.m., Sunday, July 30, at Lincoln School auditorium. She has appeared as a soprano in concert throughout Ohio and Pennsylvania, and recently sang in concert with the noted Negro baritone, Paul Robeson, who favorably commended her voice. A small admission charge will be made and the proceeds will go to the Baptist Academy located on Centerville Street. The public is invited and seating arrangements have been made by the committee sponsoring the concert." *The Marion Times Standard,* July 27, 1950.

8. Coretta Scott, "Senior Paper."

9. Coretta Scott, "Senior Paper."

Chapter 12

1. From a private conversation.

2. Coretta Scott, "Senior Paper" (unpublished paper, Antioch College Archives, 1951).

3. For a brief discussion of McGregor's life, see Gerry Jones, "Biography of Douglas McGregor," Managers Net, accessed May 15, 2011, www.managers-net.org/Biography/mcgregor .html.

4. Speaking of him later, Coretta said, "Mr. Anderson, a Negro, is one of those great souls that knows his own identity at the same time he identifies with all humanity. A versatile musician, he composes and performs in both classic and modern musical idioms. A marvelous teacher, for me, he made jazz respectable."

5. Others helped her as well. One of those was Miss Esther Oldt, a member of the Personnel Department and a trained musician. Through their shared affinity for music they developed a rapport that Coretta found encouraging and supportive.

6. Personal interview with Jessie Treichler, 1965. Julius Kiano later became Minister of Labor in Kenya West Africa.

7. Henry Wadsworth Longfellow, "Paul Revere's Ride," in Norman Foerster, *American Poetry and Prose* (Boston: Houghton Mifflin Company, 1957), pp. 790ff.

Chapter 13

1. See *Biographical Directory of the United States Congress,* found online at www.bioguide .congress.gov. Adam Clayton Power Jr. was a twelve-term African American Congressman from New York's 22nd District. He was the first African American elected from New York to the United States Congress. Prior to serving in Congress he became pastor of Abyssinian Baptist Church. During his time in Congress, he returned to preach at the church once a month. Coretta sang on one of those Sundays when he preached.

2. A classically trained singer, Hazel Scott went on to perform on Broadway and in motion pictures. In 1950, she had her own television show, one of the first African Americans to do so. She was married to Adam Clayton Powell Jr. Lena Horne enjoyed a long and productive career in both film and music spanning sixty years. From the 1930s to the 1990s, she

appeared in more than thirty motion pictures and television shows and won eight Grammy Awards.

Chapter 14

1. Benjamin E. Mays was an outspoken civil rights advocate long before the 1960s Civil Rights Era. He was president of Morehouse College in Atlanta, Georgia, while Martin Luther King Jr. was a student.

2. From a private conversation, 1966.

3. Coretta Scott King, *My Life with Martin Luther King, Jr.* (New York: Henry Holt, 1993), 68.

4. When we parted, the Kings seemed pleased that we had met. Mrs. King handed me a small gift she had carried in her purse.

Chapter 16

1. Martin Luther King Jr., *Stride Toward Freedom* (San Francisco: HarperSanFrancisco, 1986), 23.

2. E. P. Wallace, *Montgomery Advertiser,* March 23, 1955.

3. For a description of his proposed program, see King, *Stride Toward Freedom*, 25–26. See also, Charles Marsh, *The Beloved Community: How Faith Shapes Social Justice, From the Civil Rights Movement to Today* (New York: Basic Books, 2005).

4. King, *Stride Toward Freedom*, 30.

5. See Martin Luther King Jr., *The Words of Martin Luther King Jr.,* ed. Coretta Scott King (New York: Newmarket Press, 1983), 66.

6. King, *Stride Toward Freedom*, 36.

7. Martin Luther once said, "Divinity consists in use and practice, not in speculation and meditation." Martin Luther King Jr. often followed that same dictum. See Martin Luther, *The Table Talk or Familiar Discourse of Martin Luther*, trans. William Hazlitt (London: David Bogue, 1848), 179.

Chapter 17

1. In 1955, Montgomery had a population of about fifty thousand blacks and seventy thousand whites.

2. See Brown v. Board of Education, 347 U.S. 483 (1954).

3. See Plessy v. Ferguson, 163 U.S. 537 (1896).

4. In addition to complicated personal circumstances, Colvin had been charged, tried, and convicted in juvenile court of violating state segregation laws and of committing an assault in resisting arrest. The case was appealed to the circuit court where Judge Carter dismissed the segregation conviction but affirmed the assault conviction. His action deprived Colvin and her attorneys of the opportunity to appeal the segregation issue at the federal level on constitutional grounds.

5. L. D. Reddick, *Crusader Without Violence: A Biography of Martin Luther King Jr.* (New York: Harper, 1959), 9

6. According to city policy, no black could sit parallel to any white. That meant that if one white passenger needed a seat an entire row of blacks—those seated on both sides of the aisle—were required to vacate their seats even if it meant standing over seats left unoccupied on one side of the bus.

7. David J. Garrow, *Bearing the Cross: Martin Luther King, Jr., and the Southern Christian Leadership Conference* (New York: William Morrow and Company, 1986), 12.

8. Ecclesiastes 3:1.

9. "Negroes were ready for a new shuffle of the cards. Events . . . had prepared them. Basic to an understanding of Montgomery, and of King, is an understanding of this fact: Negroes already had changed. They only needed an act to give them power over their fears, an instrument to hold in their hands, and a man to point the way. Montgomery furnished all three, giving Negroes not only an act but also a remarkable fisher of men and a new ideology, nonviolence." Lerone Bennett, *What Manner of Man: A Biography of Martin Luther King, Jr.* (Chicago: Johnson Publishing, 1964), 60.

Chapter 18

1. Martin Luther King Jr., *Stride Toward Freedom* (San Francisco: HarperSanFrancisco, 1986), 39.

2. Henry David Thoreau, *On the Duty of Civil Disobedience: Resistance to Civil Government (*1849; repr., Charleston: Forgotten Books, 2008), http://books.google.com/, 12.

3. Thoreau, *Civil Disobedience,* 13.

4. Mohandas K. Ghandi, of whom King was to become a disciple, said as early as 1935, "It may be through the Negro people that the unadulterated message of nonviolence will be delivered to the world." See James J. Farrell, *The Spirit of the Sixties: Making Postwar Radicalism* (New York: Routledge, 1997), 89.

5. King, *Stride Toward Freedom*, 53–54.

6. Bennett, *What Manner of Man*, 61.

7. King, *Stride Toward Freedom*, 63.

Chapter 19

1. Other boycotts and protests had been tried before, but by Christmas the boycott in Montgomery was entering its fourth week. None of the previous boycotts in other cities had lasted that long.

2. Clayborne Carson, ed. *The Autobiography of Martin Luther King, Jr.* (New York: Grand Central Publishing, 1998), 18.

3. In perhaps one of the truly great ironies of history, white slaveholders introduced Christianity to their black slaves. Now the descendants of those slaves were using the Christian approach not only to liberate themselves but to free the master as well.

4. The most unsettling caller told Martin, "Nigger, we are tired of you and your mess now. And if you aren't out of town in three days, we're going to blow your brains out and blow up your house." Clayborne Carson, *Autobiography of Martin Luther King, Jr.*, 76–78.

Chapter 20

1. Martin Luther King Jr., *Stride Toward Freedom* (San Francisco: HarperSanFrancisco, 1986), 127.

2. Ibid., 127.

3. Ibid., 137–38.

4. Gleaned from private conversation and from a presentation I heard Coretta give at a local church not long after the Montgomery parsonage was bombed.

Chapter 21

1. Coretta Scott King, *My Life with Martin Luther King, Jr.* (New York: Henry Holt, 1993), 132.

2. Private conversation.

3. Browder v. Gayle, 142 F. Supp. 707 (1956).

4. As his career unfolded, Judge Johnson heard numerous civil rights cases. His rulings were instrumental in the desegregation of Alabama schools, but at the time of *Browder* no one knew for certain where he stood on the issues.

5. For excerpts from the transcript of the hearing, see Stewart Burns, ed., *Daybreak of Freedom: The Montgomery Bus Boycott* (Chapel Hill: The University of North Carolina Press, 1997), 59–78.

6. The International Longshoremen's Association Auditorium is located on what is now Martin Luther King Jr. Avenue. Back then, it was at the heart of Mobile's most vibrant black community.

7. Joseph Lowery was a charter member of the Southern Christian Leadership Conference (SCLC) and succeeded Ralph Abernathy as president. He was a productive leader and worked tirelessly to promote the cause of African American freedom, an effort that predated his association with Martin.

8. A successful singer and actor, Harry Belafonte was an important ally in the Civil Rights Movement. He arranged fundraisers and celebrity support throughout Martin's life. After Martin's death, he remained an ardent supporter of Coretta, offering her vital assistance at critical junctures in her life. In Friendship had been formed earlier specifically for the purpose of raising money to support southern civil rights organizations and protests.

9. Though Martin did not know it at the time, Levison was under surveillance by the Federal Bureau of Investigation (FBI). The FBI had become suspicious of Levison following his earlier brief involvement with the Communist Party. Levison was not Communist and had only broached the possibility of involvement with them because of his interest in addressing poverty and other social issues. He disassociated himself with the party when he realized

it did not stand for the kind of change he sought to support. Nevertheless, the FBI tapped his telephones and recorded every conversation. That wiretap on Levison gave the FBI access to Martin's conversations with Levison and marked the beginning of the FBI's efforts to discredit and destroy Martin. For an authoritative account of the FBI's surveillance activity, see Select Committee to Study Government Operations, "Dr. Martin Luther King, Jr., Case Study," United States Senate, Supplementary Detailed Staff Reports on Intelligence Activities and the Rights of Americans, Book III, Final Report, April 23, 1976.

Chapter 22

1. See Cabinet Paper, "The Civil Rights Program—Letter and Statement by the Attorney General," April 10, 1956, E. Frederic Morrow Records, Box 9, Civil Rights Bill, Eisenhower Presidential Library.

2. C. K. Steele, Samuel Williams, Theodore Jemison, and Medgar Evers rounded out the initial slate of officers. Though many of them have gone unnoticed, they were courageous, able leaders who gave their lives to the elimination of segregation. At the time SCLC was formed, Steele and Jemison had both conducted bus boycotts of their own. Steele would go on to lead the fight to integrate Florida's public schools. Samuel Williams was a professor at Morehouse College and one of Martin's early mentors. He later became involved with sit-ins in the Atlanta area. Medgar Evers worked tirelessly for the cause of civil rights in Mississippi. In June 1963, he was gunned down outside his home in Jackson.

3. Kwame Nkrumah was Ghana's first prime minister. He served as leader of that country and its predecessor, the Gold Coast, from 1952 to 1966. Under his leadership, Ghana gained independence from Great Britain.

4. James M. Washington, ed., *A Testament of Hope: The Essential Writings and Speeches of Martin Luther King Jr.* (New York: HarperSanFrancisco, 1991), 198.

Chapter 23

1. Tuskegee Institute, now known as Tuskegee University, was founded by the efforts of Lewis Adams and George W. Campbell. Adams was a former slave with the dream of establishing a school for newly freed slaves. Campbell, a former slave owner, was a candidate for political office who needed votes. Together they brokered a deal that put Campbell in office and established a normal school at Tuskegee. Booker T. Washington was the school's first president. The school opened for classes on July 4, 1881.

Chapter 24

1. Lillian Smith was born in Jasper, Florida, in 1897. An author and social commentator, she was an outspoken opponent of racism. Her most famous work was a novel entitled *Strange Fruit.* She died in 1966.

2. See Mitchell v. U.S., 313 U.S. 80 (1941), Morgan v. Commonwealth of Virginia, 328

U.S. 373 (1946), Henderson v. United States, 339 U.S. 816 (1950), and Boynton v. Virginia, 364 U.S. 454 (1960).

3. A subsequent group left from Montgomery on a ride bound for Jackson, Mississippi. When they arrived in Jackson, they were arrested and held in jail.

Chapter 25

1. From 1955 through September 1963, there were twenty bombings reported in and around Birmingham. See "20th Bombing Here against Negroes," *Birmingham Post-Herald*, September 16, 1963, http://bplonline.cdmhost.com/.

2. For a complete history of the group, see Amy Swerdlow, *Women Strike for Peace: Traditional Motherhood and Radical Politics in the 1960s* (Chicago: University of Chicago Press, 1993).

3. In 2006, pursuant to a Freedom of Information Act request, the FBI released some five hundred pages of records detailing their surveillance and investigation of Coretta.

4. Coretta Scott King, "He Had a Dream: Mrs. Martin Luther King Jr.'s Own Story of the Years of Struggle, Hope, Success and Foreboding," *Life* (September 12, 1969), 57.

5. Harry Belafonte, who had been kept informed of events in Birmingham, hired someone to care for the children while Coretta went to Birmingham.

Chapter 27

1. See Armstrong v. Board of Education of City of Birmingham, Jefferson County, Alabama, 323 F.2d 333 (5th Cir. 1963).

2. See Connor v. State, 153 S0.2d 787, 274 Ala. 230 (1963).

Chapter 28

1. Martin Luther King Jr., "I Have a Dream," August 28, 1963, transcript and video, http://www.youtube.com/watch?v=PbUtL_0vAJk.

Chapter 30

1. Early on, a minister friend had told Martin that Coretta should never give up her music. His wife had done that, and they both regretted it.

2. Helen Phillips was a concert and opera singer of world renown. Through the 1940s and 1950s, she appeared in concert and on stage around the world. In 1947, she became the first black to sing with the Metropolitan Opera chorus. She made her Town Hall debut in 1953.

3. The Nobel Peace Prize was established in the Last Will and Testament of Alfred Nobel, a Swedish industrialist most notable for his invention of dynamite. The Peace Prize is awarded by the Norwegian Nobel Committee and conferred in Oslo, Norway. All other Nobel Prizes are awarded at Stockholm, Sweden. Monetary awards for all Nobel Prizes are funded by the Nobel Foundation, which is located in Stockholm.

4. Coretta's travel party included Joan Daves, Christine King Farris, and Russell Goode, Coretta's accompanist.

5. Gunnar Myrdal was a Swedish economist. In 1974 he shared the Nobel Prize in Economic Science with Friedrich Hayek. Myrdal's 1944 study of race relations in the United States was entitled, *An American Dilemma: The Negro Problem and Modern Democracy*. His voice lent credibility to the African American struggle for civil rights in those incredibly bleak years prior to the Supreme Court's decision in *Brown v. Board of Education*.

6. Private conversation, December 1964.

Chapter 31

1. Voter registration examinations did not resemble a literacy test and were an inquisition designed for the sole purpose of preventing blacks from registering to vote. Registrars issued the "test" orally and were free to ask any absurd question they cared to dream up, which many did. For a vivid description of the process, see Jack H. Pollack, "Literacy Tests: Southern Style," in *Reporting Civil Rights Part One: American Journalism, 1941–1963* (New York: Literary Classics of the United States, 2003), 85–91.

2. FBI records later revealed the tape was created for the purpose of instigating marital trouble between Coretta and Martin through allegations of purported infidelity. See Select Committee to Study Government Operations, "Dr. Martin Luther King, Jr., Case Study," United States Senate, Supplementary Detailed Staff Reports on Intelligence Activities and the Rights of Americans, Book III, Final Report, April 23, 1976. No substantive evidence was ever produced by the FBI to support the allegations. Andrew Young, former executive director of SCLC gives an excellent account of this incident. See Andrew Young, *An Easy Burden: The Civil Rights Movement and the Transformation of America* (New York: Harper-Collins, 1996), 327–32.

3. Malcolm X was gunned down three weeks later, on February 21, 1965, while speaking to a crowd at the Audubon Ballroom in Harlem. Three men, all of them allegedly members of the Nation of Islam, were subsequently arrested and tried for his murder. They were convicted and sentenced to prison but later paroled. All maintained their innocence.

4. Lyndon Johnson, "President Johnson Makes an Impassioned Plea to Congress to Pass the Voting Rights Act of 1965," in *In Our Own Words: Extraordinary Speeches of the American Century*, eds. Robert G. Torricelli and Andrew Carroll (New York: Kodansha America, 1999), 262.

5. See Paul Good, "It Was Worth the Boy's Dying," in *Reporting Civil Rights Part Two: American Journalism, 1963–1973* (New York: Literary Classics of the United States, 2003), 353–55.

Chapter 32

1. Kilgore was born in South Carolina. He was a graduate of Morehouse College and Union Theological Seminary. In the 1940s, he worked in North Carolina organizing farm laborers and registering voters. Later, he was pastor of Freedom Baptist Church in Harlem. In 1972 he became the first black elected president of the American Baptist Churches USA.

Later in that decade he served as president of the Progressive National Baptist Convention. See Wolfgang Saxon, "Thomas Kilgore Jr., 84; Led 2 Baptist Groups," *The New York Times,* February 10, 1998.

2. Michael Honey, "Chasing the Dream," *The Seattle Times,* April 2, 2006.

3. Martin spoke at Bennett College in 1958. One of the people in the audience that day was a young high school student named Ezell Blair Jr. Blair was so inspired by what he heard that he joined the college students conducting the sit-ins. In 1960, he became one of the Greensboro Four, a group of protesters who conducted a highly publicized sit-in at the Woolworth's department store in Greensboro, North Carolina.

Chapter 35

1.Martin Luther King Jr., "I Have Been to the Mountaintop," speech delivered at Bishop Charles Mason Temple, April 3, 1968, transcript accessed May 15, 2011, http://mlk-kpp01. stanford.edu/index.php/encyclopedia/documentsentry/ive_been_to_the_mountaintop/.

Chapter 36

1. Now Cheyney University of Pennsylvania, it is the oldest historically black college in the United States, having been founded in Philadelphia by a Quaker, Richard Humphreys, as the Institute for Colored Youth in 1837.

2. Now West Chester State University.

Chapter 37

1. Robert Kennedy not only supplied an airplane to bring Martin's body from Memphis, he also had three extra telephone lines installed at Coretta's house. In those first few days after the assassination, we could not have managed without them.

2. Representatives from as far away as Riverside Church in New York offered their facilities for the funeral service.

Chapter 38

1. Coretta Scott King, *My Life with Martin Luther King, Jr.* (New York: Henry Holt, 1993), 314.

2. Lisa Renee Rhodes, *Coretta Scott King* (Philadelphia: Chelsea House, 1998), 135.

Chapter 40

1. Harvard Class Day is a day of events honoring the graduating senior class. It occurs the day before commencement.

2. Adapted from Genesis 37:19–20.

3. Jessie Treichler, who had worked for Eleanor Roosevelt, said Coretta's six-person mail staff handled a larger volume of mail than did Mrs. Roosevelt's eighteen secretaries.

4. I met Nixon when he called on Coretta the Sunday before Martin's funeral. I appreciated his concern for my sister but did not find him appealing.

Chapter 41

1. Luke 4:18–19

2. Before the start of the fall semester, Crozer moved to Rochester, New York.

Chapter 43

1. Since then, Atlanta University has combined with Clark College to form Clark Atlanta University.

2. Other artists included Nancy Wilson, Stephanie Mills, Ossie Davis, the Alvin Ailey Dance Company, Arthur Mitchell's Dance Theatre of Harlem, and many others.

Chapter 44

1. For a glimpse of Sweet Auburn in its heyday, see Gary M. Pomerantz, *Where Peachtree Meets Sweet Auburn: The Saga of Two Families and the Making of Atlanta* (New York: Scribner, 1996).

Chapter 45

1. The appointment was announced September 19, 1977. See Jimmy Carter, "United Nations Nomination of U.S. Representatives and Alternate Representatives to the Thirty-Second Session of the General Assembly," September 19, 1977, in "Jimmy Carter XXXIX President of the United States: 1977–1981," John T. Woolley and Gerhard Peters, *The American Presidency Project,* accessed May 15, 2011, http://www.presidency.ucsb.edu/ws/?pid= 6652.

2. See "Carter Administration Hits Repression in South Africa," *Jet,* Nov. 10, 1977, 5.

3. See UN General Assembly, Resolution 32/10, "Decade for Action to Combat Racism and Racial Discrimination," November 7, 1977. See also, UN General Assembly, Resolution 32/11, "Status of the International Convention on the Elimination of All Forms of Racial Discrimination," November 7, 1977. And see UN General Assembly, Resolution 32/12, "Status of the International Convention on the Suppression and Punishment of the Crime of Apartheid," November 7, 1977.

4. See "Mrs. King Seeks Tougher Ban Against South Africa," *Jet,* Dec. 1, 1977, 5.

5. Ruth Schachter Morgenthau was the wife of Henry Morgenthau III, whose father was treasury secretary under President Franklin D. Roosevelt. Her appointment as UN representative was announced September 14, 1977. She served as the Adlai Stevenson Professor of International Politics at Brandeis University until retirement. She died November 4, 2006, the same year as Coretta. See Dennis Hevesi, "Ruth S. Morgenthau, 75, an Adviser to Carter, Is Dead," *The New York Times,* November 12, 2006. See also, Jimmy Carter, "United Nations Economic and Social Council Appointment of James E. Baker and Ruth S. Morgenthau to Positions of the Council," September 14, 1977, in "Jimmy Carter XXXIX President of the United States: 1977–1981," John T. Woolley and Gerhard Peters, *The Ameri-*

can Presidency Project, accessed May 15, 2011, http://www.presidency.ucsb.edu/ws/index.php?pid=6629#axzz1PvroeaWc.

6. Leon H. Sullivan was born in Charleston, West Virginia. While attending seminary in New York, he worked as an associate pastor under Adam Clayton Powell at Abyssinian Baptist Church. In 1950, he moved to Philadelphia where he became pastor of Zion Baptist Church. Beginning in 1958, when Philadelphia companies proved reluctant to hire blacks, Sullivan organized a boycott he called "selective patronage." The boycott was a success and Sullivan went on to develop a number of black "self-help" ministries and entities, some of them nonprofit and some for profit. His 10-36 housing plan was enormously popular. In 1964, he founded Opportunities Industrialization Centers of America which taught job and life skills to the poor, then helped them find jobs. His unique blend of ministry and entrepreneurial flair caught the attention of General Motors, which named him to its board of directors in 1971. The African–African American Summit was but one more of his many innovative approaches to solving the problems facing blacks, both in America and around the world. Sullivan died in 2001, but his work continues through the Leon H. Sullivan Foundation.

Chapter 46

1. Coretta Scott King, "The Meaning of the Martin Luther King Jr. Holiday," Crosswalk.com, accessed May 15, 2011, http://www.crosswalk.com/faith/spiritual-life/the-meaning-of-the-martin-luther-king-jr-holiday-1241524.html.

Chapter 47

1. Antioch College Alumni Association, citation for the Horace Mann Award, June 21, 2004.

2. Betty and Walter Roberts are the parents of Julia Roberts and her brother, Eric, both of whom went on to star in numerous motion pictures.

3. The Roberts, like many who work in community theatre, were dedicated, hardworking artists who worked for the love of their craft. Their salaries were small. When Julia was born, Coretta paid the hospital bill. After Mrs. Roberts went home from the hospital, Coretta sent one of her salaried employees to Mrs. Roberts' home to assist her in caring for the infant and in doing household chores.

Chapter 48

1. See review of *Before the Mayflower,* by Lerone Bennett Jr., Books, *Jet,* March 7, 1963, 46.

2. Walter Anderson, Jessie Treichler, Frances Thomas, and Bertha Wormley remained close to Coretta throughout their lives. Walter Anderson was born on May 12, 1915. He graduated from Oberlin College Conservatory of Music, which he attended on a full scholarship. Later, he was Antioch College's first black professor. In 1946, he became the first Af-

rican American to chair a department at an all-white college or university when he was chair of Antioch's music department. In 1968 he was named director of music programs for the NEA. He died November 24, 2003.

3. Myrlie Evers-Williams was the widow of slain civil rights activist Medgar Evers. Betty Shabazz was the widow of Malcolm X.

4. Coretta had a particularly close relationship with her cousins Christine Osburn Jackson and the late Reverend E. Randal Osburn. Christine was a social activist who for many years was director of the Charleston, South Carolina, YWCA. E. Randal worked for SCLC all of his adult life and organized a strong affiliate in Cleveland, Ohio.

Additional Reading

Abernathy, Donzaleigh. *Partners To History: Martin Luther King Jr., Ralph David Abernathy, and the Civil Rights Movement.* New York: Crown Publishers, 2003.

Bailey, Richard. *Neither Carpetbaggers Nor Scalawags: Black Officeholders During the Reconstruction of Alabama 1867–1878.* 3rd ed. Montgomery, Alabama: Richard Bailey Publishers, 1995.

Bond, Horace Mann. *Negro Education in Alabama: A Study in Cotton and Steel.* New York: Athenium, 1969.

Branch, Taylor. *At Canaan's Edge: America in the King Years, 1965–68.* New York: Simon & Schuster, 2006.

Brinkley, Douglas. *Rosa Parks.* New York: Penguin Putnam, Inc., 2000.

Burns, Stewart. *To the Mountaintop: Martin Luther King Jr.'s Sacred Mission to Save America 1955–1968.* New York: HarperSanFrancisco, 2004.

Cosby, Camille O. and Renee Poussaint, eds. *A Wealth of Wisdom: Legendary African American Elders Speak.* New York: Atria Books, 2004.

Eubanks, W. Ralph. *Ever Is a Long Time: A Journey into Mississippi's Dark Past.* New York: Basic Books, 2003.

Fairclough, Adam. *Better Day Coming: Blacks and Equality, 1890–2000.* New York: Viking, 2001.

Farris, Christine King. *Through It All: Reflections on My Life, My Family, My Faith.* New York: Atria Books, 2009.

Gray, Fred D. *Bus Ride to Justice: Changing the System by the System.* Montgomery, AL: The Black Belt Press, 1995.

Jackson, Troy. *Becoming King: Martin Luther King Jr. and the Making of a National Leader.* Lexington: The University Press of Kentucky, 2008.

Johnson, Charles, and Bob Adelman. *Remembering Martin Luther King, Jr.: His Life and Crusade in Pictures.* New York: Life Books, 2008.

King, Dexter, and Ralph Wiley. *Growing Up King: An Intimate Memoir.* New York: Warner Books, 2003.

Northup, Solomon. *Twelve Years a Slave.* Baton Rouge, LA: Louisiana State University Press, 1968.

Rhodes, Lisa Renee. *Coretta Scott King.* Philadelphia: Chelsea House Publishers, 1998.

Rieder, Jonathan. *The Word of the Lord Is Upon Me: The Righteous Performance of Martin Luther King Jr.* Cambridge, MA: Belknap Press of Harvard University Press, 2008.

Sellers, James Benson. *Slavery in Alabama.* Tuscaloosa: The University of Alabama Press, 1950.

Smith, Lillian. *Killers of the Dream.* New York: Norton, 1949.

———. *Strange Fruit.* New York: Reynal & Hitchcock, 1944.

Urban, Wayne J. *Black Scholar: Horace Mann Bond 1904–1972.* Athens: University of Georgia Press, 1992.

Warren, Mervyn A. *King Came Preaching: The Pulpit Power of Dr. Martin Luther King Jr.* Downers Grove, IL: InterVarsity Press, 2001.

Works Cited

Archives

American Missionary Association Archives. Amistad Research Center. Tilton Hall, Tulane University.

Books

Beard, Augustus Field. *A Crusade of Brotherhood: A History of the American Missionary Association.* Boston: Pilgrim Press, 1909.

Bennett, Lerone. *What Manner of Man: A Biography of Martin Luther King, Jr.* Chicago: Johnson Publishing, 1964.

Burns, Stewart, ed. *Daybreak of Freedom: The Montgomery Bus Boycott.* Chapel Hill: University of North Carolina Press, 1997.

Butler, Addie Louise Joyner. *The Distinctive Black College: Talladega, Tuskegee and Morehouse.* London: Scarecrow Press, 1977.

Clark, Burton R. *The Distinctive College.* New Brunswick: Transaction Publishers, 1992. http://books.google.com/.

Carson, Clayborne, ed. *The Autobiography of Martin Luther King, Jr.* New York: Grand Central Publishing, 1998.

Farrell, James J. *The Spirit of the Sixties: Making Postwar Radicalism.* New York: Routledge, 1997.

Foerster, Norman. *American Poetry and Prose.* Boston: Houghton Mifflin Company, 1957.

Franklin, John Hope, and Alfred A. Moss, Jr. *From Slavery to Freedom: A History of African Americans.* New York: Alfred A. Knopf, 2000.

Franklin, John Hope, and Loren Schweninger. *In Search of the Promised Land: A Slave Family in the Old South.* New York: Oxford University Press, 2006.

Garrow, David J. *Bearing the Cross: Martin Luther King, Jr., and the Southern Christian Leadership Conference.* New York: William Morrow, 1986.

Good, Paul. "It Was Worth the Boy's Dying." In *Reporting Civil Rights Part Two: American Journalism 1963–1973,* 353–55. New York: Literary Classics of the United States, 2003.

Johnson, Lyndon. "President Johnson Makes an Impassioned Plea to Congress to Pass the Voting Rights Act of 1965." In *In Our Own Words: Extraordinary Speeches of the American Century,* edited by Robert G. Torricelli and Andrew Carroll, 255–59. New York: Kodansha America, 1999.

King, Coretta Scott. *My Life with Martin Luther King, Jr.* New York: Henry Holt, 1993.

King, Martin Luther, Jr. *Stride Toward Freedom.* San Francisco: Harper SanFrancisco, 1986.

———. *The Words of Martin Luther King Jr.* Edited by Coretta Scott King. New York: Newmarket Press, 1983.

———. *Why We Can't Wait.* New York: Harper & Row, Publishers, 1964.

Luther, Martin. *The Table Talk or Familiar Discourse of Martin Luther.* Translated by William Hazlitt. London: David Bogue, 1848.

Marsh, Charles. *The Beloved Community: How Faith Shapes Social Justice, From the Civil Rights Movement to Today.* New York: Basic Books, 2005.

Morgan, Joy Elmer. *Horace Mann at Antioch: Studies in Personality and Higher Education.* The Horace Mann Centennial Fund, 1938.

Peck, James. "Not So Deep Are the Roots." In *Reporting Civil Rights Part One: American Journalism, 1941–1963,* 92–98. New York: Literary Classics of the United States, 2003.

Pollack, Jack H. "Literacy Tests: Southern Style." In *Reporting Civil Rights Part One: American Journalism, 1941–1963,* 85–91. New York: Literary Classics of the United States, 2003.

Pomerantz, Gary M. *Where Peachtree Meets Sweet Auburn: The Saga of Two Families and the Making of Atlanta.* New York: Scribner, 1996.

Reddick, L. D. *Crusader Without Violence: A Biography of Martin Luther King Jr.* New York: Harper, 1959.

Rhodes, Lisa Renee. *Coretta Scott King.* Philadelphia: Chelsea House, 1998.

Shomburg Center for Research in Black Culture, New York Public Library. *Standing in the Need of Prayer: A Celebration of Black Prayer. With a foreword by Coretta Scott King.* New York: Free Press, 2003.

Swerdlow, Amy. *Women Strike for Peace: Traditional Motherhood and Radical Politics in the 1960s.* Chicago: University of Chicago Press, 1993.

Thoreau, Henry David. *Civil Disobedience.* 1849. Charleston: Forgotten Books, 2008. http://books.google.com/.

Torricelli, Robert G. and Andrew Carroll, eds. *In Our Own Words: Extraordinary Speeches of the American Century.* New York: Kodansha America, 1999.

Washington, James M., ed. *A Testament of Hope: The Essential Writings and Speeches of Martin Luther King Jr.* New York: HarperSanFrancisco, 1991.

Young, Andrew. *An Easy Burden: The Civil Rights Movement and the Transformation of America.* New York: HarperCollins, 1996.

Court Cases

Armstrong v. Board of Education of City of Birmingham, Jefferson County, Alabama, 323 F.2d 333 (5th Cir. 1963).

Boynton v. Virginia, 364 U.S. 454 (1960).

Browder v. Gayle, 142 F. Supp. 707 (1956).

Brown v. Board of Education, 347 U.S. 483 (1954).

Connor v. State, 153 S0.2d 787, 274 Ala. 230 (1963).

Henderson v. United States, 339 U.S. 816 (1950).

Mitchell v. U.S., 313 U.S. 80 (1941).

Morgan v. Commonwealth of Virginia, 328 U.S. 373 (1946).

Plessy v. Ferguson, 163 U.S. 537 (1896).

United States v. The Libellants and Claimants of the Schooner *Amistad,* 40 US 518 (1840).

Government Reports

Cabinet Paper. "The Civil Rights Program—Letter and Statement by the Attorney General." April 10, 1956. E. Frederic Morrow Records, Box 9, Civil Rights Bill. Eisenhower Presidential Library.

Department of the Interior Bureau of Education. *Bulletin: Negro Education: A Study of the Private and Higher Schools for Colored People in the United States.* 2 vols. (Washington, D.C., 1916), No. 38 and 39.

Select Committee to Study Governmental Operations. "Dr. Martin Luther King, Jr., Case Study." United States Senate. Supplementary Detailed Staff Reports on Intelligence Activities and the Rights of Americans. Book III. Final Report, April 23, 1976.

UN General Assembly. Resolution 32/10. "Decade for Action to Combat Racism and Racial Discrimination," November 7, 1977.

UN General Assembly. Resolution 32/11. "Status of the International Convention on the Elimination of All Forms of Racial Discrimination," November 7, 1977.

UN General Assembly. Resolution 32/12. "Status of the International Convention on the Suppression and Punishment of the Crime of Apartheid," November 7, 1977.

Online Sources

Alabama Legislature. "Delegates To The Constitutional Convention." Accessed May 15, 2011. www.legislature.state.al.us/misc/history/constitutions/1875/1875delegates.html.

Alabama Legislature. "Official Proceedings of the Constitutional Convention of the State of Alabama: Day Two, May 22nd." Accessed May 15, 2011. www.legislature.state.al.us/misc/history/constitutions/1901/proceedings/1901_proceedings_v011/ day2.html.

Amistad America. Accessed May 15, 2011. www.amistadamerica.com.

Biographical Directory of the United States Congress. http://bioguide.congress.gov/biosearch/biosearch.asp.

Bright, Susie. "Wise After the Fact: Coretta Scott King's Memorial." *Susie Bright's Journal* (blog). February 10, 2006. Accessed May 14, 2011. http://susiebright.blogs.com/.

Jones, Gerry. "Biography of Douglas McGregor." Managers Net. Accessed May 15, 2011. www.managers-net.org/Biography/mcgregor.html.

King, Coretta Scott. "The Meaning of the Martin Luther King Jr. Holiday." Accessed May 15, 2011. www.crosswalk.com/spirituallife.

King, Martin Luther, Jr. "I Have a Dream." August 28, 1963. Transcript and video. Accessed May 15, 2011. http://www.youtube.com/watch?v=PbUtL_0vAJk.

Martin Luther King Jr., "I Have Been to the Mountaintop," speech delivered at Bishop Charles Mason Temple, April 3, 1968. Transcript. Accessed May 15, 2011, http://mlk-kpp01 .stanford.edu/index.php/encyclopedia/documentsentry/ive_been_to_the_mountaintop/.

"Mission and History." Antioch College. Accessed May 15, 2011. http://antiochcollege.org/ about/mission_and_history.html.

"A Rich History." Karamu House. Accessed May 15, 2011. http://www.karamuhouse.org/cms -view-page.php?page=about-us.

United Church of Christ. Accessed May 15, 2011. www.ucc.org.

Woolley, John T. and Gerhard Peters. *The American Presidency Project*. Accessed May 15, 2011. www.presidency.ucsb.edu/.

Periodicals

The Antiochian. March 1967.

"Carter Administration Hits Repression in South Africa." *Jet*. Nov. 10, 1977.

Daniel, Hawthorne. "Arthur E. Morgan's New Type of College." *World's Work: A History of Our Time* 41, no. 4 (Feb. 1921), 408–9.

"Education: Retreat of a Reconciler." *Time*. May 16, 1969.

Hevesi, Dennis. "Ruth S. Morgenthau, 75, an Adviser to Carter, Is Dead." *New York Times*, November 12, 2006.

Honey, Michael. "Chasing the Dream." *Seattle Times*, April 2, 2006.

King, Coretta Scott. "He Had a Dream: Mrs. Martin Luther King Jr.'s Own Story of the Years of Struggle, Hope, Success and Foreboding." *Life* (September 12, 1969), 54–62.

Marion Times Standard, July 27, 1950.

"Mrs. King Seeks Tougher Ban Against South Africa." *Jet*. Dec. 1, 1977.

Review of *Before the Mayflower*. By Lerone Bennett Jr. Books. *Jet*. March 7, 1963.

Saxon, Wolfgang. "Thomas Kilgore Jr., 84; Led 2 Baptist Groups." *New York Times*, February 10, 1998.

Scott, Coretta. "Why I Came to College." *Opportunity: Journal of Negro Life 26* (April–June 1948): 42.

"20th Bombing here against Negroes." *Birmingham Post-Herald*, September 16, 1963. http:// bplonline.cdmhost.com/.

Wallace, E. P. *Montgomery Advertiser*, March 23, 1955.

Unpublished Works

Scott, Coretta. "Evaluation of Work at Friendly Inn Settlement." Unpublished paper, Antioch College Archives, 1947.

———. "Life Aims." Unpublished paper, Antioch College Archives, 1946.

———. "Senior Paper." Unpublished paper, Antioch College Archives, 1951.

Index

Page references in italics refer to illustrations.